The Political Economy of a Plural World

D0139990

'For thirty years Robert Cox has been at the forefront of developing a critical international political economy of modern world capitalism. A seminal thinker with an immense following, his work in the past has rarely been anything less than challenging. A dissident in a world where intelligent dissent is in short supply, here once again in a set of superb essays, Cox shows precisely why he has achieved – and why he deserves – his enviably huge reputation. A must read for anybody seriously interested in the fate of civilization before and after September 11th.'

Professor Michael Cox, *Department of International Politics, Aberystwyth*

The Political Economy of a Plural World is a new volume by one of the world's leading critical thinkers in international political economy. Building on his seminal contributions to the field, Robert W. Cox engages with the major themes that have characterized his work over the past three decades, and also the main topics which affect the globalized world at the start of the twenty-first century. The book addresses such core issues as global civil society, power and knowledge, the covert world, multilateralism, and civilizations and world order. Michael G. Schechter has written an introductory essay which addresses current critiques of Coxian theory, enabling the author to enter into a stimulating dialogue with critics of his work.

Timely, provocative and original, this book is a major contribution to international political economy and essential reading for all students and academics in the field.

Robert W. Cox is Professor emeritus of political science at York University, Toronto. He has published widely on international political economy, and his books include *Approaches to World Order*.

Routledge/RIPE Series in Global Political Economy

Series Editors: Otto Holman, Marianne Marchand (*Research Centre for International Political Economy, University of Amsterdam*), Henk Overbeek (*Free University, Amsterdam*) and Marianne Franklin (*University of Amsterdam*)

This series, published in association with the *Review of International Political Economy*, provides a forum for current debates in international political economy. The series aims to cover all the central topics in IPE and to present innovative analyses of emerging topics. The titles in the series seek to transcend a state-centred discourse and focus on three broad themes:

- the nature of the forces driving globalisation forward
- resistance to globalisation
- the transformation of the world order.

The series comprises two strands:

The *RIPE Series in Global Political Economy* aims to address the needs of students and teachers, and the titles will be published in hardback and paperback. Titles include

Transnational Classes and International Relations
Kees van der Pijl

Gender and Global Restructuring
Sightings, sites and resistances
Edited by Marianne H. Marchand and Anne Sisson Runyan

Global Political Economy
Contemporary theories
Edited by Ronen Palan

Ideologies of Globalization
Contending visions of a new world order
Mark Rupert

The Clash within Civilisations
Coming to terms with cultural conflicts
Dieter Senghaas

Global Unions?
Theory and strategies of organized labour in the global political economy
Edited by Jeffrey Harrod and Robert O'Brien

The Political Economy of a Plural World
Critical reflections on power, morals and civilization
Robert Cox with Michael G. Schechter

Routledge/RIPE Studies in Global Political Economy is a forum for innovative new research intended for a high-level specialist readership, and the titles will be available in hardback only. Titles include:

1 Globalization and Governance*
Edited by Aseem Prakash and Jeffrey A. Hart

2 Nation-States and Money
The past, present and future of national currencies

3 The Global Political Economy of Intellectual Property Rights
The new enclosures?
Christopher May

4 Integrating Central Europe
EU expansion and Poland, Hungary and the Czech Republic
Otto Holman

5 Capitalist Restructuring, Globalisation and the Third Way
Lessons from the Swedish model
J. Magnus Ryner

6 Transnational Capitalism and the Struggle over European Integration
Bastiaan van Apeldoorn

7 World Financial Orders
An historical international political economy
Paul Langley

*Also available in paperback

**Dedicated to the memory of
Harold Karan 'Jake' Jacobson,
wise scholar, inspiring teacher, loyal friend**

The Political Economy of a Plural World

Critical reflections on power, morals and civilization

Robert W. Cox

With Michael G. Schechter

Routledge
Taylor & Francis Group

LONDON AND NEW YORK

First published 2002 by Routledge
11 New Fetter Lane, London EC4P 4EE

Simultaneously published in the USA and Canada
by Routledge
29 West 35th Street, New York, NY 10001

Routledge is an imprint of the Taylor & Francis Group

Typeset in Times New Roman by M Rules
Printed and bound by
Gutenberg Press Ltd, Malta

British Library Cataloguing in Publication Data
A catalogue record for this book is available from the British Library

Library of Congress Cataloging in Publication Data
Cox, Robert W., 1926–
    Political economy of a plural world: Critical reflections on power,
    morals and civilization / by Robert W. Cox.
        p.   cm.
    Includes bibliographical references and index.
        1. Legitimacy of governments. 2. Civil society. 3. Civilization. 4.
    Counterculture. 5. Government, Resistance to. 6. Globalization. 7.
    International economic relations. 1. Title.

    JC497.C67 2002
    300—dc21   2002069949

ISBN 0–415–25290–3 (hbk)
ISBN 0–415–25291–1 (pbk)

Contents

Epilogue 189

Series editors' preface

In 1988, the late Susan Strange wrote that Robert Cox 'is an eccentric in the best English sense of the word, a loner, a fugitive from intellectual camps of victory, both Marxist and liberal'. Her review of Cox's magnum opus *Power, Production and World Order: Social Forces in the Making of History* (1987) was an early attempt to grasp Cox's thinking as independent and non-dogmatic, a characterization so different from all sorts of parochial critiques that tried to pin him down as Marxist (or attacking him for not being Marxist enough), neo-Gramscian (while sometimes chiding him for misreading Gramsci), Weberian, etc., or accused him of being reductionist, empiricist or eclectic. In this volume, Robert Cox , whilst not 'shying away' from the labels eclectic or empiricist, is most concerned with being labelled reductionist.

This is one of the important features of this book. For the first time, Cox is engaging with his critics in a comprehensive way. This takes the form of a dialogue (in Chapter 2) with some of the most important critiques of Coxian theory from Chapter 1 (selected by Michael Schechter). Three different, albeit related, strands of these critiques are reviewed. First, some key concepts in Cox's work are critically discussed: class and production, the internationalization of the state, *nébuleuse*, etc. Second, a number of issues are highlighted which have been missing or underdeveloped in the work of Cox: the military-security aspects of world order, the importance of ecology in the global political economy, and issues of transnational identity politics, including gender. Finally, Robert Cox has been criticized for being either too pessimistic or too Utopian with regard to the future of global governance. In particular the question whether the *nébuleuse* – 'the unofficial and official transnational and international networks of state and corporate representatives and intellectuals who work towards the formulation of a policy consensus for global capitalism' – can be challenged by a counter-*nébuleuse* and whether international organizations can play a supportive role in this respect is discussed.

This collection of essays is more than just a conversation between Cox and his critics though. The first part of the volume consists of a number of chapters which trace and document the gradual shift in Cox's thinking over the years, culminating in a 'new ontology of world order'. The concrete substance of this new ontology is illustrated in the second half of the book where two topics stand out: the role of a revitalized civil society (interpreted as a multilevel phenomenon) in determining the future of global governance and the prospect of generating legitimacy through the peaceful coexistence of civilizations. Both issues are analysed in the light of the present crisis of authority/legitimacy and the clash between formal and informal politics, of which the globalization of informal violence (to use Robert Keohane's term) is only the most extreme expression.

The RIPE Series in Global Political Economy is proud to be publishing this latest book by Robert Cox. *The Political Economy of a Plural World: Critical reflections on power, morals and civilization* is essential reading for those who want to know in which direction Coxian Historicism has evolved over the years and how the 'new' thinking of Robert Cox reflects more recent developments and trends in the global political economy. But its significance transcends its importance as a source for the intellectual historiography of one of the great independent thinker on global politics. The book provides the reader with a wealth of conceptual tools and theoretical insights enabling us to make sense of the present crisis of legitimacy in the global system and challenging us to think creatively and actively of ways to build a peaceful world based on the recognition of civilizational pluralism as a positive force.

Otto Holman
Marianne H. Marchand
Henk Overbeek
Marianne Franklin
Amsterdam, June 2002

Acknowledgements

In some of the chapters of this book, I have drawn upon earlier publications to which I contributed, the texts of which have been revised and edited as appropriate. In Chapter 4, I have incorporated a few passages of a chapter contributed to *Millennium Reflections Project* (2002), together with extracts from my correspondence with Lloyd Axworthy, former Minister of Foreign Affairs of Canada, concerning the war in Kosovo, published in *Studies in Political Economy* (2000). In Chapter 5 are edited extracts from my chapter in *Political Economy and the Changing Global Order* (2000), and from my chapter in *Critical Theory and World Politics* (2001). Chapter 6 is based on my article of the same title published in *Review of International Studies* (1999), and Chapter 8 is based on my article of the same title in *Studies in Political Economy* (1995). Chapter 9 is an edited extract from my article in *International Relations of the Asia-Pacific* (2001), while Chapter 10 is derived from my article in *Review of International Studies* (2000).

Together with the publishers I would therefore like to thank the following copyright holders for granting permission to use material from their work:

- Michigan University Press for permission to reproduce 'Universality, Power and Morality' from Michael Brecher and Frank Harvey, eds, *Millennium Reflections Project* (Michigan University Press: 2002).
- Studies in Political Economy for permission to reproduce correspondence with Lloyd Axworthy in *Studies in Political Economy*, Number 63 (Autumn 2000). SPE, SR 303, Carleton University, 1125 Colonel By Drive, Ottawa, Ontario, Canada K1S 5BC.
- Oxford University Press for permission to reproduce material from 'Political Economy and World Order: Power and Knowledge at the Turn of the Millennium', in Richard Stubbs and Geoffrey Underhill, eds, *Political Economy and the Changing Global Order*, 2nd Edition (Oxford University Press: 2000).
- Lynne Rienner Publishers for permission to reproduce substantially material from an essay 'The Way Ahead: Towards a New Ontology of World Orders', *Critical Theory and World Politics*, edited by Richard Wyn Jones. Copyright © 2001 by Lynne Rienner Publishers.

- British International Studies Association for permission to reproduce material from 'Civil Society at the Turn of the Millennium: Prospects for an Alternative World Order', *Review of International Studies* (Cambridge University Press: 1999), 25: 3–28. Copyright © 1999 British International Studies Association.
- Studies in Political Economy for permission to reproduce 'Civilizations: Encounters and Transformation' from *Studies in Political Economy*, Number 41 (Summer 1995). SPE, SR 303, Carleton University, 1125 Colonel By Drive, Ottawa, Ontario, Canada K1S 5B6.
- Oxford University Press for permission to reproduce material in 'Civilizations and the Twenty-First Century: Some Theoretical Considerations', *International Relations of the Asia-Pacific*, 2001, Volume 1, pp. 105–30.
- British International Studies Association for permission to reproduce material from 'Thinking about Civilizations', *Review of International Studies* (Cambridge University Press: 2000), 26: 217–34. Copyright © 2000 British International Studies Association.

Every effort has been made to contact copyright holders for their permission to reprint material in this book. The publishers would be grateful to hear from any copyright holder who is not here acknowledged and will undertake to rectify any errors or omissions in future editions of this book.

I would like to give special thanks to Michael G. Schechter not only for Chapter 1 containing analysis of criticisms of my previous work, but also for his advice and comments on my response in Chapter 2 and in other chapters of the book. Others whose advice I have benefited from in preparing this book, apart from the RIPE series editors, include Christian Chavagneux, Gregory Chin, Frank Deppe, Randall Germain, Jean-Christophe Graz, Eric Helleiner, James H. Mittelman, James Morrison and Sandra Whitworth. I have benefited much from the ideas and criticism of many others over the years. They include Mitchell Bernard, Fantu Cheru, Daniel Drache, Richard Falk, Stephen Gill, Barry K. Gills, Jeoffrey Harrod, Björn Hettne, Martin Hewson, Yumiko Iido, Harold K. Jacobson, Jacques Lemoine, James Morrison, Craig Murphy, Kinhide Mushakoji, Leo Panitch, Mustapha Kamal Pasha, Roberto Payro, Helène Pellerin, Randolph Persaud, V. Spike Peterson, Kees van der Pijl, James N. Rosenau, Mark Rupert, Yoshikazu Sakamoto, Ahmed Samatar, Timothy J. Sinclair, Marie-Claude Smouts, Georges Spyropoulos, Rodolfo Stavenhagen and Susan Strange. York University has given me a congenial and stimulating intellectual home. As always, Jessie Cox has spurred me to rethink my writing in the interests of clarity and good judgement. Natarsha Douglas prepared the final text. Of course, none of these people are in any way responsible for the resulting work.

Preface

After September 11, 2001, it became commonplace to say that the whole world had changed. Of course, this sentiment was current mainly in North America and by extension in 'the West'. The meaning was that habits of mind concerning the order of the world which had been formed by hitherto dominant power had been dramatically called into question. It was not so much that something totally new had suddenly come into existence as that a dramatic incident – the destruction of the twin towers of the World Trade Center in New York and of part of the Pentagon in Washington – had brought into full consciousness changes which had been slowly taking place for some time, but which minds conditioned to a certain sense of order had comfortably obscured.

What made the incident of September 11 so traumatic was that it demonstrated a capacity on the part of those who totally rejected established order to strike at its very heart. The symbolism of the targets required no further explanation: the attack struck at global capitalism (the World Trade Center) and the American military power (the Pentagon) that was the bulwark of globalization. 'America' is the collective noun that summarizes, for the attackers, this enemy with all its other derivative meanings – Western materialism and cultural arrogance.

The novel feature of this confrontation of powers was its assymetrical character. US military power is designed to control territory, to destroy another power's control over territory, to prevent any external attack on US territory. Prior to September 11 the next military project of the US administration was to erect a national missile defence system that could destroy missiles launched by a hypothetical 'rogue state', some unspecified hostile territorial power. But the attack of September 11 came from within US territory. Territorial confrontation gave place to non-territorial.

Yet the territorial mentality did not yield easily in the trauma. As the dust was settling on 'ground zero' where the twin towers had stood, official thoughts turned to erecting a 'perimeter' around the North American continent to filter out undesirables who might be terrorists from entering; and it linked terrorism with a territorial state, Afghanistan, and an individual leader, Osama Bin Laden, who might be found there.

The struggle dramatized on September 11 was not really over space, but rather over minds, over the legitimacy of authority within the territory of states and of the authority which governs relationships in the world as a whole. Secrecy and surprise are the weapons of the weaker party, of those who challenge the legitimacy of constituted authority. Surprise, the unexpected, defies territorial anticipation. In the first phase of this conflict, non-territorial trumped territorial power.

Subsequent pursuit of this conflict through territorial power misunderstood its nature. Land may be occupied, people killed or imprisoned, but minds will not be changed by territorial military power. The use of force only confirms and exacerbates the conviction of its opponents that the dominant power is illegitimate. The dissidents cannot be crushed because they may be anywhere and everywhere. Terror will not strike again from the same place. Individual leaders in the attack on established power will be replaced. As martyrs they may strengthen the resolve to resist.

The psychological impact of the attack on New York and Washington was to crystallize a cleavage between consent and dissent regarding the legitimacy of world authority. The military response with territorial-based military power would only further mobilize dissent. The Israeli–Palestinian conflict has demonstrated the futility of territorial power in a conflict over legitimacy. All the arts of spying, informing, torture, destruction of property, suicide bombing and imprisonment have only succeeded in perpetuating the cycle of violence in a situation where power relations are asymmetrical and legitimacy is denied, where constituted power is alien and oppressive. This could become a model for the US 'war against terrorism'.

The US (with the British) military response also opened another contradiction. The legitimacy of American power has rested upon the proposition that it has defended liberty. The use of territorial power to monitor and repress those who contest the legitimacy of constituted authority and who would strike against it would, at the extreme, require investigative, repressive and penitentiary powers destructive of the very basis of this legitimacy. September 11, within days, was followed by concern over striking the right balance between repression of 'terrorism' and respect for civil liberties. This opened the perspective that the limitations of military power might be compensated for by the construction of a regime of total surveillance. But this would negate the basis upon which America and 'the West' claimed legitimacy.

The territorial imperative persists, however, in the geostrategic realm. Bombing Afghanistan and replacement of the Taliban government may not effectively eliminate 'global terrorism', but it can alter the geopolitical relationships in central Asia that control the production and delivery of oil. The region from the Caspian Sea through Uzbekistan is the last great world reserve of oil and natural gas. Arrangements for production and for the construction of pipelines are of the greatest concern to Russia, the United States, China, Japan and southeast Asia. States and oil companies have been involved in tortuous negotiations over the production and channelling of

Central Asian oil and gas since the breakup of the Soviet Union. Russia has preferred to route the pipelines yet to be built through its territory north of the Caspian. Iran favours a route across its territory to the Persian Gulf, which the United States rejects because of its hostility to the regime in Teheran.

The United States backed the US oil company Unocal, together with its Saudi Arabian partner Delta Oil, in a project to build a pipeline across Afghanistan to a port in Pakistan. This signalled support for Turkmenistan, Pakistan and the Taliban which had gained control of Afghanistan with the help of the CIA and the Pakistan intelligence ISI. At the same time, it was a snub to Iran and Russia; they were inclined to view US support for the Unocal project as evidence of a US-CIA foreign policy which included the Taliban.

By mid-1997, US policy had shifted to advocate a 'transport corridor' from the Caspian to Turkey, avoiding Russia and Iran; but this project was less attractive to the oil companies because of its high cost, especially if the price of oil were to drop, and also because of the political turbulence in the region. From initially supporting the Taliban, the United States, following the bombing of its embassies in Kenya and Tanzania, focused on 'getting Bin Laden' and total rejection of the Taliban.

The lesson from the volatile situation in the Central Asian region was that there could be no global access to the oil and gas of this last major world source of supply without a geostrategic settlement among the major powers in the region and a resolution of the prevailing inter-ethnic and inter-religious conflict. The 'war on terrorism' which led towards control over Afghanistan and dominant influence in Pakistan could change the picture for a US government that sees the securing of oil resources as a priority concern for the future. There is still a territorial *raison d'état* behind the illusion that territorial power can eliminate 'terrorism'. The geostrategic rationale underpinning the 'war on terrorism' could extend to the targeting of Iraq and subsequently to other 'rogue states'.

But let us return to examining the phenomenon of alienation from established order and the determination of dissidents to attack established order. Throughout history there has been a pattern to challenges that have taken place to the legitimacy of dominant power – to the challenge that chaos presents to order. The main body of literature, philosophy and historiography has spoken from the perspective of order. It has given little insight into chaos, though some glimpses into chaos did come, in the Western tradition, from Heraclitus and from Nietzsche. These exceptional figures have stressed that there is a kind of order in chaos, in the permanent flux of change that includes the eternal return.

The collective actions of historical people give more practical guidance than does speculative philosophy. The challenge to established order has come about through the building of a counter-society formed around principles that contradict those of established order. Often, this begins in secret outside the disciplinary reach of existing institutions. The counter-society is peopled by the marginalized and the excluded, by those who are intellectually alienated from established order in thought, behaviour and institutions, and by those deprived of the possibility of satisfying their material needs according to the prevailing norms of social order. The counter-society emerges in secret conspiracy among some of these people, who come together in mutual understanding of their situation and a common determination to change it. They develop their own codes of behaviour, rituals and covert bonds of allegiance.

Where established society is structured hierarchically, the counter-society may be looser, allowing for more flexible action and response by its component elements. Secret societies develop the capacity to strike with surprise. Their attack may demonstrate weakness and waning legitimacy in the established order, and withdrawal of consent on the part of some of its subjects. The attack will also strengthen the resolve of others to defend order. It will accentuate the cleavage between support and dissent.

The secret society, however, lacks the organizational power to effectively replace the institutions of the existing order. Some organized but disaffected elements of the existing order, such as a portion of the military, might typically act with the support of popular forces of dissent mobilized by the secret society so as to change the regime.

The question is, then: what becomes of the secret society? Some of its members may become integrated into the new regime. Many may lapse into passive accommodation to it. For others, their marginal character and the covert nature of their activities may continue, but as parasitical upon the new order rather than as in revolutionary opposition. Parasitical covert and criminal activity can, indeed, become functional to the stabilizing of a new order. This sequence sketches a natural history of legitimacy → illegitimacy → new legitimacy. It moves through a cycle of revolutionary covert activity → compromise with elements of the old order → parasitical covert activity sustaining the new order.

This model is drawn from Chinese historical experience (see Chapter 7). The Triad and White Lotus secret societies from the seventeenth century opposed the Ming dynasty, and they defied the hierarchical Confucian social order with a more egalitarian mix of Taoism and Buddhism. In the revolution of 1911, elements from the armed forces and the bourgeoisie gained the support of the secret societies and of the popular forces that the secret societies could mobilize to overthrow the empire. Thenceforth, the triads continued as organized criminal groups which found a more or less accepted role in post-revolutionary society, occasionally useful to the political power. The model is not, of course, applicable in detail to other times and places; but it does give some heuristical guidelines for examining historical change.

Consider this pattern in relation to observed reactions to the 'incident' of September 11. President George W. Bush proclaimed 'war against terrorism'. He also proclaimed that all who were not with him and the coalition of states he intended to build up were with the terrorists. For the US administration, the cleavage was rhetorically universal and total. With the terrorists were any state that sheltered them or gave sustenance to them. This explicitly included Afghanistan under the Taliban but could by extension be held to include 'rogue states' like Iraq and Sudan and perhaps others like Syria or Iran. Where the line was to be drawn at whatever time lay with the US leadership and its understanding of what political support it could expect from other governments whose acquiescence the US leadership would deem to be necessary.

The rhetorical clarity of this cleavage between order and terrorism, between good and evil (despite the ambiguity of who exactly was to be targeted), was, however, contradicted by the existence of a vast intermediate sphere in public opinion and state policy. Many people, including some in America, although mourning the innocent people who died in the attack of September 11, felt that the 'root causes' of terrorism lay in US foreign policies that had punished and offended peoples most closely linked to the group that had launched the attack – by the US support for Israel's military power and its dominant, though isolated, position in the Middle East; and by the recurrent bombing and blockade of Iraq. But the very term 'root causes' was hurled back at any such American critics and dissenters as evidence of weak mindedness or disloyalty. Government officials warned that it was dangerous to say certain things in wartime. Commentators practised self-censorship. But some Americans continued to ask: 'Why do they hate us?'

The critical perspective was more widespread in European public opinion. It was more common for Europeans to consider that in retrospect, and despite sorrow for the loss of human life in the attacks of September 11, America had brought such an attack sooner or later upon itself. European governments, however, readily aligned themselves with the United States. *Realpolitik* governed the position of states in relation to the determination with which the world's dominant military power intended to destroy the terrorist threat.

The US government was particularly concerned to rally 'moderate' Islamic states to its cause. This, it hoped, would persuasively contradict the claims of Islamic militants that they were leading a jihad against the Satanic power and corrupting influence of America. Governments of 'moderate' Islamic states that were wary of risking reprisal from their own people by offering even token support to America hoped to gain space and time for maintaining their power with external sustenance, both financial and military, from the world super-power. Nevertheless, Pakistan and the Central Asian region risked a prolongation and deepening of turbulence as a result of the American assault.

Russia and China both found it to their interest to give at least nominal support to the US attack on Afghanistan. 'Terrorist' was the term Russia applied to the resistance in Chechnya; and support for America, including giving America access to the 'near abroad' in Central Asia for its strikes against Afghanistan, would give respite from US criticism of human rights violations in that struggle. Perhaps, also, some understanding could be reached regarding the development of the Central Asian oil reserves. China might gain similar tolerance for its repression in Xinjiang. Anti-terrorism was a marketable commodity.

Many different state interests could thus be covered by the umbrella of anti-terrorism. But although some of these were opportunistic and incidental to the immediate situation, they were joined by the solid, permanent corporate and private forces dependent upon the structure of world economic power that was sustained by US military and political power. More and more people are aware of where their own interests lie on the divide that separates those integrated with, or dependent upon, global capitalism from those who feel alienated by all that goes on under the rubric of globalization.

Many factors had contributed to the formation of dissent from the US 'war on terrorism' in public opinion, if not in government policy:

- There was resentment against the 'state terrorism' of the United States in its bombing of Iraq, Libya and Sudan, and of Israeli attacks against Palestinians including targeted assassinations and demolishing of homes and buildings.
- There was resentment against US unilateralism on ecological issues like the refusal to endorse the Kyoto protocol on global warming, the introduction of genetically modified organisms (GMOs) into the global food chain, the refusal to join in the protection of biodiversity and to cooperate in the reduction of global pollutants in deference to the interests of corporate agribusiness and the biotechnology industry.
- There was apprehension concerning the US administration's determination to control more and more of the world's petroleum resources through dominance in the Middle East and expansion into the Central Asian region, in order to assuage the insatiable thirst for energy of the American production system.
- There was resentment against US unilateralism in its refusal to join international conventions for the abolition of land mines and the establishment of an international criminal court. Nationals of other countries might be charged with war crimes and crimes against humanity in *ad hoc* international courts set up for Rwanda and for the former Yugoslavia, but no American should be subject to such charges.
- There was repugnance at the new American 'way of war' involving high-level aerial bombardment, avoidance of direct combat by US forces and use of non-US ground forces for land attack, which sends the message that American lives are of infinite value while the lives of others are expendable, especially as non-combatant 'collateral damage'.
- There was resentment against the dominance of American culture through the global mass media and the threat it posed to the maintenance of global cultural diversity.

- Above all, there was resentment against the structuring of the global economy to advance the profits of multinational corporations, sacrificing local economic autonomy everywhere, with the consequences of ecological destruction, unemployment and a widening gap between rich and poor.

This list of resentments and apprehensions defines the image of world order that the dissenters see ahead of them: the rape of the biosphere by unregulated economic expansion in which a minority of the increasingly wealthy protect themselves in fortified redoubts from the distress of the poor, where the pursuit of profit is ever-more dependent on military and police repression, and where cultural homogenization negates distinct identities. Those who see such a future inherent in the world as it is, reject it. They seek an alternative that would be more ecologically sustainable in the long run, less dependent upon force and violence, and socially more equitable and more just. They are frustrated by the impasse that the existing political, economic and social order presents to the very idea of an alternative order. They are confounded by the realization that established forms of knowledge – the 'conventional wisdom' in social science – makes it difficult even to *think* about an alternative order. The terrorist call for *jihad* is but one extreme form taken by a more general sense of frustration

These resentments and the demand for an alternative vision of the future have manifested themselves in a series of confrontations by civil society organizations and movements with governments and corporate leadership at summit conferences of the managers of the world economy, from the aborted Seattle meeting of the World Trade Organization (WTO) in December 1999, through the Quebec City summit of the Americas in April 2001, the USA–EU summit at Goteborg in June 2001, and the G8 summit in Genoa in July 2001.

In all of these instances, popular forces confronted elected politicians. Some of the politicians complained, 'Who elected the protestors?' The act of drawing this distinction between formal and informal political processes underscored the emerging gap between a vocal segment of the concerned public and the formal institutions of government. It signalled the opening of a legitimation crisis affecting both states and the institutions of global governance. The real opposition seemed to be outside of the conventional political system.

The global cleavage was increasingly to be understood as one between people even more than between states – between the beneficiaries of globalization, on the one hand, and the marginalized, the excluded and those who would refuse globalization, on the other.

This shift from states to people implied a loosening of people's sense of primary identity with a state. The notable exception was the overriding sense of identity most Americans had with their country, an identity that was manifested in patriotic frenzy after the attack of September 11. It seemed ironic that the nation-state achieved its greatest identity with the people in the nation which was the principal author and beneficiary of globalization, one of the principal effects of which has been to loosen the individual/state identity.

Elsewhere the individual/state identity was more strained, particularly among people excluded from or refusing globalization. Among these people, there has been a loss of confidence in the state as an instrument through which the hope of an alternative world could be pursued. Political party leaders appeared to them to be unable or unwilling to confront and deal effectively with their resentments against the prevailing structure of power. Formal politics for them was becoming almost irrelevant. People in this situation responded either with apathy or through action outside of formal political channels.

The grey zone between order and chaos grows greater with the decline of legitimacy. Non-violent citizen protest is flanked by those who project a certain symbolic violence, such as the 'Black Bloc' of self-proclaimed anarchists who had appeared in public protests. Police control of demonstrations became quasi-military repression with the use of chemical deterrents and live ammunition, informers and *agents provocateurs* often drawn from criminal milieux, and arbitrary arrest and detention. Organized crime expanded in parallel with globalization. Drug trafficking, the sex trade, and people smuggling flourished. These activities, while formally condemned by states, managed to benefit from a certain level of connivance on the part of state agents. Although the profits from these activities are enormous, they are not as threatening to order as is the challenge from non-formal political and social protest. The clandestine defence of the established order proceeded apace with increased investment in covert intelligence activity and covert financing of political campaigns.

How can the legitimacy gap be reduced? How might it be possible to construct an alternative order, on alternative principles, and with a new basis of popular legitimacy? This book, while providing some analysis of the genesis of the legitimacy gap through the process of globalization, focuses on two sources for an alternative order.

The first lies in the revitalizing of civil society. Legitimacy is based on popular support for political authority. Legitimacy is a power that flows from the bottom upwards. It can only come from committed, participant citizen action through a multitude of groups and associations that express citizen concern with the various aspects of community life. This can make transparent the decisions that shape public policy. The erosion of legitimacy has been nourished by the remoteness of public decision making from popular scrutiny and participation. It has been encouraged by an individualism that leads people to give their whole attention of necessity to personal and family survival and advancement, leaving the public good to professional politicians who are the more readily influenced by corporate interests and ideological sectarianism that is only too ready to fill the gap of public indifference.

The question here is, then, what are the prospects of a revival of civil society that would be sufficient to become a basis for an alternative order? To attempt an answer to this question, one has to examine the situation of civil society in the different parts of the world.

The second source for an alternative order lies in the prospect of a coexistence of civilizations, a plural world, replacing the globalization project of one single all-encompassing civilization gradually absorbing and homogenizing what is left of the cultural diversity of the world. The bottom-up process through which a rejuvenated civil society could generate the legitimating basis for an alternative global order will inevitably reflect the diversity of material conditions, historical experience, mentalities and aspirations that prevail among the world's people. These factors together shape what we call civilization. Civilization expresses the inter-subjective meanings common to a large group of people as to what is natural, just and desirable. The process of generating legitimacy will take form through a number of civilizations.

It is important to understand the formation of civilizations as a continuing process. Civilizations are not final fixed entities with a definable territorial base, destined to 'clash' with one another like sovereign states writ large. Civilizations historically have had territorial sites of origin where all of the elements that compose them once came together and prospered. But in the contemporary world we have to think of civilizations as existing in the mind rather than on a plot of land. They have all evolved considerably since their origins and the diverse minds in which they adhere have spread around the globe intermingling through the history of conquests and migrations.

So-called fundamentalisms which purport to revive the imagined ancient purity of a civilization are actually outraged responses to contemporary distress and humiliation. Rival tendencies within the same civilization seek to adjust mentalities to changed material and intellectual conditions. Conflict within civilizations is more intense than conflict among civilizations (Senghaas, 2002). Indeed, internal conflict moderates inter-civilization confrontation.

Legitimacy is embodied in civilization. Different civilizations can be defined in the emphasis they give to different principles of legitimacy. The West has put a premium on individualism. Asian societies have stressed the collectivity. Neither would altogether reject the primary principle of the other. It is the balance that makes the significant difference. Nor would either voluntarily agree to defer to the primary principle of the other. The meanings given to these respective principles of legitimacy are, futhermore, in constant evolution through the internal dialogues of civilizations. To know the meaning of any civilization at any particular moment in its development it is necessary to follow the manner in which the key dimensions of civilization may be shifting – the concepts of time and space, of individual and collectivity, of forms of spirituality, and of how these are expressed in social and economic organization. The coexistence of civilizations in a plural world will depend upon mutual understanding of how each civilization is developing and how these distinct patterns of development can be reconciled as mutually compatible.

This leads to the question of how to think about future world order, of what sort of knowledge is required to sustain the concept of a plural world. It will have to be a knowledge capable of understanding the processes of historical change.

A problem-solving kind of knowledge is useful for analysing existing conditions with a view to correcting disturbances. It is based on the collection and classification of data. The analyst, pursuing what is considered to be a 'scientific' method by analogy with the physical sciences, takes position as an independent external observer of the data. The knowledge produced is regarded as 'objective' or 'positive', which means that the analyst allows observation of the object (data) to determine the conclusions. Of course, this does not take account of the fact that the analyst is part of the social world observed and not separable from it, that the subjectivity of the analyst's position determines the questions asked and the kind of data examined, and that the analysis plays a role in restoring equilibrium to the existing order. These implications can be ignored as irrelevant to the purpose of a kind of knowledge that is useful for correcting dysfunctions and maintaining order in the whole.

A different kind of knowledge is required in order to understand how historical change has come about and how change can be bought about. This kind of knowledge deals with facts, i.e. 'mades' not 'givens'. The Latin languages are clearer concerning this distinction. *Factum* derives from the Latin verb to make, just as *datum* does from the verb to give. The fact incorporates intention and action; it has a meaning to be discovered. The fact is not only observed from without, but challenges you to understand it from within as the consequence of human activity (Collingwood, 1946). Data are just there; they have no meaning in themselves. They are not selves, but mere phenomena.

Positivism is synchronic: the social world is given. Enquiry about its meaning is pointless: it is just there. The historical method is diachronic: the social world is meaningful – it is good for some and bad for others and conflict over its preservation or change evokes strong passions – and it is 'made' by collective action over time.

The historical method – historicism for short, in juxtaposition to positivism – has been a steady current in European thought, although since the eighteenth-century Enlightenment it has often been given less respect than the scientific pretensions of positivism.

In relatively stable times, the problem-solving approach of positivism seems all that is necessary to cope with disturbances to the social order. When the social order – both local and global – is beset by crisis, when its meaning is challenged and its legitimacy is questioned, then the historical method is called upon for explanation. We have to look into minds to discover the divergent meanings that different people see when confronting the same events. The simplistic term 'terrorism' will not do in so far as it obscures the complex meaning of September 11, 2001.

Collective human action generates certain habits and patterns of behaviour, institutions and ideas that, in their consistent 'fit', together become durable for a time as historical structures. Positivism, which has an aversion to 'wholes', ignores the existence of historical structures in its analysis of discrete data. Historicism, which likes to look from the whole into its various parts, enquires into the origins of historical structures and the possibilities of structural transformation.

The genius of Giambattista Vico produced the most complete and coherent exposition of historicism in European thought. It is worth while to return to his work, written in the early eighteenth century, as a foundation for thinking about the transformation of world order at the beginning of the twenty-first century. Of course, other civilizations have produced comparable works of genius in the perception of historical change. I think particularly of Ibn Khaldun, Vico's predecessor by three centuries, writing in the after-glow of the peak moment of the Islamic civilization that among other things introduced medical science and Greek philosophy to a more backward European society. But Vico will do to introduce a way of thinking leading to the themes of this book: understanding the transformation of historical structures, the making of revolutions, and the possibility of a plural world of coexisting civilizations.

Let me now move from the general question of knowledge appropriate to the study of historical structural change to the particular genesis of this book. Perspectives are rooted in time and place. Thought is individual but it has a context. It evolves in the author's experience of the historical world, and of the structures and events that prompt enquiry. It may be influenced also by the perspectives of others who are responding at the same time but in a different way to these historical structures and events. It is therefore proper to consider a book as a stage in a process in which the author has developed thinking over some years through a changing social and political milieu, and has absorbed criticism of the ongoing work from others as well as in self-criticism and reconsideration.

The structure of this book treats of the matters discussed in this preface but in the reverse order. It begins with an analysis of critiques of my previous works prepared by Professor Michael Schechter of Michigan State University. It continues with my reflections on these criticisms and how they and other events have stimulated a transition to modified perspectives and different themes.

There follows a discussion of Vico's thought and how that thought has been interpreted by others as a basis for understanding structural transformation and the coexistence of a plurality of civilizations. The historicist approach derived from Vico leads directly to the question of power and values in politics and society.

Next, comes a discussion of globalization as the salient dynamic of the contemporary world; and the challenge which the consequences of globalization pose for imagining a new ontology of world order that is better able to diagnose the key problems in the world of globalization.

Finally, the book moves from diagnosis to therapy, with a discussion of the conditions for an alternative order: the revitalization of civil society and the conception of a plural world of coexisting civilizations.

1 Critiques of Coxian theory

Background to a conversation

Michael G. Schechter

The purpose of this essay is quite straightforward. It is also very unusual, almost unique. Thus this needs to be made explicit and explained. In this essay I will recount, summarize and synthesize various critiques of some of the major works of Robert W. Cox. The intent behind this unusual undertaking, especially in a volume containing Cox's own works,[1] is to allow Cox to begin an explicit published conversation with some of his critics, aimed at clarifying, elaborating, rethinking and revising earlier arguments. Chapter 2 of this volume gives him an unusual opportunity to systematically and explicitly address his critics' concerns,[2] something that seems particularly important as few of his critics publicly acknowledge how his thoughts have evolved over time.[3]

As will become evident shortly, some of the critiques of Cox's work seem to contradict each other. Scholars' readings of his work and their criticism of it oftentimes seems to reveal as much about the critics' own ideological, epistemological and ontological predilections as about his. Critics have sought to classify Cox's work in well-known categories such as Marxist, Gramscian, Weberian, or the Frankfurt School, and then have criticized him for deviating from their understanding of what is proper to these currents of thought. Cox's critics have examined his work in the perspective of his perceived neglect of issues important to the critics' own priorities – military-security issues, feminism, and ecology, for instance, and of how he fails to meet the criteria of positivism, neo-realism, or post-modernism. Some time ago, Susan Strange wrote that Cox 'is an eccentric in the best English sense of the word, a loner, a fugitive from intellectual camps of victory, both Marxist and liberal.'[4] That probably sums up his own sense of who he is.

As will be shown, Cox has also been criticized for his perceived pessimism with regard to agents of change such as intergovernmental and non-governmental organizations while others have read into his work an excessive, even utopian, optimism about prospects for structural change in world political economy. He has further been seen as someone who, while being critical in his social-political analysis, lacks commitment or purpose with regard to outcomes and the pursuit of change.[5]

Conceptual critiques go to the heart of his work. Is he too state-centric or does he not give adequate attention to the state? Is he too focused on class relations? Does he see globalization too much as an impersonal process (courting the notion of inevitability) rather than a project of states? Is he reductionist, seeing everything economistically as based on production, to the exclusion of cultural forces and of an understanding that all human activity is conditioned by the state of the biosphere?

This chapter is organized around these points of criticism of Cox's work. The reader of this book will see that many of the criticisms of gaps in Cox's coverage of world affairs are answered in the contents of the present volume – including the emphasis on ecology, civil society, and on culture and civilizations – and that Cox has also advanced his effort to explain his epistemological and methodological roots, though perhaps not to the satisfaction of all of his critics. The point is that his thinking has evolved beyond the phase it was in when many of the criticisms were made. This volume is intended then, in part, to mark a further stage in that evolution. While self-reflection may be the primary inspiration for the development of thinking, criticism is an important stimulus.

One additional point about this chapter must be added. Its substantive focus is wholly unreflective of the commentary in the vast literature that refers to Cox's published work. Most of that literature is quite laudatory. Cox is generally recognized, even by some of his harshest critics,[6] as a major figure in contemporary International Relations theory, a founder of modern-day International Political Economy, and the first major scholar to apply critical theory to the study of International Relations.[7] James H. Mittelman's and Martin Griffiths's summary judgments are illustrative of this more characteristic commentary:

> Cox's work allows for the posing of new questions and perspectives on the complexities and contradictions of our age, based upon his particular synthesis of historical understanding and sociological imagination. Coxian studies are beginning to occupy a recognized place in the global 'scientific' community of international relations scholars, notably on the critical flank. Cox has helped to shape the sense of where its problems lie, what its appropriate methods might be, and the kinds of criteria that might be appropriate for evaluation in the human and social sciences.[8]

> The work of Robert Cox is, in conclusion, a major contribution to the rise of critical theory in the study of international relations. From his base at York University, he has inspired many students to rethink the way in which we should study international political economy, and it is fair to say that Gramscian historical materialism is perhaps the most important alternative to realist and liberal perspectives in the field today.[9]

More than mere classificatory confusion

Much ink has been spilled on trying to classify Cox's work. Perhaps this is just, as Cox is said to have invented the term 'neo-realism', a term that some so labeled have quickly shunned.[10] While most call Cox a Gramscian of some sort or another or some variant of a critical theorist, he prefers to call himself a historical materialist.[11] Mittelman writes of Coxian historicism;[12] Brown has called him 'a fairly conventional Marxist (Marxist-Leninist even) contending that his historical-materialism while explicitly based on a rejection of positivist accounts of Marxism seems much closer to these sources than he is, perhaps, conscious of.'[13] Martin Shaw, however, refers to Cox as 'bowdlerizing' Marxism.[14] John Adams calls Cox's Marxist variant 'watery'.[15]

Behind the quest for categorization of his work – something a review of the whole of Cox's work clearly defies[16] – often are substantive disagreements with his perspective. For example, those who have chosen to refer to Cox as a *neo*-Gramscian, a *new* Gramscian[17] or a member of the Italian School of International Relations,[18] are not simply making the obvious point with which Cox readily concurs, namely that Antonio Gramsci was mostly concerned with national politics and thus applying Gramsci's concept of civil society and hegemony to the global scale requires a lot of 'reading into' Gramsci. Rather, some of them at least dissent from Cox's interpretation of Gramsci. Hazel Smith, for example, seems to concur with Peter Burnham's criticism that the neo-Gramscian literature (in which both Smith and Burnham always include Cox) 'offers little more than a version of Weberian pluralism oriented to the study of international order.' Stated even more forcefully, she characterizes Burnham's critique as seeing the 'neo-Gramscian approach' as 'barely distinguishable from a sophisticated neo-realist account.' She continues, this time more in her own voice: there is 'some controversy as to whether the concepts utilized by the neo-Gramscians can be considered as recognizably "historical materialist" in the Marxist sense,' even though they are self-professedly historical materialist.[19] Randall D. Germain and Michael Kenny, whose concern is more with those who do not 'take stock more fully of the bountiful literature on Gramsci's work and engage with it,'[20] provide an interesting critique of the 'new Gramscians' downplaying of 'one of the central insights provided by Gramsci with regard to hegemony, namely, that dominant and subaltern classes engage in a series of material and ideological struggles which change the very nature of the terrain under contestation.'[21] But the most extensive critique of Cox for having fallen 'short of a more thorough Gramscian analysis' is by Bob Jessop and Ngai-Ling Sum. They suggest that Coxian analyses tend 'to prioritize the (material) power-institution side' of the 'trialectic' of production, institutions and ideas by:

> (a) over-privileging class over non-class identities and interests in the analysis of power and institutions; (b) under-examining 'ideas' (even the ideas central to economic hegemony and governance) – seeing them in

largely ideational terms rather than as both practical and discursive in nature, attributing their production primarily to intellectuals rather than exploring the complex articulation of folklore, popular common sense, specialized disciplines, science and philosophy, and regarding them as relatively fixed rather than as inherently polysemic and unstable; and (c) largely ignoring the complex co-constitutive relationship among ideas, power and institutions in favor of a largely juxtapositional analysis of different factors that were often ideal-typical terms.[22]

Some of those who refer to Cox as a critical theorist (where the 'c' and 't' are intentionally lower cased) rather than a Critical Theorist do so because, from a Habermasian perspective, Cox is seen to be 'belittling' 'the significance of communicative action, which boasts a separate logic and dynamic of development.' From this perspective, Cox is understood to be arguing that the inter-subjective dimension is 'derivative of the production of material life,' admittedly, however, where production is broadly conceived to include the production of ideas, institutions and social practices. Jürgen Haacke, in particular, suggests that because Cox locates the potentiality for political change in 'the paradigm of production', in the post-positivist era, he opens himself up to the (perhaps unfair) charges, leveled against 'other Marxists' of lacking 'imagination.'[23] The fact that Cox may not understand himself to be working within the tradition of the Frankfurt School seems largely irrelevant to such critics.[24]

In a somewhat similar vein, when Martin Shaw refers to Cox as a 'bowdlerized' Marxist, he is not simply suggesting that Cox has omitted the violence and class conflict of Marx, but that Cox has in some important way distorted Marx. Moreover, Shaw is concerned about the 'trend' that Cox set for Marxist-influenced international theorists 'in failing to refer to Marx's own writing on the state' – with its conception of this institution as comprising 'bodies of armed men.'[25] Indeed, Cox is accused of not even granting states the 'residual' military-security role that neo-liberal institutionalists like Joseph S. Nye and Robert O. Keohane did.[26] Military power in Cox is seen as merely a function of political economy.[27] In a similar vein, Andrew Linklater notes that, contra Giddens, Cox doesn't discuss the 'apparent vulnerability' of historical materialism to realist criticism (meaning the threat of violence in international relations and the continuing nuclear threat).[28]

Critiques coming from various schools of international relations thought

While it may be difficult to appropriately or fairly pigeon-hole Cox's eclectic approach to International Relations, the lack of a consensual label has certainly not prevented those identifying themselves in one school of international thought or another from finding fault with one aspect or another of Cox's work.

Central amongst these critics have been those whom Cox labels neo-realists, including John Mearsheimer and Kenneth Waltz. While the former's criticism of critical theory is among the most vociferous, its value for us is diminished because he lumps together under that rubric a wide variety of scholarship, including Cox's, but also work by constructivist theorists who are generally distinguished from critical theorists.[29]

A bit more surprising has been the relative quiet, at least in direct and published forms, of self-proclaimed positivists.[30] Mittelman's earlier explanation for mainstream North American scholars' scant written commentary on Cox's work is worth recounting and supplementing. Mittelman suggests that it may be because there is such a gulf between mainstream North American political scientists' epistemologies and Cox's or because Cox 'challenges the ontology, political orthodoxy and ethical silences of neoliberalism.'[31] Other possibilities include Steve Smith's suggestion that some positivists are now hesitant to publicly embrace and defend all of the key elements of positivism that Cox has identified and critiqued in their work:

> If positivism can be defined as accepting four main features – naturalism, empiricism, belief in patterns existing in social phenomena, and the value/fact distinction – then I would argue that most North American international relations theory has happily jettisoned the last two of these, but retained the first two as foundational epistemological positions.[32]

Although its muted and unpublished form may be surprising, the substance of positivists' criticism is not. Critical theorists like Cox are criticized for failing to adhere to one of the cardinal rules of social science, i.e. searching for recurrent themes in a quest for identifying general or universally valid laws by doing valid and replicable research. Thus critical theorists' work is seen as lacking the essential ingredients for cumulative research. Moreover, critical theorists' work is seen as reinserting into the International Relations agenda moral judgments and political purposes (i.e. returning to the sort of work that was seen as typifying the earliest pre-behavioral social scientists in general and students of international organization in particular).[33] Of course, Cox's most frequently cited aphorism may be applicable here: 'Theory is always *for* someone and *for* some purpose.'[34]

The criticism of Cox's work from feminist and ecological theorists, including eco-feminists, has been more public, but still somewhat muted. Oftentimes it seems to take the form of a kind of saddened resignation. That is, here is the scholar whose approach more than any other has opened space for their own work, and who, like they, has gone outside the traditional discipline to seek what they believe are more appropriate methodologies and who, like they, have largely turned from problem-solving epistemological stances.[35] Yet, Cox himself (and many of those following in his footsteps) is portrayed as not having focused enough attention on issues key to them (i.e.

the plight of the marginalized – ethnic minorities and especially women, and the environment). In part at least, Steve Smith seems to believe that that is almost inherent in scholarship like Cox's that looks at international or world orders (i.e. the structural aspects of his scholarship). Smith sees such 'readings' of the nature of International Relations as often largely omitting questions of race, ethnicity, and gender 'since they are not presumed to be parts of any international order.'[36] Some environmental scholars, however, have taken note of 'progress' in Cox's most recent work. Still they do not see him as recognizing ecology as an autonomous actor in world politics, one not mediated through the state. Eric LaFerrerière speaks of Cox's work most directly:[37]

> while Cox's work is in line with ecoradical thinking, the ecological significance of his historicism must be drawn out. Ecology was literally an afterthought to Cox's path-breaking book [*Production, Power, and World Order: Social Forces in the Making of History*],[38] and while Cox has dealt with the issue more directly since then [as in 'Perspective on Globalization'],[39] it is far from central to his argument. For instance, in his report to the United Nations University, Cox did not include environmental issues among the key global developments of the 1990s,[40] though he did suggest that they should receive more attention.[41]

What LaFerrière believes to be the key issue – and one he doesn't find specifically addressed in Cox's work – is 'can and should an ethic be derived from nature and, if so, what should it be?'[42]

Sandra Whitworth's comments typify those of feminist scholars sympathetic to a critical perspective. She argues that International Political Economy (IPE) and critical International Relations scholars have been unable to focus their attention on gender 'because even in its more sophisticated forms there has been an almost exclusive emphasis on production, work, exchange and distribution.' Cox, in particular, is found to consistently stress 'the importance of ideas in his theoretical work, and yet falls back to more straightforward class analyses in his empirical work.'[43] Without explicitly naming names but in a volume devoted to Cox's contributions to the field of international studies, W. Spike Peterson summarizes her (quite similar) views: 'In short, whatever the innovative contributions of these [critical and postmodern] theorists, however dissident, disruptive or deconstructive their inquiries, it is remarkable how they fail to disturb – much less dismantle – andocentric premises.'[44] Steven Bernstein makes a similar argument about Cox's work, but doesn't limit it to the gendered aspects. After praising Cox's 'historicism' for identifying 'agency in social movements as a potential source of counter-hegemony or a basis for alternative hegemonic blocs,' and thus not falling prey to what he sees as the traditional Gramscian argument that 'ultimately rests on an overly blunt explanatory scheme where classes empowered by the current mode of global production ultimately triumph,' Bernstein asserts that Cox's 'applied research still gives primary causal weight to economic variables. It cannot account for ideational or institutional change independent of economic forces without important subsidiary ideational explanations.'[45]

Other criticism of Cox's work, including that by some feminist scholars, comes from a post-modernist perspective, an approach with which Cox is not particularly sympathetic. Jim George, who takes the postmodernist position 'seriously' notes, however, that even from this perspective Cox's sophistication often deflects criticism. George begins by noting that from a postmodernist perspective, 'there *are* some themes in Cox's work that could be interpreted as consistent with a metanarrative reading of historical materialism and the historical development of a repressed critical rationality.' But, interestingly, George doesn't leave it at that. He continues: 'On close reading, however, Cox's *Production, Power and World Order* is a more sophisticated argument than this, with its detailed discussion of the relationship between production, social class, and political power, warranting serious and sustained study before any conclusion is reached regarding Cox's modernist status.'[46] Of course, one of the key problems with Cox's work from a post-modernist perspective is his 'assertions about normative values and progress in history' and his reliance on 'uncritical assumptions about criteria of judgment that collapse critical theory back into Marxist or liberal idealism.'[47]

Some more generalized and often contradictory concerns

Cox's undue pessimism

Scholars from a variety of different schools of international thought have taken issue with what they see as Cox's pessimism about the contemporary world order and the possibilities for transcending it. They explain this in a variety of ways. Some go so far as to explain his lack of faith in contemporary intergovernmental organizations by his own experiences as an administrator at the International Labour Organisation (ILO). Gareau opines that Cox acquired a 'jaundiced view' of international institutions after having spent years at the ILO, just as Gramsci before him concerning the League of Nations. Cox is seen to have overgeneralized about intergovernmental organizations' hegemonic legitimizing roles from the fact that he saw the ILO as being controlled by a hegemonic United States government acting through that institution's bureaucracy.[48] Building on the work of Frederick H. Gareau, Philip Nel and his colleagues argue that multilateral organizations 'at specific junctures in history, try and challenge the hegemonic discourse.'[49] Gareau seeks to support this argument by arguing that, contrary to what Cox alleges:

> third world forces have taken control of the United Nations General Assembly away from the first world, at least temporarily, and used it, for

example, to legitimize the New International Economic Order. Moreover, third world pressure led to the establishment of the United Nations Conference on Trade and Development, which has often acted against the ongoing hegemony. Of course, the Soviets also set up anti-hegemonic institutions, such as the Warsaw Pact and the Council for Mutual Economic Cooperation.

Gareau goes on to make similar arguments about the League of Arab States and the Organization of African Unity, the latter understood to have 'also predictably' 'legitimized the Southern position on the world economy and delegitimized that of the North.'[50] While many of his examples seem quite dated – even UNCTAD has changed its institutional ideology of late – his argument may still be worth pondering, especially as he claims that Gramcsi's and Cox's distorted views on the hegemonic legitimizing roles of intergovernmental organizations is contributing to a 'legacy' that must be revised.

Others simply see the world as evolving in ways Cox had not anticipated when he wrote or they simply see the world differently than does he. For example, after noting Cox's observation that the democratizing elements within an emerging global civil society are not particularly strong or well organized,[51] Tim Shaw and his colleagues argue 'that the highly symbolic *fin-de-siècle* debacle of the "battle for Seattle" suggested that institutions like the WTO [World Trade Organization], let alone the Multilateral Agreement on Investment (MAI) cannot take civil society [including its demands for democratization of global governance] for granted.'[52] Some suggest they now need to heed the calls of people like Ralph Nader and become more democratic and transparent.[53]

Nel and his colleagues focus on the 1995 extension of the Non-Proliferation Treaty (NPT) and the 1997 Land Mines Treaty (i.e. the Convention on the Prohibition of the Use, Stockpiling, Production and Transfer of Anti-Personnel Mines and on their Destruction) to 'demonstrate the continuing value of existing and emerging spheres of multilateralism.'[54] That is, they believe that Cox has prematurely given up on the 'old multilateralism'.[55]

Laura Macdonald moves on to international non-governmental organizations and so-called global civil society. She sees as a 'danger' in Cox's work, his 'tendency to portray global civil society in one-dimensional terms without recognizing the forms of contestation against the transnational capitalist hegemony that already exist.' She sees Amnesty International, Greenpeace and OXFAM as 'prototypes' for future grand transnational coalitions linking together some of the most powerful actors in civil society, including churches, political parties and trade unions (not all part of everyone's understanding of civil society, I might note).[56] She realizes that these prototypes are, as yet, too specialized, small, temporary or poor to challenge the existing hegemonic order. But she urges that the criteria for evaluating success not be too stringent, so that energy will be devoted to thinking of ways to create new linkages.[57] Thus, Macdonald seems to be suggesting that Cox has underestimated the degree to which global civil society and the 'new multilateralism' is already operative, alongside the old multilateralism or perhaps that his pessimistic observations have simply been overtaken by events.

Michael Cox writes from a different political perspective than Macdonald and with a view towards Robert Cox's most recent writings. He sees them as having much in common with others of the 'left', who have real problems coming to terms with the fall of the Soviet Union. He argues that the left has tried to compensate for the fall of the Soviet Union by understating its impact on the essential nature of the international system. In this context, he sees Robert Cox as portraying the evolving world order as pretty much like what it was prior to 1989: 'the rich remain rich, the poor South remains the poor South and the US remains in control.' He continues along this theme by noting that Cox sees the basic structures of the Cold War continuing in the shape of high military spending, the operation of intelligence services and an unequal distribution of power among various states. The cause of this unwillingness to accept the fundamental changes that have occurred in the world order is explained in terms of Robert Cox's lack of 'a coherent vision of what he is for, especially post-USSR': he's seen as a 'well-informed rebel without a political cause,' sensitive and insightful in what he is against, but without a clear vision about what he is for.[58]

Cox's undue optimism

Waltz portrays Cox's intellectual project as not coming to grips with the problems of the day. He argues that while he has 'no quarrel with Cox's concern with counter and latent structures, with historical inquiry, and with speculation about possible futures, however [Richard] Ashley and Cox would transcend the world as it is; meanwhile we have to live in it.' In addition to this generalized rejection of the utopianism of critical theory (as contrasted to problem-solving theory), Waltz expresses a more specific reservation about Cox's speculations about emerging world orders: 'The likelihood of their realization will vary not only with changing production processes and social forces, which he emphasizes, but also with distributions of capability across states, which I emphasize.'[59] A similar view is expressed in Hampson's review of Cox's *New Realism*. Fen Osler Hampson focuses in on one of the potential agents of change to a possible new world order that Cox has written about: an evolving global society or a 'new multilateralism'.[60] Hampson *opines* that some might find the 'bottoms up' approach to multilateralism (i.e. Cox's new multilateralism) 'utopian.'[61]

John J. Mearsheimer isn't very specific about what he finds lacking, or indeed as a superior alternative to the normative aspects of Cox's work. Mearsheimer understands critical theorists as challenging and subverting realism, expecting 'to create a more harmonious and peaceful international system,' one 'in which all states consider war unacceptable practice, and are not likely to change their minds about the matter,' and there do not appear to be any 'troublemaker states.' But, he adds, 'the theory itself says little about either the desirability or feasibility of achieving that particular end.'[62]

A more nuanced and detailed criticism of Cox's optimism/idealism comes from Roger D. Spegele, who sees Cox's 'robust globalism' as failing 'to persuade us that it is a reasonable non-utopian and practical project.' He contends that Cox 'seems far too sanguine about [the] power to change the world by intellectual means alone, and far too willing to give up the very emancipatory goals which have distinguished Marxism from forms of left-wing positivism.' His critique focuses on what he sees as a lack of an account in Cox about how people's awareness of the present social divisions generated in the production process move through stages to practical conditions that are better:

> Identifying economic and social contradictions is of dubious benefit if it does not at the same time create motivational energies to change them. Merely alluding to the possibility of space for counter-hegemonic movements, in the face of the obvious obstacles which common sense suggests stand in the way of their development, does not suffice. On a classical Marxist understanding – not defended here – dialectical theory is inherently radical in so far as it engages in self-criticism as a way of preparing revolutionary agents to bring about revolutionary change. But theory, for Cox, evidently is only about making people 'aware' of what the world is like, providing them with reasons and 'hoping' they will act upon them rather than, for example, transforming their self-understandings so that they *will* act to eradicate their suffering. But in stripping theory of its inherent radicalism in the evident interest of providing a more satisfactory 'scientific' conception on international politics, we lose all purchase on providing a basis for a belief in the movement from a condition of alienation to a condition in which things are radically better; we sacrifice emancipation, and thus call into question the critical/emancipatory goal which Cox offers as the *raison d'être* of his theory.[63]

Specific conceptual critiques

Residual 'state-centrism' or too much of a believer in the 'retreat of the state'?[64]

Martin Shaw, for one, argues that Cox sees civil society in national terms, a perspective that is too limited.[65] William I. Robinson, while acknowledging Cox's path-breaking work on the transformation and internationalization of the state, social forces and his critique of the inadequacy of core-periphery distinctions, still wonders if Cox (and some other neo-Gramscians) might still suffer from state-centrism in some places in their writings.[66] Leslie Sklair, who also praises Cox (and Stephen Gill) for grappling creatively with the issue of state-centrism and the possibility of various forms of globalization, concludes that 'they [Cox and Gill] do not . . . make the extraordinarily difficult decisive break with state-centrism which is necessary if we are to move forward. The concept of transnational practices and its political form, the TCC [transnational capitalist class], is but a first step towards achieving this.'[67]

A similar theme provides the leitmotiv for some of the ecological critiques of Cox's work. Gabriela Kütting, for example, argues that while Cox makes the link

> between unconstrained productive forces and the limited power of regulatory intervention through state actors, highlighting the incompatibility between what he calls production structure and ecological requirements . . . he continues to see the impacts of the state system and sovereignty as the primary issue rather than the effect on the environment or the effect of environmental degradation on global society.

For Kütting, at least, this means that 'Cox's critical approach still operates within the traditional concerns of the international relations (IR) discipline – that is, mostly concerned with actors and their ability to change outcomes or structures in the international or global arena.' This is counterposed against an 'alternative critical approach' that focuses 'not only on the actors in the international system but also on environmental degradation itself. Thus it broadens the IPE discourse on the environment by linking effectiveness to ecological rather than political concerns.' Kütting believes this 'alternative' approach would lead to different questions than posed by Cox's more traditional, actor-focused statist approach. For example, it would ask about the interaction among markets, civil society and equity issues, not limited to an assessment whether one accord succeeded, but focused on what were the sources of change, which may or may not have been totally tied to the accord.[68]

One of Linklater's concerns with Cox's work seems to run in the opposite direction.[69] He raises the 'question' of whether Cox's analysis understates the peripheral role of weak *states* in the international political system. While acknowledging Cox's insights on the peripheral role of dominated classes (domestically and internationally), Linklater's concern is that Cox may be making 'national security politics' of peripheral states too reducible to the 'international politics of class relations.'[70] This follows from Linklater's contention that more attention needs to be paid to the degree to which peripheral states possess autonomy from the internally or externally dominant class.[71] Thus Linklater's concern seems to be that Cox *understates* the residual power of the state in the international system. Laguerre raises a related issue. He is concerned by what he sees as Cox's separation of civil society from political society, seemingly defining them as always playing separate roles. Using the (thus far abortive) construction of democracy in Haiti to exemplify his point, Laguerre argues that the sources of democracy included actions 'imposed' from above by the state as well as from the grassroots and the Diaspora, two important arms of civil society. Thus, from Michel Laguerre's perspective, it is necessary to recognize that sometimes the distinction between civil and political society is blurred and that 'they are equally involved in various forms of transnational relations because their interests are intertwined.'[72]

Further on this point, Burnham contends that Cox's works on globalization may 'underplay the extent to which "globalisation" may be authored by states and regarded by state agents (both liberal market and social democrat) as one of the most efficient means of restructuring labour-capital relations to manage crisis in capitalist society.' This is what some call globalization as a project rather than as a process. Burnham explains this failing in Cox's work – looking at globalization more as a process than as a statist project – as derivative of 'his failure to develop a coherent theory of the state and its relationship to class.'[73]

Reductionism

Most of the authors who accuse Cox of being 'reductionist' do it the same way, i.e. noting that his work is very sophisticated and that he obviously tries to avoid falling into the trap of reductionism. Spegele's critique exemplifies this. First, he cites Cox's introduction to his book, *Production, Power, and World Order*, emphasizing the word 'all' to underscore his point: 'Production creates the material basis for *all* forms of social existence.' Thus, Spegele, who refers to Cox as a 'production Marxist', concludes that production is 'the ontological basis to which everything else is ultimately reducible.' But, Spegele quickly adds: 'To be sure, Cox tries to avoid reductionism by appealing to dialectical or reciprocal relations between "power" and "production."' Spegele continues, however: 'Cox's attempt to avoid reductionism fails to obviate his explicit efforts to reduce social reality to materialistically conceived Leibnizian monads.' The key variable Cox uses to explain change in international relations – patterns of production and modes of production – are both 'anchored in production relations.' Thus, Spegele suggests, 'on this reading, Cox's theory is grounded in metaphysical realism, an already discredited and eminently discardable monistic metaphysics.'[74]

John M. Hobson argues similarly. He contends that even though 'since Gramsci, neo-Marxists have attempted to delink themselves from Karl Marx's *Preface to A Contribution to the Critique Political Economy*, in which he first explicitly outlined the "base-superstructure approach", they can only do so at the level of rhetoric. That is because the "base-superstructure model" is and must be fundamental to, or the "ordering principle" of, any Marxian political economy approach.' This, Hobson believes is 'especially true of Cox's so-called multi-causal approach in which he argues that there are three levels of analysis – production relations, forms of state and world orders –

between which there can be no one-way determinism.' While Hobson suggests that Cox's approach may sound multi-causal (i.e. Weberian), it isn't: 'for each of these three levels of analysis is actually defined *in the first instance* (never mind the 'last') in *pure class* terms. In short, a Gramscian or Coxian approach negates reductionism *only at the rhetorical level . . .*'[75]

E. Fuat Keyman echoes and extends this line of criticism:

> Cox's Gramscian critical theory tends both to be class reductionist in its employment of the concept of hegemony and to involve patriarchal and Eurocentric gestures in its privileging the categories of class over non-class identities. Class reductionism occurs as Cox takes the concept of mode of production, defined in terms of the existing relations of production, as the 'essence' of international relations.[76]

Keyman elaborates:

> The problem occurs in Cox's critical theory, due precisely to his conception of production defined *only* in terms of social classes. When reflected on the concept of hegemony, class dominance and its relation to the state becomes the key to understanding the reproduction of the state/civil society complex. In this way, intersubjectivity is reduced to production. In terms of consent, hegemony becomes inseparable from the notion of 'false consciousness' with regard to the subordinated groups. With regard to the dominant classes, hegemony corresponds to the ideas, values, and consciousness of those classes.[77]

Keyman concludes:

> The reduction of difference to identity (class) prevents Cox's Gramscian international relations theory from fully coming to terms with the significance of the practice of inclusion/exclusion in the way in which hegemony is constructed at the level of intersubjectivity. To be precise, neither Cox nor the Gramscian school in general takes into full account the discourses of masculinity and Eurocentricity with which the regime of modernity operates as a process of othering.[78]

Such exclusionary discourse is seen to pervade contemporary international relations theory, including where the 'third world' is othered. Thus, it's Keyman's position that unless Cox's work can be freed of its class reductionism, it cannot address the production of a counter-hegemonic discourse that is needed to develop counter-hegemonic blocs.[79]

Ronald J. Diebert accuses Cox of 'employing economistic categories of Marxist thought.' Diebert believes that Cox's 'recent rediscovery' of Innis's writings are a hopeful sign that he might adopt a more 'sophisticated materialist approach – one that privileges neither material, technology, nor cultural factors.'[80] It's that sort of approach that Diebert finds, 'apropos at a time when the unintended consequences of modern industrialism are materializing in ozone depletion and global warming, and when earth-circling satellites and webs of fibre-optic cable bind the planet together in a hyper-media environment.'[81]

Misleading or overstated dichotomies?

One of the most frequently recounted of Cox's dichotomies relates to his distinction between 'problem-solving' and 'critical theory'.[82] Most scholars find the distinction illuminating and do not question or seek to qualify it.[83] But others who find it thought-provoking also believe it a bit too sharply delineated.[84] Germain, for example, argues that not simply can both approaches make useful contributions to International Political Economy (and International Relations theory more broadly), but an approach that combines the two might, in some instances, be most illuminating. Although he assumes that Cox does not agree that 'combining the two is desirable or even possible,' Germain seeks to demonstrate such a synthetic approach, one that carefully 'nests' the 'narrow [problem-solving] view into its broader and more historical or sociological cousin' [critical theory].' He does this, for example, in his work on the European Monetary Union.[85]

Burnham is also concerned about this self-same dichotomy, but he argues that the relationship between problem-solving and critical theory has not been adequately addressed or resolved in Cox's work. He connects this with the difficulty of combining Weberian and Marxian methodologies, something that apparently troubles him about Cox's work.[86] The challenges inherent in Cox's reliance on both Marx and Weber are also something featured in Mittelman's writings about Cox's scholarship.[87] Burnham extends this critique. He seems generally bothered by Cox's eclecticism. He argues, seemingly disdainfully, that 'in many respects Cox seems to endorse the view that different methodologies can be selected legitimately to study different chronological periods . . .'[88]

Another widely cited and important contribution of Cox to the study of International Relations relates to his use of Gramsci to better differentiate conceptions of hegemony (ensuring that the term isn't always understood simply as a synonym for power dominance).[89] Aida A. Hozic's innovative research on Siliwood – the hybrid sector that weds Hollywood and Silicon Valley – takes issue with the two conceptions of hegemony that Cox has distinguished, contending that the

> construction and reconstruction of successful hegemonic blocs is neither a simple issue of power nor one of the public/private distinctions *per se*. Rather, hegemony appears to depend, first and foremost, on the ability to draw (or blur) the boundaries themselves, i.e. on the ability to create obscure power lines – cognitive, normative or economic – and to

keep them independent of political structures and visible and well-known instruments and institutions of domination.[90]

Conceptual confusions or substantive disagreement?

As noted before, few contemporary scholars of International Relations are directly quoted as often as is Robert W. Cox. In no small measure that's because of the conciseness of his prose and his ability to turn a phrase. Still, there are those who believe that some of his key concepts are unclear. Andrew Baker falls into this small group. He contends, for example, that 'the internationalization of the state' is 'quite a vague and ill-defined concept as far as identifying the specific role of particular international forces in state transformation. The concept of the "internationalization of the state" suffers from a lack of empirical grounding.' It is ambiguous, imprecise and possibly 'overblown' (i.e. the role of domestic factors and ideas in explaining the transformation of the state may be understated).[91] Martin Shaw also finds the same concept 'internally weak.' Cox is seen by him to devote 'no real attention to the structural changes in state power itself.' That's because the state is seen as adjusting to the exigencies of the world economy of international production, the threat or onslaught of globalization and little else.[92] Shaw argues, as a consequence, that Cox and other critical international theorists have 'abandoned the state to realism – a serious mistake because realists have never had more than a superficial understanding of these problems.'[93]

A few of Cox's critics share Baker's concern with Cox's 'caricature of the state' as a 'transmission belt.' Baker contends that the metaphor 'fails to capture the complex relationship between the state and the so-called globalization process.' The concept seems to mask the bureaucratic complexity of central state agencies, which have proven capable of restructuring themselves 'in terms of objectives and hierarchies . . .' Whilst the global economy may exist outside of and beyond the state, it simultaneously exists beneath it and within it. In sum, Baker concludes, the 'concept of "the internationalization of the state", with its references to transmission belts, does not capture the way in which transnational economic structures cut across and interact with the state in sufficiently explicit fashion.'[94] Jan Aarte Scholte also contends that Cox 'exaggerates insofar as his metaphor [of the transmission belt] could imply that the post-sovereign state has lost all sight of its "internal", territorial constituency.' Rather, Scholte argues, the 'state has often been a site of struggle between territorial and supraterritorial capital.' He supports his contention by suggesting that, especially in the most industrialized parts of the world,

> various states have responded to contemporary globalization with intensified trade protection in respect of certain domestic economic sectors. Likewise in the name of guarding domestic interests, immigration

controls have rarely been as tight as they are at the end of the twentieth century, aided in particular by the new information technologies that have in other respects dissolved borders.[95]

Even Leo Panitch – who praised Cox's *Production, Power and World Order* as challenging the dominant realist approach to International Relations in a way comparable only to the impact of Miliband's *The State in Capitalist Society's* challenge twenty years earlier to the pluralist approach to comparative politics – finds the transmission belt imagery 'perhaps too brittle'. As an alternative to Cox's imagery and related contention, Panitch would

> argue instead that the role of states remains one not only of internalizing but also of mediating adherence to the untrammeled logic of international capitalist competition within its own domain, even if only to ensure that it can effectively meet its commitments to act globally by policing the new world order at the local terrain . . . What needs to be investigated is whether the important shifts in the hierarchy of state apparatuses really are those which bring to the fore those most involved with the international 'caretakers of the global economy', or whether a more general process is at work, determined more from within the state itself, whereby even those agencies without such indirect international links, but which nevertheless directly facilitate capital accumulation and articulate a competitiveness ideology, are the ones that gain status, while those which fostered social welfare and articulated a class harmony orientation lose status.[96]

But Panitch is not done with his critique. He sees Cox's work as containing 'an unresolved antinomy.' On the one hand, there is an image of an increasingly centralized supranational management structure (the *nébuleuse*), founded on ideological consensus among the elites that populate transnational institutions and forums. On the other hand, there is the image of an unregulated system of international finance, owing in part to the inability of states to coordinate their policies. Thus, Panitch contends that it might not be entirely off the mark to portray Cox here as having a certain empiricism, rather than looking for more orthodox and neater patterns of determinations.[97]

Burnham argues that Giddens's account (portrayed as drawing on Althusser) 'carries a sophistication which eludes the neo-Gramscian presentation.' He specifically has in mind Cox's understanding of ideology, which Burnham understands 'as a set of shared notions of the nature of social relations or as collective images of the social order.' Burnham elaborates on the problems he sees with this characterization:

> An analysis of 'beliefs about' how society is constituted obscures a focus on the ideological effects of material practices. The notion of a 'dominant ideology' consisting of shared beliefs legitimating a social order is thoroughly discredited on both empirical and theoretical

grounds . . . In its place is the understanding that in principle some of the most potent forms of ideological mobilization 'do not rest upon shared beliefs (or shared normative commitments); rather they operate in and through the forms in which day to day life is organized.'

He traces the origins of this understanding of the ideological effects of material practices to Marx's observation that capitalist reproduction is achieved largely through the 'dull compulsion of economic relations.'[98] These critiques, in particular, leave one wondering if the goal was to get Cox to clarify this concept or whether the point was simply to argue against them.

Omissions or disagreements over what should be emphasized

One of Cox's closest personal and intellectual friends was the late Susan Strange. They were, of course, both participants in the refounding of the study of modern day International Political Economy. But their scholarship had significant differences; not least of all was the fact that Strange was very much a problem solver and a critical thinker, but not a critical theorist.[99] Like Cox, she wrote that International Political Economy is comprised of dominant structures. 'But where Cox identified production, knowledge and institutional structures, Strange identified four structures: including financial, production, knowledge and security structures. Moreover, she gave primacy, at least until late into her life, to financial structures,' a formulation that separated her from Marxists and Cox.[100] Differences over Cox's seeming omission or insufficient attention to so-called 'security structures' is hardly unique to Strange; others have remarked on it directly.[101] Strange never demanded an explanation in writing nor did she query Cox in any of her writings on what he thought of the primacy she placed on financial structures.

Burnham is more direct about what he sees as missing from Cox's work. He contends that 'labor markets are neglected and viewed as external to the politics of economic adjustment and restructuring.' He explains this as resulting from a tendency to 'fetishize' markets 'as discrete, technical, economic arenas and the overwhelming tendency to view them in terms of trade, finance and the application of new "technology".' While he generally associates this tendency with liberal and realist analyses of International Political Economy, he finds it also in the works of critical theorists like Cox, who, he argues, 'separate social reality into rigid categories and look for external links between artificially disaggregated phenomena.' He contends that ultimately Cox's view tends to 'fail to grasp the complex organic set of social relations which is the global economy.'[102]

In lieu of a conclusion

Given the purpose of this essay, it would seem inappropriate to write a conclusion. The immediate purpose of this essay was to recount, summarize and synthesize some of the key critiques leveled against some of Cox's published work. Obviously, this essay could not hope to be comprehensive nor have critics actually commented, at least in accessible published formats, on all of Cox's writings, some of which appear for the first time in this volume. The longer-range and more important purpose of this essay was to set up a conversation between Cox and some of his critics. Not simply is this essay intended to encourage Cox to reflect on other scholars' readings of his various writings, but it is also intended to encourage others to join in this conversation with Cox.

As this essay evidences, Cox's work has been both praised and critiqued by people from a wide variety of schools of social and political thought. His work has also been read in almost as many ways as it has been categorized. Indeed, some of the critics seem to contradict each other, for example, about whether Cox's work is too state-centric or whether he has accepted wholeheartedly the notion of the 'retreat of the state.' Others seem to complement each other, as in the concern about whether Cox has too little faith in the old multilateralism, be that UN related agencies or old and so-called new social movements. Perhaps the most critical statements are from those who see Cox's work as being reductionist: materialist, classist, economistic. Even that criticism, like that by feminists and ecologists, is almost always accompanied by praise for his sophistication, his courage and his accomplishment in expanding the space for intellectual dialogue, discussion and debate. Hopefully, in its own way, this chapter and especially the one that follows it will be read in this vein.

Notes

1 An important precedent to this essay can be found in Sinclair's discussion of the 'reception and criticism' to Cox's work in Sinclair's chapter in the first collection of Cox's writings. Timothy J. Sinclair, 'Beyond International Relations Theory: Robert W. Cox and Approaches to World Order,' in Robert W. Cox with Timothy J. Sinclair, *Approaches to World Order* (Cambridge: Cambridge University Press, 1996), p. 12–14. See also James H. Mittelman, 'Coxian Historicism as an Alternative Perspective to International Studies,' *Alternatives*, 23, No. 1 (January–March 1998), and Stephen Gill and James H. Mittelman, 'Preface,' in Stephen Gill and James H. Mittelman, eds, *Innovation and Transformation in International Studies* (Cambridge: Cambridge University Press, 1997).

2 For an earlier example of this, see Cox's comments on his thinking about the 'world events of 1968': 'Retrospectively, I can see a gradual but fundamental shift in my thinking. . . .' Robert W. Cox, 'Influences and Commitments,' in Robert W. Cox with Timothy J. Sinclair, *Approaches to World Order* (Cambridge: Cambridge University Press, 1996), p. 26. Interestingly, Haacke seizes upon this as evidence that Cox admits that some of his work is 'normatively suspect.' Jürgen Haacke, 'Theory and Praxis in International Relations: Habermas, Self-Reflection, Rational Argumentation,' *Millennium: Journal of International Studies*, 25 (Summer 1996): 273.

3 This seems particularly surprising given that many of his most important earlier works were collated in a prior collected volume, introduced by an insightful and

highly original essay by Timothy Sinclair that highlighted the evolution of Cox's thought. Moreover, Jim Mittelman has also authored an important, sympathetic overview of Cox's major intellectual contributions and the evolution of his thinking. Sinclair, 'Beyond International Relations Theory.' Mittelman, 'Coxian Historicism.' For an interesting exception, see Eric LaFerrière, 'International Political Economy and the Environment: A Radical Ecological Perspective,' in Dimitris Stevis and Valerie J. Assetto, eds, *The International Political Economy of the Environment: Critical Perspectives, International Political Economy Yearbook* Vol. 12 (Boulder, CO: Lynne Rienner, 2001), p. 213

4 Susan Strange, 'Review of *Production, Power and World Order: Social Forces in the Making of History, International Affairs*,' 64, No. 2 (Spring 1988): 269–70.

5 In this regard, it's interesting to note, Robert Cox and Lloyd Axworthy, 'Correspondence: The Crisis in Kosovo,' *Studies in Political Economy*, 63 (Autumn 2000): 133–52.

6 Such as Peter Burnham and Hazel Smith. See, for example, Burnham's 'The Politics of Economic Management in the 1990s,' *New Political Economy*, 4, No. 1 (March 1999), and Smith's 'The Silence of the Academics: International Social Theory, Historical Materialism and Political Values,' *Review of International Studies*, 22 (April 1996).

7 Burch underscores how impressive this is by noting that most 'Marxians' or 'those similarly affiliated are typically relegated to the margins of the discipline.' Kurt Burch, 'Constituting IPE and Modernity,' in Kurt Burch and Robert A. Denemark, eds, *Constituting International Political Economy*, International Political Economy Yearbook Vol. 10 (Boulder, CO: Lynne Rienner, 1997), p. 40 n.4.

8 Mittelman, 'Coxian Historicism.' p. 89.

9 Martin Griffiths, *Fifty Key Thinkers in International Relations* (New York: Routledge, 1999), p. 118.

10 Robert O. Keohane, 'Realism, Neorealism and the Study of World Politics,' in Robert O. Keohane, ed., *Neorealism and Its Critics* (New York: Columbia University Press, 1986), p. 16.

11 Robert W. Cox, 'Postscript 1985,' in Robert O. Keohane, ed., *Neorealism and Its Critics* (New York: Columbia University Press, 1986), p. 249. Griffiths refers to him as a 'theoretical iconoclast.' *Fifty Key Thinkers*, p. 114.

12 Mittelman'Coxian Historicism.'

13 Brown sees the 'substantive content' of Cox's work as 'disappointingly conventional – an uneasy mix of Leninist theories of imperialism and neo-Marxist dependency theory.' Chris Brown, *International Relations Theory: New Normative Approaches* (New York: Columbia University Press, 1992), p. 202.

14 Martin Shaw, *Theory of the Global State: Globality as an Unfinished Revolution* (Cambridge: Cambridge University Press, 2000), 84–5.

15 John Adams, Review of *Production, Power and World Order, Annals of the American Academy*, 501 (January 1989): 224–5.

16 Especially if one takes into account some of Cox's academic writings published in the early 1970s, most notably *Anatomy of Influence* (New Haven, CT: Yale University Press, 1973). That classic work in the field of International Organization, co-authored with Cox's close friend the late Harold K. Jacobson, is still cited in many works by positivists. Indeed, its 'Framework for Inquiry' is included in the latest edition of positivist Paul F. Diehl's International Organization reader: *The Politics of Global Governance: International Organizations in an Interdependent World*, 2nd edn. (Boulder, CO: Lynne Rienner, 2001).

17 This is the term adopted by Germain and Kenny who include many whose chief acquaintance with Gramsci seems to be through reading Cox's work. Randall D.

Germain and Michael Kenny, 'Engaging Gramsci: International Relations Theory and the New "Gramscians",' *Review of International Studies*, 24 (1998): 3.

18 The 'Italian School' (in quotes in the original) is the term used by Stephen Gill, who credits it to 'an anonymous reviewer.' 'Epistemology, Ontology and the "Italian School,"' in Stephen Gill, ed., *Gramsci, Historical Materialism and International Relations* (Cambridge: Cambridge University Press, 1993), p. 21. Germain and Kenny make explicit that Cox 'does not consider himself to be a member of any "school", Gramscian-inspired or otherwise,' noting that his work has involved prolonged engagement with the thought of Vico, Sorel, Carr, Braudel and Collingwood as well as with Gramsci, 'Engaging Gramsci,' p. 4 n. 3. Cox details some of the key influences on his work in 'Influences and Commitments.'

19 Smith, 'Silence of the Academics': 202 and 202 n.

20 Even though this is the thrust of their argument, they concur with Cox that one needs to go beyond Gramsci to understand key aspects of the contemporary world order. This is obvious to them, for example, in terms of Gramsci's conception of civil society, one that excluded 'some of the central locations and relations of social power within modern societies, including the arena of gender relations, the institution of the family, and the realm of voluntary, non-commercial activities that increasingly characterizes how people experience and participate in social life.' They also see Gramsci's conception of 'resistance' as 'shallow and undertheorized.' 'Engaging Gramsci,' p. 19.

21 'Engaging Gramsci,' p. 18. They believe that a 'welcome corrective' to this view of 'hegemony of largely a one-directional power relationship [where] hegemony is fashioned by this elite transnational class on its own terms and then forced or imposed on subaltern classes has come only in the recently edited volume written in honor of Robert and Jessie Cox.' 'Engaging Gramsci', pp. 18, 18 n. 68, and 20. The volume alluded to is: Stephen Gill and James H. Mittelman, eds, *Innovation and Transformation in International Studies* (Cambridge: Cambridge University Press, 1997) and the relevant discussion appears to be in Fantu Cheru's 'The Silent Revolution and the Weapons of the Weak: Transformation and Innovation from Below,' p. 156 in that volume.

22 Bob Jessop and Ngai-Ling Sum, 'Predisciplinary and Post-Disciplinary Perspectives,' *New Political Economy*, 6 (March 2001): 94–5. Jessop and Sum concede, however, that Cox's more recent work has 'has begun to correct these problems in two ways: first by adopting a more faithful Gramscian analysis and/or taking a Foucauldian cultural turn in dealing with ideational issues; and, second, by providing a more rigorous analysis of the institutional mediations involved in the organization, articulation and embedding of production and political domination.' They specifically single out Cox's incorporation of 'otherness' into his work on civilizations and his discussion of the new world order in terms of the 'new medievalism.' Nevertheless, they conclude, from their own 'paradoxical pre- and post-disciplinary perspective the Coxian school has failed to deliver its full potential.'

23 Haacke, 'Theory and Praxis', pp. 273–4.

24 Because his often-cited epistemological distinction between problem-solving and critical theory appears to draw on Max Horkmeier and Habermas, he is seen by some, like Linklater and Haacke, as working within the Frankfurt School ambit. Linklater sees Cox's discussion of problem-solving approaches as resembling the Frankfurt School's attack on positivism. Andrew Linklater, *Beyond Realism and Marxism: Critical Theory and International Relations* (New York: St. Martin's Press, 1990), p. 28. Haacke, 'Theory and Praxis,' pp. 273–4

25 While not blaming or crediting Cox with setting the 'trend,' Deudney contends that 'the leading contemporary schools of Marxist International Relations theory remain focused on capitalism and do not contain developed treatments of security

issues.' He includes Cox in his references. Daniel Deudney, 'Geopolitics as Theory: Historical Security Materialism,' *European Journal of International Relations*, 6, No. 1 (2000): 87.

26 See, for example, Robert O. Keohane and Joseph S. Nye, *Power and Interdependence*, 3rd edn (New York: Addison-Wesley Educational Publishers, 2001), ch. 9.

27 Glassman makes a related point. After taking note of Cox's insights into the role of IGOs in an imperial state system (i.e. working symbiotically with expansive capital and collaborator governments), Glassman goes on: 'But it is equally important to note, in an era when capital has the appearance of being a power unto itself . . . the imperial system has historically been underwritten by the use of military power.' Jim Glassman, 'State Power Beyond the "Territorial Trap": The Internationalization of the State', *Political Geography*, 18 (August 1999): 684.

28 *Beyond Realism and Marxism*, p. 31.

29 While obviously open to criticism, Smith's division of the 'current situation of international theory' into three theoretical clusters is helpful here in explaining why Mearsheimer's criticism, which seems to focus on works such as those by the social constructivist Emanuel Adler, is not very helpful to us. Smith suggests that 'there is *rationalism*, containing the bulk of neorealist and neoliberal, as well as some Marxist, work . . . *reflectivism*, which broadly consists of the post-positivist approaches of critical theory, postmodernism, and feminist and gender theory,' and *social constructivism*, 'which attempts to bridge the gap between rationalism and reflectivism, basically by adopting a very "thin" version of the epistemology of the latter.' He places Cox in the reflectivist category; he also notes that because Cox ultimately places 'the ideational as secondary to the material' in his work on world order, he is 'more of a historical materialist than a constructivist,' Steve Smith, 'Is the Truth out There? Eight Questions about International Order,' in T. V. Paul and John A. Hall, eds, *International Order and the Future of World Politics* (Cambridge: Cambridge University Press, 1999), pp. 103–4.

30 Young, for example, in alluding to Cox's critique of neo-realism, argues that there is no need to engage in 'stale debates. Surely, we are all interested in exploring the relative weight of material conditions and institutions – not to mention ideas – as determinants of collective outcomes at the international level.' Oran R. Young, 'System and Society in World Affairs: Implications for International Organizations,' *International Social Science Journal*, 144 (June 1995): 200–1. See also Keohane's critique of 'reflective' approaches, where he would obviously categorize Cox. Robert O. Keohane, 'International Institutions: Two Approaches,' *International Studies Quarterly*, 32 (1998): 379–96. Michael Brecher is one of the several positivists who have written to Cox over the years, expressing concerns about Cox's work.

31 'Coxian Historicism,' 74. For a clear view of Cox's position, see Robert W. Cox, 'Realism, Positivism, and Historicism,' in Robert W. Cox with Timothy J. Sinclair, *Approaches to World Order*.

32 Smith, 'Is the Truth out There?,' p. 100.

33 Martin J. Rochester, 'The Rise and Fall of International Organization as a Field of Study,' *International Organization*, 40, No. 4 (Autumn 1986). Friedrich Kratochwil and John Gerard Ruggie, 'International Organization: A State of the Art on an Art of the State,' *International Organization*, 40, No. 4 (Autumn 1986).

34 Robert W. Cox, 'Social Forces, States, and World Orders: Beyond International Relations Theory,' in Robert W. Cox with Timothy J. Sinclair, *Approaches to World Order*, p. 87.

35 J. Ann Tickner, 'You Just Don't Understand: Troubled Engagements Between Feminists and IR Theorists,' *International Studies Quarterly*, 41 (December 1997): 619–20.

36 Smith, 'Is the Truth out There?', 102–3 and 108–9.
37 Eric LaFerrière, 'A Radical Ecological Perspective,' in Dimitris Stevis and Valerie J. Assetto, eds, *The International Political Economy of the Environment: Critical Perspectives*, p. 213. See also Jonathan Hughes, *Ecology and Historical Materialism* (Cambridge: Cambridge University Press, 2000).
38 (New York: Columbia University Press, 1987).
39 In James H. Mittelman, ed., *Globalization: Critical Reflections*, International Political Economy Yearbook Vol. 9 (Boulder, CO: Lynne Rienner, 1996).
40 Robert W. Cox, 'An Alternative Approach to Multilateralism for the Twenty-First Century,' *Global Governance*, 3, No. 1 (January – April 1997): 103–4.
41 Cox, 'An Alternative Approach,' pp. 109–10. LaFerrière also notes that Mittelman ignores the issues in discussing Cox's scholarly contribution, although he concedes that both Cox and Mittelman discuss ecology (or environmentalism) as an element of globalization or as agents of resistance to globalization. 'International Political Economy,' p. 213.
42 Eric LaFerrière, 'Emancipating International Relations Theory: An Ecological Perspective,' *Millennium: Journal of International Studies*, 25, No. 1 (Spring 1996): 55.
43 Sandra Whitworth, *Feminism and International Relations: Towards a Political Economy of Gender in Interstate and Non-Governmental Institutions* (New York: St. Martin's Press, 1994), pp. 54–5.
44 W. Spike Peterson, 'Whose Crisis? Early and Post-Modern Masculinism,' in Stephen Gill and James H. Mittelman, eds, *Innovation and Transformation in International Studies*, p. 186.
45 Bernstein calls for a 'socio-evolutionary explanation' instead, one which 'attempts to retain some of Cox's epistemological insights without being limited by Gramscian foundations.' Steven Bernstein, 'Ideas, Social Structure and the Compromise of Liberal Environmentalism,' *European Journal of International Relations*, 6, No. 4 (2000): 504 n. 22.
46 Jim George, *Discourses of Global Politics: A Critical (Re)Introduction to International Relations* (Boulder, CO: Lynne Rienner Publishers, 1994), p. 182.
47 Kimberly Hutchings, 'The Nature of Critique in Critical International Relations Theory,' in Richard Wyn Jones, ed., *Critical Theory and World Politics* (Boulder, CO: Lynne Rienner Publishers, 2001), pp. 83 and 85.
48 Frederick H. Gareau, 'International Institutions and the Gramscian Legacy: Its Modification, Expansion, and Reaffirmation,' *The Social Science Journal*, 33, No. 2 (1996): 224 and 226. For Cox's views, see, for example, Robert W. Cox, 'Labor and Hegemony,' in Robert W. Cox with Timothy J. Sinclair, *Approaches to World Order*, 'Labor and Hegemony: A Reply,' in Robert W. Cox with Timothy J. Sinclair *Approaches to World Order*, and Robert W. Cox, 'Multilateralism and World Order,' in Robert W. Cox with Timothy J. Sinclair, *Approaches to World Order*.
49 Philip Nel, Ian Taylor and Janis van de Weshuizen, 'Multilateralism in South Africa's Foreign Policy: The Search for a Critical Rationale,' *Global Governance: A Review of Multilateralism and International Organizations*, 6 (January – March 2000): 44.
50 Gareau, 'International Institutions:' 227.
51 See, for example, Robert W. Cox, 'Introduction', in Robert W. Cox, ed., *The New Realism: Perspectives on Multilateralism and World Order* (London: Macmillan Press Ltd for the United Nations University Press, 1997).
52 Timothy M. Shaw, Sandra J. MacLean and Maria Nzomo, 'Going beyond States and Markets to Civil Societies?,' in Thomas C. Lawton, James N. Rosenau and Amy Verdun, eds, *Strange Power: Shaping the Parameters of International Relations and International Political Economy* (Burlington, VT: Ashgate, 2000), 394.

53 An alternative foreshadowed by Cox himself, it should be added. 'Introduction,' *The New Realism*, p. xviii.

54 Nel, Taylor, and van de Weshuizen, 'Multilateralism': 56. Martin Shaw also argues that Cox has underestimated the role of increasingly responsive to civil society IGOs as agents of global transformation, for example, to a more democratic world. *Theory of the Global State*, pp. 263–5.

55 One place where Cox explains his position is, Robert W. Cox, 'Reconsiderations,' in Robert W. Cox, ed., *The New Realism*, pp. 253ff.

56 See, for example, Louis D. Hunt, 'Civil Society and the Idea of a Commercial Republic,' in Michael G. Schechter, ed., *The Revival of Civil Society: Global and Comparative Perspectives* (London: Macmillan Press, Ltd., 1999).

57 Laura Macdonald, 'Mobilising Civil Society: Interpreting International NGOs in Central America,' *Millennium: Journal of International Studies*, 23 (Summer 1994): 276–7.

58 Michael Cox, 'Radical Theory and International Disorder after the Cold War,' in Birthe Hansen and Bertel Heurlin, eds, *The New World Order: Contrasting Theories* (New York: St. Martin's Press, 2000), pp. 202–3 and 213. For Cox's own discussion of the continuities in the post-cold war era see, for example, 'Reconsiderations,' *The New Realism*, pp. 249–59.

59 Kenneth N. Waltz 'A Response to My Critics,' in Robert O. Keohane, ed., *Neorealism and Its Critics*, p. 338.

60 See, for example, Cox, 'Introduction', in *The New Realism*, p. xix.

61 Fen Osler Hampson review in *International Journal*, 52, No. 4 (Autumn 1997): 735.

62 Whereas he frequently cites Cox's work, most of this criticism of idealism seems directed at social constructivist scholars like Adler. John J. Mearsheimer, 'The False Promise of International Institutions,' *International Security*, 19, No. 3 (Winter 1994/5): 38–-41.

63 Roger D. Spegele, 'Is Robust Globalism a Mistake?,' *Review of International Studies*, 23 (1997): 224.

64 The phrase 'retreat of the state' was popularized by Susan Strange. *The Retreat of the State: The Diffusion of Power in the World Economy* (Cambridge: Cambridge University Press, 1996).

65 Martin Shaw, *Theory of the Global State*, pp. 263–5.

66 William I. Robinson, 'Beyond Nation-State Paradigms: Globalization, Sociology, and the Challenge of Transnational Studies,' *Sociological Forum*, 13, No. 4 (December 1998): 587.

67 Sklair doesn't claim to have achieved this breakthrough either, but is working toward it. Leslie Sklair, 'Social Movements for Global Capitalism: The Transnational Capitalist Class in Action,' *Review of International Political Economy*, 4, No. 3 (1997): 521 and n. 8.

68 Gabriela Kütting, 'A Critical Approach to Institutional and Environmental Effectiveness: Lessons from the Convention on Long-Range Transboundary Pollution,' in Dimitris Stevis and Valerie J. Assetto, eds, *The International Political Economy of the Environment*, p.182.

69 Burnham also contends that 'it is a fallacy . . . to suppose that the importance of the nation state in the world order has diminished with the rapid international-ization of capital. The starting point for a productive analysis of the international order is thus the recognition of the durability of the nation state . . . ,' something he doesn't see in neo-Gramscian approaches to world order that seek 'to replace state center frameworks with a study of class forces and their operation in national/international contexts.' 'Neo-Gramscian Hegemony and the International Order,' *Capital and Class*, 45 (Fall 1991): 86–7. See also his 'Politics of Economic Management,' especially n. 16.

70 A contrast between Cox and Ayoob on this point might shed some light on Linklater's contention. See, for example, Mohammed Ayoob, *The Third World Security Predicament: State Making, Regional Conflict, and the International System* (Boulder, CO: Lynne Rienner Publishers, 1995).

71 Linklater, *Beyond Realism and Marxism*, pp. 31 and 116.

72 Michel Laguerre, 'State, Diaspora, and Transnational Politics: Haiti Reconceptualised,' *Millennium: Journal of International Studies*, 28, No. 3 (1999): 645–6.

73 Burnham, 'Politics of Economic Management,' 39.

74 Spegele, 'Is Robust Globalism': 221.

75 John M. Hobson, 'For a "Second-Wave" Weberian Historical Sociology in International Relations: A Reply to Halperin and Shaw,' *Review of International Studies*, 5, No. 2 (Summer 1998): 357. See also, John M. Hobson, 'The Historical Sociology of the State and the State of Historical Sociology in International Relations,' *Review of International Political Economy*, 5, No. 2 (Summer 1998): 297. There, he calls upon Cox 'to shed his Marxist skin and embrace a Weberian approach in order to realize fully his otherwise laudable objectives.'

76 E. Fuat Keyman, *Globalization, State, Identity/Difference: Toward a Critical Social Theory of International Relations* (Atlantic Highlands, NJ: Humanities Press, 1997), p. 119.

77 Ibid., p. 120.

78 Ibid., pp. 121–2.

79 Ibid., p. 122.

80 See, for example, Robert W. Cox, 'Thinking about Civilizations', *Review of International Studies*, 26, No. 5 (December 2000): 10 n.

81 Ronald J. Deibert, 'Harold Innis and the Empire of Speed,' *Review of International Studies*, 25, No. 2 (April 1999): 289.

82 Robert W. Cox 'Social Forces,' pp. 88–91.

83 See, for example, Kenneth N. Waltz, 'A Response to My Critics,' in Robert O. Keohane, ed., *Neorealism and Its Critics*, p. 338.

84 See, for example, Keyman, *Globalization*, pp. 114–15.

85 Randall D. Germain, 'In Search of Political Economy: Understanding European Monetary Union,' *Review of International Political Economy*, 6, No. 3 (Autumn 1999): 391 and 397 n. 2. See also, Michael G. Schechter, '*Our Global Neighborhood*: Pushing Problem-Solving to Its Limits and the Limits of Problem-Solving Theory', in Martin Hewson and Timothy J. Sinclair, eds, *Approaches to Global Governance Theory* (Albany: State University of New York Press, 1999).

86 Burnham, 'Politics of Economic Management,' 39.

87 See, for example, James H. Mittelman, 'Rethinking Innovation in International Studies: Global Transformation at the Turn of the Millennium', in Stephen Gill and James H. Mittelman, eds, *Innovation and Transformation in International Studies*.

88 Burnham, 'Politics of Economic Management', 39.

89 Robert W. Cox, 'Gramsci, Hegemony, and International Relations: An Essay in Method,' in Robert W. Cox with Timothy J. Sinclair, *Approaches to World Order*.

90 'The insertion of Hollywood into discussions of hegemony . . . [also] clearly shifts debates about US economic and military power onto debates about culture, play and entertainment. . . .' Aida A. Hozik, 'Uncle Sam Goes to Siliwood: Of Landscapes, Spielberg and Hegemony,' *Review of International Political Economy*, 6, No. 3 (Autumn 1999): 289 and 299–300.

91 Baker is also troubled by Cox's notion of '*nébuleuse*'. He contends that little empirical research has been done to address the niche roles of various branches of *nébuleuse*, their relationships with the state, the social basis of this, and how the so-called "Washington consensus" is continuously being adjusted, modified, and fortified.' Andrew Baker, '*Nébuleuse* and the "Internationalization of the State" in the UK? The Case of HM Treasury and the Bank of England,' *Review of International Political Economy*, 6, No. 1 (Spring 1999): 80 and 96.

92 Shaw notes that Cox recognized the EEC as a major instance of internationalization of the state, but 'this too was defined in purely economic terms.' Martin Shaw, *Theory of the Global State*, pp. 84–5 and 263–5. Michalak and Gibb also contend that Cox's work on globalization seems to emphasize the decline of the state and underemphasize the rise of continental integration into trading blocs, portrayed as not simply an economic phenomenon and, at least, potentially one that will strengthen statist actors relative to social forces. Wieslaw Michalak and Richard Gibb, 'Trading Blocs and Multilateralism in the World Economy,' *Annals of the Association of American Geographers*, 87, No. 2 (1997): 264.

93 Martin Shaw, *Theory of the Global State*, p. 265 n.

94 Baker, '*Nébuleuse*': 80 and 96.

95 Jan Aart Scholte, 'Globalisation and Governance,' in Patrick J. Hanafin and Melissa S. Williams, eds, *Identity, Rights and Constitutional Transformation* (Broofield, VT: Ashgate, 1999), pp. 140–1.

96 Leo Panitch, 'Globalisation and the State,' in Ralph Miliband and Leo Panitch, eds, *The Socialist Register – 1994* (London: The Merlin Press Ltd, 1994), pp. 68 and 73.

97 Ibid, p. 73.

98 Burnham, 'Neo-Gramscian Hegemony,' pp. 84–5.

99 A. Claire Cutler, 'Theorizing the "No-Man's-Land" between Politics and Economics,' in Thomas C. Lawton, James N. Rosenau and Amy C. Verdun, eds, *Strange Power*, p. 170.

100 Ibid., 167-168.

101 See discussion above on page 4 and the related notes (n 25–8).

102 Burnham, as quoted in Cutler, 'Theorizing,' 169.

2 Reflections and transitions

Theorizing is a continuing process in which there are no final fixed positions. Theory follows history – as Hegel wrote: 'The owl of Minerva spreads its wings only with the falling of the dusk.'[1] Theory evolves through controversy among distinct views of 'reality', each a particular perspective in time and space. Two principal factors shape theory. One is the objective movement of history which is continually throwing up new combinations of forces that interact with one another. The other is the subjective perceptions of those who contemplate these forces with a view to understanding and acting upon the movement of history.

The previous chapter has analysed criticisms of my earlier writing. There have been important changes in the world since my writing of the 1960s, 1970s, 1980s and early 1990s. My own perceptions of 'reality' have changed, in some respects concerning matters pointed out by my critics. I put quotation marks around 'reality' to indicate that there is always a subjective element in a dialectical relationship between the analyst and the object of analysis. History shapes the consciousness and perceptions of the analyst; and the analyst's mind shapes its mode of apprehending the movement of history.

Thus, my critics may perceive a different 'reality' from the one I have written about. We all look at the same objective movement of history but we apprehend it in different perspectives. To understand each critique fully it would be necessary to enter into each critic's perspective. I shall not attempt to do that here so as to respond to critics one by one. I shall try rather to address a number of the specific points of criticism with a view either to clarifying what I meant to say or to indicate how my perceptions have changed and are changing. I shall not stand in judgement over the different perspectives on reality some of my critics may have.

On labelling

In this kind of exercise, one is usually reduced to dealing with schools of thought as a shorthand for perspectives. My critics try to classify my work as being in certain currents of thought, and as Michael Schechter pointed out in Chapter 1, they often have difficulty in doing so, certainly in agreeing about it. For my part, I have difficulty seeing myself in identities they have conferred upon me, although I can usually understand why they have placed me where they do. I try to see from which bodies of theory or opinions my critics look upon my work. In this concern for intellectual identities, there is a serious risk of Eurocentrism (I include America within this range of mentalities). Most of the criticism discussed here comes from currents of theory of European and American origin; so the debate risks becoming confined to this milieu, a milieu which encourages a strong tendency to think of itself as universal.

I was thus struck a short while ago in meeting a Japanese scholar who perceived an affinity of my work with that of Nishida Kitaro, a Japanese Buddhist philosopher of the 1930s whose work took the form of a dialogue with Western philosophy.[2] Nishida saw the world in terms of peoples and individuals reflecting the world they experienced through the individuality of their own cultures. This Japanese scholar's perception of my work's affinity to that of the Buddhist philosopher is at least as legitimate as the perception by some of my critics of its affinity to Marxism, even though these perceptions seem to be totally contradictory.

To what extent am I a Marxist? I think most of those who pride themselves on having a deep knowledge and commitment to Marxism as a philosophy and methodology would not regard me as a proper Marxist; and this is clearly shown by some of the comments reported in Chapter 1. On the other hand, some who have no Marxist pretensions or who harbour perhaps an antipathy to Marxism do label me as Marxist, even Marxist-Leninist.[3]

Marxism is a very ambiguous label. There is a sense in which it means a commitment to political action and to a vision of world history unfolding into the future. There is another sense in which it signifies a method of social analysis; and the latter meaning bifurcates into either a rigorous ontology reflecting fundamental 'truth' or the more flexible form of heuristic hypotheses for enquiry. In the latter form, it is almost possible to say that we are all Marxists now, given the demonstrated usefulness of many Marxist (or perhaps better, Marxian) models for understanding social processes. For my part, I would shun the Althusserian notion that there is fundamental truth in Marxism[4] and would rather favour Fernand Braudel's notion that Marx has provided some historical hypotheses which may prove to be useful for understanding some historical problems but are not so useful for others – Braudel's metaphor was that of a ship that sails well in some waters but founders in others.[5] A proper Marxist would probably regard this attitude as empiricism.

I have used the term 'historical materialism' which some equate with Marxism or, if they are Marxists themselves, consider Marxism to be the only valid version of it. Georges Sorel, a heterodox Marxist, asked what historical conditions were conducive to the adoption of certain collective sentiments, certain eschatological visions, certain myths, by certain groups of people (Sorel, 1971). Max Weber, whose work seems to be anathema to most self-proclaimed Marxists, enquired in his sociology of religion into how certain forms of religious belief corresponded to the material conditions of existence of the groups that espoused them. Gramsci in his thinking about ideology, culture and social class clearly distinguished his own historical materialism from historical economism (or what we might call 'vulgar Marxism', the economic determinism of ideas). There are obviously varieties of historical materialism most of which do not imply that ideas are determined by economic relations, but rather that there is a relationship between ideas and material circumstances that is to be investigated.

A good part of the quarrel between Marxists and Weberians has to do with the distinction between the synchronic and the diachronic. Looking at the synchronic dimension (space rather than time) can lead to seeing the world or society as a system of interrelated parts with a tendency to equilibrium. Looking at the diachronic dimension (time rather than space) leads naturally to enquiry into the ruptures and conflicts that bring about system transformation. One might say that Weber is a good guide to the former – the technique of expressing the complexity of existence in the form of ideal types – and Marx a better guide to the latter by offering patterned explanations for social, economic and political transformation. But ultimately, time and space are not separate and opposed categories; they are aspects of the same thing and both techniques of analysis are necessary for understanding social life. Jean Piaget argued, convincingly for me, the need to link the two modes of explanation, the diachronic and the synchronic, the genetic and the functional, in order to arrive at a fully satisfactory explanation (Piaget, 1965).

I have no pretensions to the title of Marxist, though I admire many scholars who legitimately have that title. I think it takes a long time to become a Marxist and I have not devoted enough time to it. That is partly because I have found many other sources of inspiration along the way. In terms of theory, the first was R. J. Collingwood. Collingwood pointed me in the direction of Vico. I would not object to the statement that Vico provides the foundation of my theoretic thinking as it has emerged, with the qualification that it took me quite a long time before I came to appreciate his work and this appreciation is superimposed upon other approaches to theory I had already absorbed.

Vico was concerned with social transformation and he saw class struggle as the driving force. He also examined social change through the transformation of mentalities; and he pictured historical change in terms of a sequence of synchronic slices (of course he did not use the word 'synchronic') in which law, social custom, family relations, economic practice and religion formed interrelated patterns. In other words, he combined the diachronic and the synchronic, the genetic and the functional long before those terms appeared.

The second major inspiration was Georges Sorel. Sorel rejected any metatheory of history of the Hegelian or Marxist kind, any view that the historical outcome was in some way predetermined. But he was very concerned about historical change, and how it came about. From Marx and from Vico and from his own field experience as an engineer of the *ponts et chaussés*, he saw class struggle as the key to understanding social change and to acting for it. His focus was on how people came to understand antagonistic social relationships in which they were involved and how they could be stimulated to act, to pursue a 'march towards deliverance'. His reflections on social myths looked into the imaginations of primitive Christians and of his contemporary proletarians; but the social myth was a feature of many other historical and contemporary groups. The content of the myth is less important than its mobilizing power for sharpening the lines of conflict and stimulating action for change.

Gramsci, whom I came to read much later, elaborated the analysis of class and class conflict and of the mental imagery that gives social groups self-awareness and an understanding of where they stand in society and how they must act for their emancipation. He built upon Vico, Marx, and Sorel without swallowing holus-bolus a total system derived from any of them.

Along the way, I have drawn upon the works of others. One was Karl Polanyi, his notion of the social embedding of the economy and of society's reaction to the attempt to dis-embed the economy and to make society subject to its dictates. Polanyi's theory leans perhaps too far in the functionalist, synchronic direction and lacks a full appreciation of the role of conflict in change; but it gives a useful model for tracing the *potential* for conflict and change. Another was Fernand Braudel from whom I derived the method of historical structures. Both Polanyi and Braudel wrote in a world intellectual milieu influenced by Marx, but both demarcate their work from his.

Many of my critics have put a Gramscian, or more commonly 'neo-Gramscian', identity upon me; and some have chided me for offering an incorrect interpretation of Gramsci. To that, I would say that there can be different readings of Gramsci as of any major thinker, readings conditioned by the perspective and preoccupations of the reader. The pertinent question is not: Did I correctly understand Gramsci? Rather, it is: Do the inferences which I have drawn (perhaps incorrectly, but I am not ready to admit that) from Gramsci help towards understanding the historical phenomenon that is the object of my enquiry? The concern should be with the adequacy of Cox's understanding of the world rather than with the adequacy of his understanding of Gramsci.

There is little to be gained by pursuing the issue of fixing a label on my intellectual identity. I do not shy away from the word 'eclectic'. The problem facing anyone who seeks to define the 'problematic' of the contemporary world is to draw upon and in so far as possible integrate modes of understanding from different sources so as to yield a result that both explains adequately and orients action. That is the only valid test, not whether you follow correctly some pre-established model. It is more useful to leave intellectual identities aside and address the question of what are the important things to focus upon.

Key concepts

Class

I have been criticised for focusing in my previous work too exclusively upon class and for being 'reductionist' about production. There is merit in both criticisms but perhaps they are overstated and should be put in context. My book *Production, Power and World Order: Social Forces in the Making of History* (Columbia University Press, 1987) grew out of a study of labour relations. As it developed in my mind and with the benefit of critical comment by others, labour relations became less an object of enquiry in itself and more an angle of vision upon society and the world as a whole. This was not an attempt to *reduce* the whole of social affairs and historical change to labour relations and the production process, but to use that point of departure, that perspective, for the exploration of the wider world. Of course, the point of departure conditions what you see, and it is quite legitimate to point out that I missed some things that were important at that time, and which I, in retrospect, recognise to have been neglected. Furthermore, the intervening fifteen years have brought about changes in the world that have given me a somewhat different view of the things it is important to focus upon, an adjusted ontology, something I address in Chapter 5.

Class is, however, a historical constant. Marx did not invent class analysis. Vico before him, as mentioned, saw class struggle as the dynamic of history. Disraeli was aware of its impact in nineteenth-century Britain. Class analysis is not *per se* Marxism, although perhaps Marxists are most comfortable with it and do it best.

Marx analysed class in the context of nineteenth-century Britain, and by extension to the capitalist world of that time. His particular time-and-space-conditioned analysis (one might say because of its very elegance and rhetorical persuasiveness) has become frozen in the thinking of some of his successors, when they might better have re-examined the meanings of class in different spatial and subsequent temporal conditions. The essence of class is social dominance and subordination. It can be expressed and experienced in the forms of gender, race, caste, status group and other identities, all of which converge into the relations of the production process, although they have many other manifestations as well. Feminist and post-colonial scholars, in particular, have found my earlier work insufficiently attentive to their concerns and have gone far to make up for the deficit.

Within capitalism the class relationship has many variations. Marx's historical writings showed this more, perhaps, than his economic analysis in *Capital*. Since Marx, the meaning of class within capitalism has evolved and it is important to keep pace with changes in production relations to understand the changing lines of conflict. André Gorz (1982) writes of Marx's proletarians that they have become integrated into capitalism, no longer capitalism's nemesis – part of the problem more than its solution. When

Jimmy Hoffa Jr. says North American workers are (or should be) primarily concerned with protecting their jobs from being shifted into the Third World, he reveals a line of conflict among workers *within* capitalism. The question of class begs fundamental rethinking.

Production

In the opening sentence of my 1987 book, I wrote: 'Production creates the material basis for all forms of social existence, and the ways in which human efforts are combined in production processes affect all other aspects of social life, including the polity.' In itself, the first part of the sentence is trite. Everything has to have a material basis in order to exist really, i.e. other than in thought. Even thoughts, however, which have no material existence for the immediate thinker, originate from experiences of the individual, the community, or of the distant reaches of early humanity (e.g. Vico's myths and Jung's archetypes) which were *produced* in certain material conditions. 'Production' refers to a process rather than to a set of existing things, i.e. products. It refers to the diachronic rather than the synchronic dimension of reality. What began for me as a study of existing organization for the production of goods and services became conceptually expanded to include the production of institutions, law, morality and ideas.

Of course, the set of existing things – the synchronic distribution of forces – is the condition in which the production process takes place. What has been produced conditions what is being produced. The distribution and redistribution of things produced – of wealth and skills and ideas and of the material means of coercion in their concrete embodiments – is in itself a production. The moving of material productive resources and labour to create new environments for production is itself production. So is the creation of the mental climate, the habits and attitudes, in which material production takes place.

The distribution of existing things can be inventoried as something observed from outside. The production process is more mysterious; it can only properly be understood from inside by a historical mode of enquiry.[6] This distinction can be applied to the sphere of military, economic and administrative capabilities. These are all part of the set of existing things and, of course, they condition what can be done and what is done. Production put them there; and they define the power relationships in which further production will take place.

There is an analogy in a bifurcation that has taken place in historiography. Historians have traditionally studied the power holders – the courts and chancelleries and those who challenge them. During the twentieth century a different tack was taken by a group of historians – the *Annales* school in France were exemplars – who focused attention on the basic structures of society, demography, food, housing, the daily activity of people, *les gestes répétés* in Braudel's words. They conceived the movement of history as taking place at different levels. On the surface is *l'histoire événementielle*, events history, that which is recorded in the newspaper. Below that, and conditioning events, is 'conjunctural' history, influences that, operating in the medium term, create the milieu in which action takes place, such as an economic cycle, a pattern of social organization, a scientific paradigm, or a prevailing ideology. These two levels rest upon and are in turn conditioned by the *longue durée*, i.e. those enduring (but not eternal) structures that are taken to be the natural order of things such as the state system, capitalism, social hierarchies and language. The three levels interact. Events have to be explained in the context of conjunctures, and both ultimately have to be related to the *longue durée*. Events can be viewed in the synchronic dimension. Conjunctures and the *longue durée* have to be understood in the diachronic dimension.

The state

There is confusion among my critics as to the role of the state in my work. Some see my writing as too state-centric, others as insufficiently aware of the central importance of the state, yet others as lacking a full appreciation of 'structural changes in state power'. I am shy of discussing '*the* state' and of offering 'a coherent theory of the state and its relationship to class'. '*The* state' may be seen as a Eurocentric concept – a vestige of the Western imperialism that spread a certain concept of political authority around the world. I prefer to adopt a historical approach, to consider the development of varieties of political authority arising in different times and places in the context of the variety of influences – economic, social, cultural, internal and external – that shape political authorities. I have used in preference to 'state' the more cumbersome term 'state/society complex', that is to say the institutions of authoritative rule in relation to the balance of social forces that can sustain or undermine them. In this perspective, there are different forms of political authority, or, to revert to the term of common currency, different forms of state; and these different forms have different degrees of autonomy in relation to their external environment – the inter-state system and the world economy – and different degrees of control in relation to their society.

The inter-state system embraces at any one time the range of political authorities accorded the status of states. Two useful fictions are purported to lie at the basis of this system: the sovereign equality of states and the concept of anarchy as postulating the nature of relationships among them. These notions facilitate the management of conflict and cooperation among the units and the creation and functioning of international organizations. They obscure the perception that the actual relationships among the constituent units are hierarchical or clusters of hierarchically arranged units.

The broad context in which states are shaped includes, below the state, the society which may sustain it; and, above or beyond the state, the external environment that influences its form and behaviour. It is more complicated than that. External influences penetrate states not only directly, but also through the domestic society; and forces within domestic societies participate along with states in shaping the external political and economic environment.

In describing the 'internationalizing of the state', I have referred to the unofficial and official transnational and international networks of state and corporate representatives and intellectuals who work towards the formulation of a policy consensus for global capitalism as a *nébuleuse* – something that has no fixed and authoritative institutional structure, but which has emerged out of discussions in bodies like the Trilateral Commission, the World Economic Forum meetings in Davos, the regular meetings of central bankers, of the OECD, IMF, World Bank and WTO, and the G7 and G8 summit conferences and their preparatory meetings.

Management of global capitalism is a multilevel process, determined at the national level by the balance of social forces within states, at the transnational level by an evolving ideology (neo-liberalism) produced by business schools, journalists and other intellectuals, at the international level by those institutions that develop officially endorsed policy guidelines, and again at the national level by the translating of these guidelines into concrete measures of national fiscal and monetary policy. Much more empirical work is needed to give a fuller picture of the complexity of the policy process of global capitalism.[7]

I have been justly criticized for using the metaphor of a 'transmission belt' to describe the impact of economic globalization upon states. This metaphor has lent itself to giving the false impression of a totally external force impacting upon states from without and perhaps of an all-powerful centralized directorate of global capitalism. It may obscure the role of the balance of social forces within the state and of the potential for resistance to globalization from hostile social forces. I hereby withdraw this misleading metaphor.

The *nébuleuse* is challenged by other social forces that arise within domestic societies and increasingly coordinate their resistance to globalization and which elaborate alternative visions of what the future might look like. If the *nébuleuse* expresses the consensus of forces promoting global capitalism, something like a counter-*nébuleuse* is emerging in opposition. The balance between these two sets of forces is determined by struggle within society from local to global levels.

I would not want to create the impression that the *nébuleuse* is a steadily and progressively centralizing force. The very looseness that the term implies contains the prospect of inconclusiveness and discord. What it does imply is a commitment to continue dialogue towards the solution of problems encountered in the common interest of capitalism as an institutionalized process. There is no 'antinomy' between the fragility of international finance and a possibly more robust trading system. This is a problem internal to capitalism in which different fragments of capitalism have difficulty in reaching agreement, but which they continue to address together through the *nébuleuse*.

The development of the *nébuleuse* does not mean that the organization of global capitalism has passed out of the hands of states over to a new supra-state global mechanism, a central committee of global capitalism that directs state policies. It means that the dominant forces at work at different levels – local as well as global – concur in giving priority to competitiveness in the global economy and in precluding interventions by whatever authority that are not consistent with this aim.

Military and police power

It has been objected with some justification that I have not given due weight to the military factor in world power relations.[8] Any underestimate of the importance of military power would be particularly distorting with regard to the last decade of the twentieth and first decade of the twenty-first centuries when military actions have been in the forefront of world events. The salience of the military in this period should be seen in the context of the changing balance between military and economic forms of power during the last half-century.

During the post-war decades and the Cold War period, the United States aided in the economic recovery of western Europe and Japan as counter-weights to Soviet military and ideological power. As the European and Japanese economies grew in relation to the US economy and US productivity, they remained dependent upon US military protection. At a certain point in the 1970s, economic support by Europe and Japan for the United States (by financing a growing US payments deficit) became a quid pro quo for maintaining this protection. The Vietnam War was a turning point as the war was financed by the US payments deficit because other countries were willing to hold unlimited amounts of US dollars. When General de Gaulle signalled that France was no longer prepared to assist the United States in this way to conduct a war which he disapproved of, the consequence was severance of the dollar's link to gold and the shift of the international financial system to flexible exchange rates. But Germany and Japan continued to support the US payments deficit in return for US military presence.

In the 1980s, the inability of the Soviet economy to keep pace with the United States in the arms build-up during the Reagan era, along with its inability to shift from extensive to intensive growth, was a principal cause of the collapse of the Soviet Union. This left the United States in an uncontested position of military supremacy. The greater depth of the US economy gave the United States the military and political advantage; but at the same time the United States had become more dependent on European and Japanese economic cooperation.

Thenceforth, US military power served as the bulwark for enforcement of an American concept of world order which was shared in varying degrees by other governments, particularly members of NATO. This was a neo-liberal global economic order into which Europe and Japan were becoming increasingly integrated and which was potentially extending to the rest of the world. The post-Cold War conflicts (war in the Gulf, in the Balkans and in Afghanistan) have had the common feature of suppressing threatened disturbances to this vision of global order. US military power assumed leadership in NATO-centred coalitions to re-establish order. The fact of US predominance in military power enabled the United States to require economic as well as military and political support from allied powers. The relative decline of US economic power compared to its position in the post-war era, along with the supremacy of US military power, converted the aid relationship of the early post-war years into a tributary relationship. The US administration commanded decisions about the use of military power to which allies contributed economically and sometimes militarily.

This system had its stresses and strains. In both western Europe and Japan there were concerns about military dependency on the United States. The possibility of an independent European military capability not controlled by a US-dominated NATO alliance aroused concern in Washington. So did the aspirations on the part of some Japanese to become more independent of the United States in foreign policy – aspirations by Japanese pacifists who resisted Japanese involvement in US-led military ventures, and by Japanese nationalists who aimed to create a national military capability comparable to Japan's economic status in the world. Other US allies would also be apprehensive lest a US administration overreach coalition consensus by extending military interventions, for instance into Iraq in the guise of the US war against terrorism, and by risking political and strategic destabilization in the Middle East and Central Asia.

The war against terrorism has brought with it the spectre of a new police power reinforcing military power. Preventive arrest and detention together with extensive powers of surveillance generate the image of an emerging panopticon state and society.[9] Police have been using violent methods and pre-emptive strikes against protesters in mass demonstrations. The manipulation of consent through the casting of military and police action as the pursuit of high moral principles, the evoking of patriotism to exclude or marginalise dissent, and the erecting of new 'Star Chamber'-type judicial proceedings to punish offenders, together contribute to the transformation of state and society from a politically liberal towards an authoritarian, disciplinary and repressive collectivity.

Legitimacy

A critical question about the 'state/society complex' is the extent to which the state is securely sustained by its population. Conditions range from a population that is broadly participant in the political process and regards its political institutions as the natural order of things; and a population that looks upon political authority and its agents as alien and predatory. To assess the range of situations between these extremes is to pose the *legitimacy* question.

The condition of civil society is a first point of enquiry towards answering the legitimacy question. 'Civil society', like the state, is also in origin a Eurocentric concept. Initially, it referred to the bourgeois order, the realm of private interests which the state existed to regulate in the general interest. Now civil society is seen as being distinct from both state and corporate power in so far as these two are perceived to be integrated in a comprehensive authority structure. The term civil society is now more commonly reserved for autonomous groups (autonomous in relation to both state and corporate power) capable of expressing and pursuing collective aims of social improvement and emancipation. Some of these groups aim to influence state policy, some have humanitarian, ecological or peace concerns at the global level, and some organize protection and welfare at the local level.

Civil society understood in this sense competes for public support with exclusionary and xenophobic populism. It exists also alongside a national and transnational realm of covert activities, including intelligence services and organized crime, which cumulatively penetrates public institutions and influences public policy in an occult manner.

An active civil society may make politicians more accountable and encourage public confidence in the efficacy of the political process. Civic action and protest may also come to be seen as an alternative to a failing political process. The causes of declining legitimacy may range from outright suspicion of the state and its agents, to apathy on the part of the self-satisfied, and to a disdain for the official political process when it comes to be seen as the plaything of a discredited political class that appears incapable or unwilling to remedy the ills of society or is just mired in corruption. Declining legitimacy undermines political authority from within. The decline is accelerated by public perceptions that transnational corporate power and international finance which are unaccountable to the public really determine the conditions in which people live and the future prospects of the planet.

The condition of legitimacy varies enormously. In the United States, the Constitution is enshrined in the hearts of the people while the political process, so long as prosperity prevails for at least the half of the population which bothers to vote, appears often as a form of public entertainment rather than as an engine of change. In Italy, a wise but cynical population tolerates a manifestly corrupt political leadership, relying heavily for its welfare upon the strength of family and social connections and the ability of these connections to secure their share of the state's largesse. In Japan, a momentarily charismatic personality breaks on to the political scene to inspire a (perhaps naive) hope that a moribund political gerontocracy can give place to a revival of national energies and economic recovery. In the poor countries of the world, people continue to fend for themselves and attempt to organize their welfare locally apart from and despite the state. Confidence in international organization is eroded by scandals and failures in peace-keeping operations, by the perception that attempts to invoke an international rule of law are thinly veiled exercises in great power dictation, and by the subordination of those forums that are open to a wide expression of views to those narrowly constrained by dominant powers. Just about everywhere legitimacy is a problem. My point is that dealing with this problem is the condition for political order at the local, national and world levels.

The future of global governance

Critics differ as to whether I have been optimistic or pessimistic in my assessment of the prospects for social and political change. Discussion of a new 'bottom-up' multilateralism, a movement from civil society, both national and transnational, to provide the grounding for a transformed form of global governance is considered by one critic to be 'utopian'. It *would* be utopian if it were an intellectually constructed plan for institutional change. The thinking that came out of the United Nations University programme on multilateralism that I coordinated was rather an attempt to see beyond the sclerotic, politically biased and often malfunctioning existing international institutions by addressing the problem of the social basis for an alternative order. What shape that order might take could only be discerned in the process through which the challenge to the existing order became stronger until it, in its turn, might become dominant. The likelihood of that coming to pass in the foreseeable future is, of course, moot. Therein lies the charge of pessimism, which I accept. A pessimist sees the constraints that define the limits of the possible, the strong bonds that hold the existing order together, and the influences that orient its direction of development. The pessimist as critic also looks for the contradictions in the status quo that might become triggers of change and focuses on how desirable change might be pursued realistically.

The more pertinent criticism is that I have lacked a coherent vision of what I am for, that I am a 'well-informed rebel without a political cause'. This is a more serious challenge than the charge either of undue optimism or of pessimism. I hope that this book may respond, at least in part, to that justifiable criticism. The path I have trodden in life may explain an apparent lack of commitment to causes. Twenty-five years as an international civil servant can remove one from a sense of primary identity with nation or class, and also arouse some scepticism about the efficacy of international organizations. Another twenty-five years in academia can hone the critical faculty and confirm a feeling of distance from active political and social engagement. My life experience does not fit me well for the role of what Gramsci called an 'organic intellectual'. There is no social group with which I feel a special solidarity and identity and to which I owe a preferential consideration. I am an observer, not a representative. The role of critic comes naturally to me, the role of advocate perhaps less so. Yet I am not content merely to analyse the historical process. I also want to put that analysis to the service of historical change.

The biosphere

I have moved on in my perception of the world since writing the texts that have been the main object of criticisms. Two concerns stand out. The first is the fundamental importance of the biosphere for survival. Ecology was forgotten in Marxian theory. Marx's appropriation of the labour theory of value makes man the creator of all value and the master of the universe. Karl Polanyi, following the physiocrats, brought nature back in as a source of value. It is only relatively recently that some economists as well as ecologists have recognized that economic logic and the logic of biology and life are distinct and, under the currently evolved modes of thought of both disciplines, contradictory.

Before we think of international relations or international political economy we have to think of the larger whole in which these activities take place. That larger whole is the biosphere. The sum of human activities takes place within the biosphere which is the condition for the existence of life. The economy, as one sphere of human activities, thus needs to be regulated so as to sustain the biosphere. To understand this is to understand humanity as part of nature, as interdependent with other forms of life and life-sustaining substances.[10] What I am *for* is an economy embedded in society, to use Polanyi's metaphor, and a society self-conscious of its embeddedness in the biosphere. Whether this is achievable, given the priority accorded to short-term interests in politics, is another question; but it sets a goal.

Civilizations

The second concern which has come to prominence in my thinking since I wrote those works which form the basis for the bulk of the criticism reported in Chapter 1 is about civilizations in world order.[11] My concern here has coincided with a revival of interest in civilizations in international relations literature. I think this revival got off to a false start by picturing civilizations, much in the manner of neo-realist Cold War inspired literature, as large territorially based political entities that 'clash' with one another. The concept of a civilization in the 'clash' thesis is of a finished structure with a political authority (the state that exercises leadership in the group of peoples constituting the civilization) and a territorial grounding. The prescriptions derived from that perception were similar to those for dealing with Cold War conflict – US leadership of the West, reinforcing the 'Western' cultural unity, the strengthening of NATO, and, to underpin all that, maintaining the predominantly Caucasian-Christian character of the United States perceived to be threatened by submersion in an influx of other peoples (Huntington, 1996).[12]

The other way of looking at civilizations is as historical process, the continuing evolution of the ways in which different groups of people perceive the world. This process proceeds through dialogue and debate, sometimes violent, among different cultural orientations, all of which crystallize the sentiments of social groups and orient them in different directions. Islamism (or what Western media often call Islamic fundamentalism) is not the revival of an archaic consciousness. It is quite modern, an expression of the revolt of people touched by economic modernization and at the same time excluded from or recoiling from it. There are other competing currents within Islamic societies, some more adjusted to existing world-economy practices and the existing political power structure. These other concepts of Islam are manifest in some places and repressed in others. There is an ongoing competition for the shaping of an Islamic mentality which is conditioned by the material conditions and power relationships affecting Islamic collectivities.

The same reasoning applies to Western civilization, whether one calls it Judeo-Christian or something else. Some tendencies in Western civilization are essentialist and exclusive; others more relativist and open to influences from other civilizations. Social conflict manifests itself in alternative views of the world and of the future. Similarly, the world views of Chinese and Japanese people are not homogeneous but are expressed in different tendencies.

All of these 'civilizations' are contested spheres of inter-subjectivity. That is to say, civilizations exist in the mind rather than on the ground, consisting of shared assumptions about the natural order of things. It is possible to characterize such civilizational tendencies, in a shorthand for a particular historical time and place, as *types* of inter-subjectivity coherent with the people's conditions of existence. This can be useful for comparative understanding; but it misses the potential for development. To grasp this potential it is necessary to understand more about the parameters that shape the mentalities which constitute civilizations and how movement in the parameters can change the quality of civilizations. That is a question I begin to address in the later chapters of this book.

International organization

What role does international organization play in regard to both present problems and long-term outcomes? I have been chided for seemingly underestimating the potential of the United Nations and its agencies in particular. What I see in the present world context is a hierarchy of international institutions in which the UN system has been marginalized with respect to effective action on major political and economic issues. Kosovo made it clear that the United States with the (often reluctant, but nevertheless acquired) support of its main allies would take its own decisions on military security matters when it felt necessary, bypassing the UN Security Council. The world economy agencies (IMF, WTO and World Bank) function as part of what I called the *nébuleuse* that tries to generate a consensus for the management of global capitalism among governmental and corporate powers in which the United Nations takes a subordinate but compliant place.

It is true, as some critics have pointed out, that the UN institutions provide a forum for the less powerful to voice their protests against the prevailing power structure. The demand for the New International Economic Order (NIEO) was given as an instance. However, as things now stand, the NIEO and similar initiatives from the less powerful have been aborted or diverted. That fact does not negate the importance of UN agencies as sites in which dominant power can be contested; but it does suggest scepticism about the prospects of effecting structural change in the short term through these agencies. For the longer term, they are places where the less powerful can raise consciousness about their grievances and can mobilize opinion.[13]

This is why I think that empowering the voices of the weaker and the marginalized in the long run will depend upon the strength of social movements at the base of society. Change in the way the world is organized and run at the top will only come about through pressure from below. 'Reform' in the discourse familiar within the United Nations usually means increasing efficiencies of management in the 'top-down' perspective of the dominant powers. I advocated a 'two-track strategy': continuing to use the existing institutions to highlight issues affecting the less fortunate while at the same time putting effort into the building of a civil society that is both nationally based and transnational in its orientation. This has been called 'globalization from below'.

This being said, there is no inevitability about this happening. I cannot subscribe to any 'progressive' theory of history. History is what we make it. What is certain is that there will be change over time in the basic structures of social life. The only sphere in which change is cumulative (and might be called 'progressive' in that sense) is in technology. What people have learned about how to make things they cannot unlearn other than through a total collapse of civilization – and that could happen unless humanity learns how to avoid destroying the biosphere. But in matters of morality there are no firm guarantees against regression to barbarism as the twentieth century has amply demonstrated. One can only continue the struggle through civil society for greater equity and tolerance of diversity. The 'war to end wars' of 1914–18 and the 'never again' of Nuremberg were fond hopes, ill-founded in historical experience, as the populations of the African Great Lakes region among others have good reason to know.

Concentrated global power

Since the last decade of the twentieth century and the proclaimed end of the Cold War it has become obvious to many that there has been a major change in the structure of world order. The United States has become the pivot of a military and economic system anchored in the Western NATO alliance with tentacles extending selectively into the rest of the world. US military power sustains the neo-liberal economic order managed by the *nébuleuse*. It contains, and if necessary punishes, disruptive forces. The United Nations has been brought into a subordinate relationship; and a tangle of other international and regional organizations and agreements deal with a host of functions in a manner generally consistent with the complex central power.

This new complex but coherent power constellation has affirmed certain norms of behaviour which it is prepared to enforce – norms which are not without ambiguity, for example democracy, and not without selectivity in enforcement, for example against genocide. The power constellation has also created judicial procedures for trial and judgement (which, nevertheless, are not applicable in practice to agents of the core power and its allies).[14] There is some confusion between the role of the United States as leader of coalitions dedicated to enforcing general principles, for example defence of the territorial integrity of Kuwait in the case of the Gulf War, and as defender of its particular national interests, for example protection of its oil supply in the same case.

In a relatively short period of time, this power structure has fought three wars (against Iraq, Serbia and Afghanistan) and has opened the prospect of more to come.

Two books were published in the year 2000 which identified this new power structure and each gave it a different new name. Martin Shaw (2000) stretched the concept of 'state' to cover the phenomenon which in its existing form he called the 'western state' and in its potential form the 'global state', a telos that would have substantially encompassed the whole world. Shaw regarded this as a benign development which offered the vision of a social democratic world much in the image of Britain's New Labour.

The other book by Michael Hardt and Antonio Negri (2000) evokes very much the same picture of a global authority with America as its core which encompasses potentially the whole world. While Shaw's description is very much in political and institutional terms, Hardt and Negri are more concerned with the philosophical and psychological underpinnings of world power. They see the European renaissance between 1200 and 1600 as having turned away from the transcendence of God and divinely ordained hierarchies, towards a liberating immanence of human creative potential. Transcendence was, however, quickly restored in the form of state sovereignty. The ultimate form of transcendence in our time is 'Empire' (the title of their book). 'Empire' is not imperialism in the sense of the nineteenth-century expansionist European nation-state. It is more analogous to the Roman empire, a complex political authority that through its communications system extended its law and shaped minds and society throughout the known world. They recall St Augustine's image of the dialectic between the City of God (transcendence) and the earthly city (immanence); and they define the task of the present as to negate the transcendence of today's 'Empire' so as liberate the immanence of the 'multitude', i.e. the variety of human potentialities. Hardt and Negri are anarchists. They see Empire as something to be deconstructed, not embellished by social democratic political authority.

The task of deconstruction is broad and deep. Economic globalization strives to eliminate all other forms of economy and in doing so exacerbates inequalities and weakens the biosphere upon which all life depends. Awareness of these consequences mobilizes people in a variety of acts of resistance that have only begun to achieve coherence at the global level. The obstacles are considerable. Consent to the order of 'Empire' is constructed through a pattern of economic rewards and disincentives. The media in information and entertainment propagate norms and ideas that sustain authority,[15] and institutions of learning propagate a knowledge system that makes it difficult to think and discuss alternative worlds. The whole is reinforced by a punitive and disciplinary system that builds conformity. Power is not just institutionalized authority; it shapes and reproduces mind and body; it is what Hardt and Negri, echoing Foucault, call biopower, which implies that the task of deconstruction begins with the mind and the body.

Where Shaw foresees a simple progression towards the 'global state', Hardt and Negri cling to hope in a historical dialectic that contains the potential for a transformation of 'Empire', much as Marx foresaw the transformation of capitalism once it had exhausted its historical mission. For them, in historical terms, globalization is a 'good thing' in so far as it clears away relics of transcendence from the past, particularly the idea of state sovereignty. The notion of a dialectical process that calls globalization into question points in a direction that Shaw's analysis does not pursue. Recent research on globalization has explored forms of resistance, not just in the very public protests at summit meetings of the global economic managers, but also in the depths of societies.[16] I see the primary task of critical scholarship today as to clarify resistance to globalization and 'Empire' today so as to help create a more coherent counter-force.

I am less convinced than Hardt and Negri that all of the past must be swept away, and more convinced that cultural continuity and development will be the basis for people in different parts of the world to pursue different paths towards emancipation. Immanence can draw upon the past. Breaking the monolith of 'Empire' can reveal a new potential diversity of life and social organization. The roots of potentially coexisting civilizations are still alive and may flourish into a plural world.

There is a struggle within European societies between the Atlanticist and the autonomous European views of the future. These options are linked to a struggle over the form of capitalism – the Anglo-American versus the social market or social democratic forms. The Kosovo War highlighted the opposition of state and public opinion in Russia, China, India and much of what used to be called the 'Third World' to the prospect of a NATO-led consolidation of world power. George W. Bush's war against terrorism will reveal other cleavages. The 'all who are not with us are for terrorism' attitude of dominant power provokes dissent.

Within societies all across the world, in the West as well as the non-West, opposition has been mobilizing in increasingly demonstrative confrontations against the economic and military manifestations of this concentrated power. These evidences of resistance express rejection of the Western version of a unitary political and economic global governance. They constitute a demand for pluralism, for the possibility that societies can follow different paths of development. The alternative to globalization is not a 'clash' of civilizations, each defending its supposedly essential cultural integrity from foreign subversion, indeed, globalization is most likely to provoke that 'clash'. The alternative is the continuing evolution of coexisting civilizations reacting to and borrowing from each other in their internally guided development. Just as biodiversity is the condition for the healthy development of all species, so cultural diversity is the condition for the health of civilizations.

3   Vico, then and now

When I was studying history at McGill University in the 1940s, it was still possible to think of history in the manner of Lord Acton's approach to the editing of the Cambridge Histories: that industrious research would ultimately succeed in compiling all the facts needed to make a definitive universal history. Acton not only had confidence in the ability of the professional historian to know the facts with indisputable clarity, he also confidently subjected those facts to the judgement of a universal moral law.

Yet the events of the twentieth century undermined confidence about facts and challenged the universal validity of moral judgements. The mid-century point was particularly crucial in urging a rethinking of what history was and what it was about. World War II marked a number of structural changes in the world that called for historical explanation: the emergence of new centres of power in a post-European world order, the revolt against the West in the political process of decolonization, the revived practice of genocide in the heart of Western civilization, all raised questions as to what kinds of facts would be conducive to understanding history and what kinds of moral judgements would be pertinent.[1]

A critical student of history in the 1940s might justifiably wonder about how history could help to understand what was happening in the world, and to ask what was the nature of historical knowledge. Such questions led me at that time to read works of the Oxford historian and philosopher R. J. Collingwood (1942, 1946), and also Oswald Spengler's *Decline of the West* (1939). Both, in different ways, put me on a route that led later on to Vico.

Collingwood was much influenced by the Neapolitan historian and philosopher Benedetto Croce; and it was Croce who contributed in a major way to a revival of interest in his Neapolitan antecedent of the early eighteenth century, Giambattista Vico. Croce (1955) is remembered for his aphorism that all history is contemporary history, that is to say that people in different times and places look to the past in the light of the problems they confront in their present.[2] Contrary to Acton's ideal, people need different histories in relation to the different worlds in which they live. In other words, history is not something external to the historian-observer. The historian is a part of history, a re-maker of history, the self-conscious link between the problems of the present and the past that makes them intelligible.

Vico[3] asserted as much in his critique of Descartes, who served in many ways as counterpoint to his own thought. Descartes had a low opinion of history which he thought to be a very imprecise, uncertain study. He was more admiring of mathematics and physical sciences. But applied to history, Descartes's concept of mind, the *cogito*, was a mind possessed of a universal rational capability which received the impression of the observable external evidence research could turn up. Acton had inherited this viewpoint.

Vico's view was very different. For him there was no such thing as a universal rational mind; nor do we know history as something external to the human mind. People can know history because people have made history; and the making of history is also the making of human minds and the transformation of mind through the process. As he put it, knowledge of history is 'to be found within the modifications of our own human mind' (*NS*, 331).

The rational mind that Descartes assumed to be universal was for Vico itself the product of late historical development. Its historical contingency could only be understood as a stage in the history of mind. Similarly, human nature was not a universal through time and space that could be used by political philosophers like Hobbes as a postulate for deducing theories of political and social order. Human nature was a changing product of history, made and remade by people. All this represented a sharp challenge by Vico to the universalism of the north European Enlightenment – a challenge which went very largely ignored for a century and more in the supreme self-confidence of the Enlightenment.

To say that history is the history of the 'modification of mind' is not to espouse a philosophical idealism that sees all of history as shaped by ideas. For Vico, mind is transformed by reaction to the changing material conditions of existence, or, as he put it, 'the human necessities or utilities of social life' (*NS*, 347). This process of the development of mind began, in Vico's imaginative reconstruction, with a thunderbolt that inspired in the most primitive creature the idea of a god; and it continued among evolved human beings in the reshaping of political order through class struggle.

Mind is the avenue of access to understanding how such material influences have provoked the reshaping of society. The problem for the historian is how to imagine the mental processes of people whose minds are differently constituted from the historian's own, and in this way to be able to reconstruct mentally their world and their actions. Vico called this capacity *fantasia*. Others have called it imaginative reconstruction. Collingwood (1946) called it rethinking the thought of the past.

Some postmodernists have questioned the possibility of doing this; or have even condemned the very attempt as an imperialist usurpation of other people's identity. But to deny this possibility is to deny history, and by implication to remain bound by one's own particular perspective on the world and one's own historically conditioned judgemental apparatus. Vico was aware of the difficulty when he said that it had taken him full twenty years to begin to conceive how the most primitive people at the dawn of time might have perceived their world (*NS*, 338). Perhaps he was wrong in the way he reconstructed it. But the effort was fruitful and a guide to future historians.

Spengler's monumental work was not derived from Vico. If Spengler appealed to any antecedent, it was to Goethe (Spengler, 1939, I, pp. 25, 49 fn.).[4] But he was trying to do something which Vico also had attempted. He was trying to discern a pattern in the developmental stages of mind and society, changes that came from within the different human communities whose trajectories have constituted historical civilizations. This aspect of Vico's work is more controversial. Even Collingwood had little sympathy for it; and professional historians generally have kept their distance from it and from Spengler and other systematizers like Toynbee.

Vico found these developmental patterns not in the intentions of historical actors but in the aggregate consequences of their actions. Vico called his vision an 'ideal eternal history'. He wanted to marry Plato's static notion of eternal ideas which would constitute the ideal state to the more dynamic Christian notion of a Divine Providence revealed through history. Others, after Vico, tried to do the same thing by using secular imagery. Adam Smith invoked the 'invisible hand' and Hegel the 'cunning of reason' to mark the distinction between the pursuit of particular motives and the aggregate consequences which result.

Vico's aim was to produce a total science of humanity, or at least to sketch out hypotheses that could be developed into such a science.[5] The centrepiece of this science was a history of mind. It began with the most primitive awareness of *Self* among bestial creatures struggling for their own survival. The sense of self, Vico thought, must have come about by opposition to a threatening *Other*. A thunderbolt generated the image of an angry god – a deity imagined as expressing sentiments which the bestial creature found within himself. The creation of religion thus lay at the beginning of mind's development. It was elaborated in poetry and myth, the original languages that bound people together in what today we might call inter-subjectivity, that is to say, shared symbols and a vision of their world that enable people to communicate meaningfully with one another and to act in concert.

In this original creative stage of language, Vico concluded that people were not capable of abstraction; everything was concrete and particular. But from that focus on the particular emerged what Vico called 'imaginative genera' or 'imaginative universals', often the name of a god or of a hero that came to express certain qualities. These imaginative genera contained the germ of what, with the dawn of reason, would become concepts, the intellectual tools that rational humans use to represent and act upon their world.

The transformation of mind for Vico was accompanied by changes in all other aspects of social life – in human nature, in language and religion, in political, social, economic and legal structures, and in language. He saw a synchronic coherence in all these aspects of collective life. They all changed in concert, one with another. Spengler had the same vision of coherence in transformation; he perceived different aspects of social life – political structures, mathematical knowledge, sexual relations and architecture – as interrelated in an overall process of historical change. This was a Vichian idea whether or not Spengler was conscious of it.

Both also saw the developmental cycle passing its peak into a point of decline and decay. Vico called this moment of decadence the 'barbarism of reflection' which would come about through 'each man thinking only of his private interests' (*NS,* 1106). Reason would degenerate into an instrumental manipulation that would fragment community, leading to a competition of all against all that would be worse than the initial barbarism of the senses.[6]

The implication of his 'ideal eternal history' was that after a long period of social disintegration, of entropy, a revival of culture and civilization could come about through a new burst of creative energy in a new era of poetry and myth. Yet Vico hesitated to reach this conclusion about his own time. He deviated from the predictive potential of his own science of historical process to offer instead the possibility that a monarchic regime might protect society against its self-destructive tendencies, maintaining order while allowing for pursuit of private interests. Perhaps this was a relapse into optimism, perhaps a prudent deference to the status quo.

My starting point was to think about how particular historical circumstances – the late 1940s in my own case – can prompt questions about the meaning of history and the nature of historical knowledge. I would now like to pursue this kind of enquiry into the circumstances of Vico's life and times that conditioned the writing of *The New Science*; and then, to consider the circumstances, in subsequent ages including our own, that have stimulated revival of an interest in Vico's work.

Vico's world

At the beginning of the eighteenth century when Vico lived, Naples was the fourth city of Europe, after London, Paris and Istanbul. Its population of about half a million was about the same as that of Madrid, the chief city of the most recent imperial power. The great Mediterranean empires of the recent past were all in decline. Naples' one-time central position in the politics of a Mediterranean world was a thing of the past. Naples and neighbouring Sicily were subject to the interplay of external political forces – Spain, France, the Papacy and Austria. Naples lacked effective control over its own political destiny. Yet pride in the past and nostalgia for lost independence remained as an undercurrent, a latent challenge to foreign rulers.

Neapolitan society was lopsided. The vast majority of the rural population were serfs on landed estates. The city of Naples was overcrowded. The very poor were about a quarter of the urban population, many of them homeless. (Braudel, 1979, I, pp. 467–70). The capital drew into itself the surplus wealth produced elsewhere in the kingdom by peasants, seafarers, miners and artisans. This surplus was enjoyed by a dominant class of courtiers, large landowners and high-ranking ecclesiastics, flanked by officials, judges and lawyers amongst whom justice was bought and sold. The Church owned two-thirds of the landed property of the kingdom, the nobility owned two-ninths, and one-ninth was left to poor smallholders. A substantial part of the surplus was transferred as ecclesiastical revenues to Rome to maintain the life-style of cardinals of the Church. This became one of the major issues in the city during Vico's lifetime, exacerbating a long-standing animosity of Neapolitans towards Rome. There was an impoverished petty bourgeoisie among whom Vico must be counted. His annual salary of 100 ducats as professor of rhetoric at the University of Naples did not suffice to support his family. He made out by giving private lessons, and by writing commissioned works and ceremonial texts for noble families.

The intellectual and cultural life of the city nevertheless remained vibrant. Five centuries earlier the court of the Hohenstaufen Emperor Frederick II at nearby Palermo had been the most intellectually brilliant in Europe. Roman, Greek and Arab thought collided in open discussion. Frederick himself, perhaps the most remarkable man of his time in Europe, was fluent in French, German and Italian, Latin, Greek and Arabic (Runciman, 1958, p. 20). His critical free-thinking spirit is epitomized in his saying that the three great imposters of history were Moses, Christ and Mahomet.[7] The Pope condemned him as Anti-Christ.

Naples, in Vico's time, although subject to a more repressive political and ecclesiastical orthodoxy, retained something of that intellectual ferment. Its subterranean spirit was irrepressible.

An Italian writer of the twentieth century, Curzio Malaparte, in his novel *La Pelle* (*The Skin*) evoked this aspect of the eternal Naples in a conversation he imagined with an American colonel of the Allied forces invading southern Italy in 1943. This colonel was in peacetime a professor of literature in a great American university, a lover of Europe and of the European Enlightenment. Naples, Malaparte told him, was

> that terrible, wonderful prototype of an unknown Europe, situated outside the realm of Cartesian logic . . . the most mysterious city in Europe. It is the only city of the ancient world that has not perished like Ilium, Nineveh and Babylon. It is the only city in the world that did not founder in the colossal shipwreck of ancient civilization. Naples is a Pompeii which was never buried. It is not a city: it is a world – the ancient pre-Christian world – that has survived intact on the surface of the modern world.

There is, indeed, something pre-Christian in Vico's thought, despite his frequent protestations of Christian piety. And there is also a hint of post-modernity that suggests an observer of the passage of the civilization within which he lived.

Riots broke out in Naples when Ferdinand of Aragon tried to impose the

Spanish Inquisition in 1508, and again when Philip II made the same attempt in 1565. But the Inquisition was installed in the city nevertheless, and remained until it was abolished two years after Vico's death. The state also insisted on deference to established order in the publication of opinions (Stone, 1997).[8] Seventeenth-century Europe, following the wars of religion and the repression of Islam in Spain, broadly endorsed the idea that the state should enforce moral and religious uniformity. The principle of *cuius regio eius religio* consecrated in the Treaty of Westphalia could be regarded as the political dogma of the era.

Although repression on grounds of opinion was not extreme in Naples in Vico's time, it could be dangerous for an author to provoke authority. A contemporary of Vico's, the historian Pietro Giannone, who wrote the first of the great Enlightenment histories, which became a model for Gibbon's *Decline and Fall of the Roman Empire*, fell foul of the Inquisition, was forced into exile, found refuge first in Vienna, then in Geneva, and finally ended his days a prisoner in Milan (Stone, 1997, pp. 211–13).[9] A French Benedictine scholar who visited Naples at that time reported a popular song which went: 'If you talk they'll send you to the galleys; if you write they'll send you to the hangman; and if you're silent they'll send you to the Holy Office of the Inquisition.' Nevertheless, popular songs and unorthodox opinions proliferated. If the state and the Inquisition aimed to quash these, they obviously failed. The enduring spirit of Neapolitans was too much for them.

The life of a scholar required considerable ingenuity in practical matters apart altogether from intellectual issues. Vico managed to court favour with the powerful in a modest way through the several changes of regime that happened during his productive years. He was deferential to a succession of rival political authorities. Ultimately, at the close of his career, his discretion was rewarded in his appointment as court historiographer with a stipend doubling his meagre professorial salary (*Autobiography*, p. 204).[10]

Vico's relationship to ecclesiastical orthodoxy raises more complex questions. The *New Science* could be read as posing a challenge to Church doctrine. In the text, Vico proclaims his Catholic piety.[11] But was he being sincere or ironic? Irony plays a key role in Vico's theory of language. In *The New Science* he writes that irony is a mode of speech characteristic of the age of reason. Metaphor had been characteristic of the heroic age, when poets spoke in what Vico called 'true narrations', expressing themselves directly, without dissimulation. In the more evolved – and more decadent – era of reason, people would toy in ironic ambiguity with truth and falsity. So it is an obvious question whether Vico practised irony in his own work.[12]

One instance that gives rise to this question is the separation Vico made between the history of the Hebrews and the history of the gentiles. The Hebrews, he wrote, had revelation direct from God. The gentiles came to religion on their own by an historical process of discovery – a discovery initiated by the mythic thunderbolt. We might say that, according to Vico, for the gentile peoples, God did not create man, rather men created the gods. In

Vico's words, 'it was fear which created gods in the world, not fear awakened in men by other men, but fear awakened in men by themselves' (*NS*, 382, 191). This is a fairly good definition of alienation, the creation by people of a power which thenceforth rules over them.

The meaning of 'gentile' shares this ambiguity. In one sense gentile means non-Hebrew. (Vico as a philologist classifies people by language.) But Vico, who wrote in Latin before he came to compose *The New Science* in Italian, always used words in their etymological sense.[13] The adjective 'gentile' comes from the Latin 'gens' or people. One can infer that the *New Science* is about the whole of the human race and that the exception he makes for the Hebrews has meaning only as a theological precaution to escape Church censure for his analysis of human history.

An important section of *The New Science* is Book III, 'The discovery of the true Homer'. In it Vico undertakes a critical analysis of the Homeric canon and concludes that it could not have been written by one person; and that Homer was a collective name, an imaginative universal, for the creators of the poetry of the Greek people through the early stages of their history. Biblical criticism was alive and well in Vico's time, notably in the work of Spinoza which was condemned by the Catholic Church. Vico's thesis on Homer could well be read as a suggestion that the Old Testament, by analogy, recorded the mythology of the Hebrew people. Moses, like Homer, would not have been a real person, but rather the name under which the early Judaic poetry was collected.

Vico did affirm the necessity of piety and religion for the maintenance of the state. This might signify his own sincere belief in divine sanction for public institutions. It could also be taken as a rule of political wisdom derived from his analysis of human affairs. His research taught him that poetry and myth create the solidarity needed to sustain organized communities.

The debate remains alive today as to whether or not Vico affected piety as a cover for the heterodox implications of his *New Science*.[14] Of course, no one can know. Should we care? We may perhaps be forgiven for setting aside concern for Vico's eternal soul and turn to consider the impact of his work on subsequent thinking about human affairs.

Vico and revolution

In an irony typical of Vichian thought, this prudently conforming scholar reappeared on the European political scene one hundred years after the publication of the definitive edition of *The New Science* in the guise of a revolutionary. The French historian Jules Michelet discovered the book in 1824 and was so impressed that he learned Italian to make an abbreviated French translation of the work.

Like Vico, Michelet was a relatively poor *petit bourgeois*. His father was a printer who had suffered under the censorship of Bonaparte. Vico had been a bookseller's son. Michelet could not have been much impressed by Vico's protestations of piety and deference to authority. He was a child of the French Revolution and an anti-clerical.

Michelet took from Vico the idea that the people – that collective noun – is the principal actor in history. *Le peuple*, for Michelet, is a mystical unity, not the messy confusion of conflicting parties or the passivity and withdrawal of individuals concerned only with survival, but the embodiment of Rousseau's General Will that can do no wrong. Michelet's legacy in France is the myth of the Revolution in the Jacobin tradition – the unity of the State, secularism (*laïcité*), and the mission to carry the spirit of the Revolution to Europe and the world. Michelet's revolutionary universalism is, of course, inconsistent with Vico's historicism but Michelet's history constructs a new heroic age in the spirit of Vichian poetry (Wilson, 1940, pp. 3–35; Geyl, 1955, pp. 56–90).

Marx, for his part, a little later, was struck by Vico's insistence that human history is intelligible because it has been made by men. Vico had written that the origin of human institutions, religious or secular, are to be understood through 'a severe analysis of human thoughts about the human necessities or utilities of social life' (*NS*, 347).

But Marx's appropriation of Vico here was one sided. Marx was keenly aware of the radical social restructuring produced by the industrial revolution. He saw material production as the primary cause in relation to which mentalities and institutions were consequences. Vico had a more organic view in which religion, language, morals and economic and social organization were an interactive whole. If there were to be any primary element for Vico – who could not have had any experience of the social consequences of industrialism – it would be *language*, not as cause of the whole, but as the key to understanding of the whole and to linking its various components together. And, behind language, *religion* was, in Vico's thinking, what bound people together into community.

Looking back, we can see a greater affinity between Marx and Vico in the role of class struggle as the driving force of history. Marx did not pick Vico up on this; but a highly original and heterodox figure in the Marxian tradition, Georges Sorel, did so at the turn of the nineteenth to twentieth centuries. Sorel built upon Vico an explicit theory of revolution for his time (Sorel, 1896).

Two Vichian ideas were fundamental in Sorel's thinking. One was the idea of the *ricorso*, of the recurrence of a creative spirit that could revive a decadent society. Sorel represented primitive Christianity as a Vichian *ricorso*; and he envisaged socialism as the *ricorso* to be made in his own time.

The other Vichian idea that Sorel appropriated was myth, the collective image, the social poetry evocative of strong passion, that mobilizes creative energy into action (Sorel, 1941). He saw the eschatological myth of a second coming as the driving force behind primitive Christianity. He looked to the myth of the general strike as the collective image that would inspire revolutionary action in the early twentieth century.

Sorel differed from both Michelet and Marx on one important point. Michelet and Marx both saw history as the story of progress. This was consistent with the common sense of their era. The European Enlightenment did not admit of any regression to tenebrous times. The French Revolution heralded the continual expansion of liberty. The Industrial Revolution brought with it the idea of continuous material growth. European empires carried these ideas around the globe. The nineteenth century deified Progress with a capital 'P' (Bury, 1955). It was only in its last decades that a combination of economic downturn, imperial rivalries and ideological challenges called the idea of Progress into question.

Sorel did not believe in progress. He attacked the idea in what he perceived to be its roots in the Enlightenment (Sorel, 1947). In this he was closer to Vico who reflected the classical view of history as cyclical. But Sorel also rejected a cyclical view of history along with Vico's ideal eternal history. For Sorel there was no general pattern in history. We lived in a Heraclitan world of perpetual change without any predetermined direction. The important thing was to understand how change could be brought about; and for this Vico's myth was crucial.

Vico was no activist. He was content, as a survivor in troubled times, to have discovered the key to understanding history. He did not aspire to change history. Sorel did; and affirmed Vico's psychological discovery of the role of social myths as the means.

Vico and liberalism

Vico has also influenced the development of liberal thought in the twentieth century through two seminal thinkers, Benedetto Croce and Isaiah Berlin. Classical liberalism derived from the European Enlightenment. It was grounded in the postulate of the autonomous individual endowed with natural rights who lives in a society which is a web of contracts, and who is animated by a capacity for rational choice sustained by private property.

Vico's view was very different. For him human nature is not fixed and uniform, but constantly being transformed through history; and rights are not inherent, but are won through historical struggles. Moreover, society has priority over individuals. Society constitutes the setting in which people act, and collective action by people can change society. So Vico starts with different assumptions from those of Enlightenment liberalism.

There is a tension between two aspects of Vico's thought. On the one hand, there is his emphasis on human agency and the possibility of understanding history by the imaginative reconstruction, through *fantasia*, of individual and collective historical actions. On the other, are the aggregate consequences of human activity which differ from the aims of the historical actors, and which, not being willed by people, Vico attributed to Divine Providence.

Benedetto Croce, much influenced by Hegel, evoked a world spirit, a movement towards liberty inherent in the historical process – a kind of immanent deity. Isaiah Berlin, who was sceptical about inherent historical forces, leaned towards Vico's emphasis on people's capacity for choice and action.

Berlin's interest in Vico emerged from a study of counter-Enlightenment thought. He saw Vico's major achievement as raising the issue of pluralism by rejecting the monism of Enlightenment universalism. Vico's discovery of the true Homer demonstrated his general point that ideas and values have to be understood in relation to their cultural and historical context and the stage of development of the human mind in which they appear. Timeless values, by implication, have no place in historical judgements.

By making cultural pluralism the foundation of his liberalism, Berlin faced the predicament of the relativist implications of historicism: How can one affirm any principles as having universal value? And if you cannot, what grounds are there for moral choice? He was obliged to agree with the counter-Enlightenment and post-modernist critique that there can be no foundation for *absolute* values. He rests his own liberal convictions simply upon principles that seem to him inseparable from his own humanity. Beyond that there are customs and practices concerning which we expect to find wide differences (Berlin, 1991, p. 205).[15]

One might retort that our sense of our own humanity is itself a historical construct. To which Berlin would reply, quoting Schumpeter, that 'to realise the relative validity of one's convictions and yet stand for them unflinchingly, is what distinguishes a civilized man from a barbarian' (Berlin, 1958, p. 57).

Through Berlin, the Vichian tradition confronts the spectacle of a plurality of civilizations.

Vico and civilizations

The events of the 1940s, I suggested at the beginning, called for a new look at world history. The same can be said for our own time, more especially since September 11, 2001. We now are experiencing, on the one hand, the apparent submergence of distinct cultural identities under a global economic and communications web supported by seemingly insuperable military force. On the other hand, we experience resentment and resistance, such as we saw at Seattle, Quebec City and Genoa, against the would-be monolithic globalized civilization and the military and police power behind it. We are also being made forcefully aware of the assertion of other identities – gender, ethnicity and religion – in the face of dominant globalizing forces, and of concern that unregulated globalization will damage the biosphere upon which all life depends. 'Global terrorism', as the dominant discourse names it, is only one, if the most extreme, form of resentment and resistance.

There are, moreover, signs that the 'barbarism of reflection' and the extremes of irony have gone a long way in the dominant civilization to sap confidence in public institutions and the sense of social solidarity, and to exalt the pursuit of private interests. Vico's indicators of decline are manifest.

Civilization, in Vico's analysis, does not succumb to external attack. Its solidarity erodes from within.

The main choice we confront today concerns the coexistence of civilizations, which is the alternative to one homogeneous globalized civilization. In this regard there is a significant silence in Vico's work – a silence about Islam, a civilization bordering upon his own. The history of Naples, Sicily and southern Italy during the centuries leading up to Vico's time was one of the encounter between Islam, Christianity and the memory of imperial Rome. I referred earlier to the court of Frederick II at Palermo in the thirteenth century as the site of a free exchange of ideas among Islamic, Christian and free-thinking scholars of the Epicurean tradition of Rome. Saracen troops fought for Frederick and for his bastard son and successor Manfred for control of southern Italy in resistance to the Papacy and its French allies (Runciman, 1958, p. 92).

That era of the open encounter of civilizations was long past. By the late seventeenth and early eighteenth centuries Islamic influence had been repressed in Europe. One might look back to Thomas Aquinas, who had been a scholar at the University of Naples, and whose critique of Averroes (or Ibn Rushd by his Arabic name) in the late thirteenth century marked both the heritage of Islamic philosophy in Christendom and its ostracism. Subsequently, the ostracism was reinforced by Papal and Spanish ascendency in southern Italy. But one might assume that although the Islamic culture which had introduced Greek philosophy and medicine to western Europe was repressed, it was not entirely extinguished. In the historical imaginations of Vico and his contemporaries the past undoubtedly still lived, even if some parts of it were censored from consciousness.[16]

One Islamic writer of the fourteenth century, Ibn Khaldun (1967), produced a work that had striking similarities to Vico's *New Science* almost 350 years earlier. Ibn Khaldun was born in 1332 in Tunis, son of a distinguished family that had migrated from Seville before the Spanish *reconquista* took possession of that city. He was highly educated in the Islamic and Greek classics including Aristotle and Averroes. As a young man he achieved prominence in the turbulent diplomacy and politics of North Africa. His abilities were recognized in a wider world. His counsel was sought by Pedro the Cruel of Castile, the conqueror of Seville, and by Tamerlane, the Mongol conqueror of Damascus; but Ibn Khaldun discreetly avoided such compromising associations. His political projects in North Africa failed and he withdrew from active politics, like Machiavelli in Florence more than a century later, to reflect upon the nature of politics and society through the study of history. The result was his *Muqaddimah* or prolegomena to world history, completed in 1377. The aim of this study was to set forth a new science of human civilization and social organization.

Civilizations, for Ibn Khaldun, were born, grew and declined in a cyclical process. Civilization emerged from savage nomadic peoples whom he described as on a level with 'wild, untameable animals and dumb beasts of prey' (Ibn Khaldun, 1967, p. 93). Among such people, the warrior band developed a sense of solidarity – Ibn Khaldun's word was *'asabiya* which has been rendered by his translator into English, perhaps not entirely adequately, as 'group feeling'. The moral cohesion of *'asabiya* enabled a people to found a political authority, a state or dynasty. Political authority, in turn, encouraged production and trade in a settled urban mode of life. Gradually, however, the affluence generated by urban life would undermine the ascetic solidarity of the primitive founders and social decay would follow. A revival would require a new spirit of *'asabiya* to be aroused by a new prophet; or, if this did not happen, the likely alternative for a decadent society would be foreign conquest.

Ibn Khaldun had personal experience of four coexisting civilizations. His research bore directly on the Arab and Berber civilizations of North Africa. His travels and political activity brought him into contact with the European Christian civilization, and the Asian Mongol civilization of the invaders from the east. He was well aware of the trade links by sea across the Mediterranean and over the desert from the Sudan. His education had introduced him to the sciences of ancient Greece and he reflected with regret upon the absence of records of similar knowledge from the Persians, Copts, Chaldeans, Syrians and Babylonians (Ibn Khaldun, 1967, p. 39).

The schema of the rise and fall of civilization which he constructed from this knowledge has many similarities to that which Vico later represented as his ideal eternal history.

The point is that in two coexisting and distinct civilizations whose cycles were operating on different time scales – the peak and decline of Islam preceding by several centuries Vico's vision of the crisis of European consciousness in his own time[17] – similar visions of the civilizational process were expressed by perceptive scholars. Both were suggesting that civilizations have a common form and that they rise and decline through a similar historical process. They also understood that each civilization was unique in its cultural manifestations and posed to the others a challenge to be understood.

* * *

In conclusion, let me return to that eccentric, solitary genius, Giambattista Vico. He presented himself in his *Autobiography* (p. 132) as a marginal, of 'melancholy and irritable temperament', a stranger in his own land.[18] He discreetly preserved his intellectual autonomy in the midst of powerful political, social and ecclesiastical forces. He thought of himself as a devout Catholic, or at least wished to be perceived as such, yet his New Science contained serious challenges to orthodox belief. He resisted being assimilated to a 'group' or 'school' in the intellectual debates of his own time and place (*Autobiography*, p. 133). His thought remained obscure and neglected, a potential resource for future times.

During the next 250 years he was discovered and rediscovered by a variety of schools. What these revivals of Vichian thought had in common, in a negative sense, was rejection of Enlightenment universalism and positivist scientism. In a positive sense, they were all concerned with the moral basis of society, and with the sense of solidarity and the creative spirit required to found and sustain a social order.

Vico's challenge for our own time is that we endeavour to understand a plural world of coexisting civilizations. His thought can be a help to understanding and living with diversity. The first requirement is to achieve a consciousness of our own relativity – the particularity of our own historical conditioning. The next is to be able to enter empathetically, through what Vico called *fantasia*, into the mental processes of another civilization.

This sense of civilizational pluralism brings us back to Vico's starting point: his criticism of Descartes. Where Descartes, as representative of Enlightenment thought, posited a single rational truth known in the mind of a single human nature, Vico, posited a variety of human natures and of truths formed by distinct histories. The issue is universalism versus historicism. Vico's inspiration urges us to accept the vision of a plurality of cultures and civilizations, each with their own truths, and to search for compatibilities and reconciliation among them. It alerts us against succumbing to the homogenizing force of a single global civilization which would reduce cultural diversity to Disneyesque folklore.

4   Universality, power and morality

'International order' and 'international solidarity' will always be slogans of those who feel strong enough to impose them on others.

In politics, the belief that facts are unalterable or certain trends irresistible commonly reflects a lack of desire or lack of interest to change or resist them.

(E. H. Carr, 1946, pp. 87, 89)

Politics, as E. H. Carr emphasized, is always a compromise between power and morality. Power relations change through history. The dominant political authority (state or empire) of one era gives place to another. The same applies to power relations between races and genders. What is sometimes more controversial is that morality also changes over time and varies over space, that different peoples in different times and places have different sets of values, and that claims to universality in moral judgement are ultimately dependent upon the dominant power of one group over others. This is not a finding of cynical international relations theorists of the twentieth century. It was clearly articulated by Blaise Pascal (1623–1662), a convert to Jansenism whose deep moral convictions rested on conscience rather than Cartesian rationalism – 'the heart has reasons that reason knows not of'. Among the fragments of his *Pensées* we can read:

> Truth on this side of the Pyrenees becomes error on the other side . . . Custom creates the whole of equity, for the simple reason that it is accepted. It is the mystical foundation of its authority; whoever carries it back to first principles destroys it . . . We must not see the fact of usurpation; law was once introduced without reason, and has become reasonable. We must make it regarded as authoritative, eternal, and conceal its origin, if we do not wish that it should soon come to an end.
>
> (*Pensées*, fragment 294)

And further:

> Justice is subject to dispute; might is easily recognized and is not disputed. So we cannot give might to justice, because might has gainsaid justice, and declared that it is she herself who is just. And thus being unable to make what is just strong, we have made what is strong just.
>
> (fragment 298)

For Pascal political morality was an oxymoron. The truth you knew in your heart was incommensurate with the variability of the conventional order. Morality was an individual thing. Custom, the practices shaped by power relations through history, was of another order. Hegel made such a distinction between *Moralität*, the obligation to bring about something which does not exist (what you know in your heart to be right), and *Sittlichkeit*, custom or what obliges you to bring about what already exists (Taylor, 1979: 83–4). The same distinction lurks in Vico's separation of divine revelation from historically constructed 'common sense'. Pascal denounced the casuistry of the Jesuits which purported to resolve an ethical case of conscience by interpreting religious dogma so as to compromise with particular circumstances. He would not defer to what we now call 'community standards' as the test of what is right. Putting Pascal beside Vico, what the heart knows confronts what history has constructed. These are two separate things which do not brook being confused one with the other.

When political leaders appeal to universal moral principles they participate, perhaps on occasion unwittingly, in the historical construction of or reinforcement of 'community standards'. This is a matter of power determining right and wrong. If Pascal and Vico were correct in pointing out that the practices and values of communities are historically constructed and thus differ in time and place, there can be no basis for affirming one moral code as absolute and universal.

At one extreme, political leaders mobilize power to enforce what they proclaim to be the one and only true ethical system. At the other extreme is the recognition that no ethical system has absolute and universal validity and adjustments among rival systems depend upon the relative strength of contending powers. The first approach is a powerful tool for mobilizing people behind a cause. The second is more useful in working out an accommodation of a conflict in which there is no clear winner; it may achieve a certain relative justice that allows all parties to pursue their own values in peaceful coexistence. Either way, power determines the verdict. Neither extreme, in the realm of politics, impinges upon the convictions of the heart. People of conscience know right and wrong independently of power relations. But when a political leader purports to make a conviction of conscience into an instrument of political power, it is prudent to be wary lest politics degenerate into fanaticism, self-delusion, or hypocrisy.

Moral relativism is considered to be evil by monotheistic religions, by ideological zealots and by well-meaning altruists. Attempts to invoke universal principles of morality in politics require careful scrutiny. One may be attracted by the hope for a world in which all can agree upon what is good and what is evil; but one should be cautious to avoid the myopia of unconsciously restricted world views and the manipulative disingenuousness of politicians who use moral claims in the pursuit of particular interests. The relationship of morality to power is the key problem in a critical approach to politics.

Critical theory, morality, and structural change

The critical analyst goes through a double process of historical thinking. The first phase is self-consciousness of one's own historical time and place which determines the questions that claim attention. The second phase is the effort to understand the historical dynamics that brought about the conditions in which these questions arose and what constraints and opportunities they present for change.

The broad consensus of the European Enlightenment (e.g. in both Hobbes and Rousseau) was that human nature was universal and unchanging in time and space, and that political truths could be deduced from this construction. The Enlightenment, by and large, had a low opinion of history as an inferior, imprecise kind of knowledge. The natural sciences were the model in which scientists were observers of physical phenomena whose regularities could be demonstrated to be universal laws. The assumption of a universal human nature opened the way to explore the possibility that human activity in history and society could be treated like the phenomena of physical nature by social scientists who would take up the position of external observers and catalogue human activities in search of universal laws. During the nineteenth century this attitude towards science came to be called positivism.

Positivism deals with data, i.e. 'givens'. Historicism deals with facts, i.e. 'mades', which presume a maker with a purpose. For the positivist facts become data. This implies a double distortion. First, the actor (or the complex of thoughts, emotions and pressures that converge in the act) is removed from the action. Only the effect is left. The event observed by the actor becomes the impact or consequence of something that remains undisclosed. Second, the event is abstracted from its complex context, from all those linkages, affiliations and antagonisms that give meaning to an event. The positivist approach envisages the construction of a science of human affairs based on the observation, classification, comparison and correlation of data which have been torn out of the whole set of relationships in which they occur.

Already in the eighteenth century a dissident strand of European philosophy challenged the hegemony of the Enlightenment and its positivist heritage. In this dissident perspective the study of history and society was understood to be fundamentally different from physical science. Kant, of course, made the distinction between the phenomena which were the objects of scientific observation and the 'thing-in-itself' which could not be known. Giambattista Vico, before Kant, reversed the Enlightenment view about the supremacy of natural science over what we would now call social science by affirming that a thing could only be truly known by its maker. For Vico (see Chapter 3), the physical universe could be known truly only in the mind of God, its maker, whereas human history was intelligible to the minds of human beings who are the makers of history.

Nineteenth- and twentieth-century theorists like Wilhelm Dilthey, Benedetto Croce, R. G. Collingwood and Martin Heidegger pursued the analysis of historical thought as a distinct tradition. This led initially to the sense of a dichotomy between the world as nature and the world as history. The same distinction between positivism and historicism emerged within Marxism in the thought of Antonio Gramsci.

For Vico, there was enough similarity among human minds for one mind to be able empathetically to reproduce the mental processes of another so as to be able to understand a mind differently shaped by history. Today, an extreme post-modernist position would deny that possibility, affirming that human natures have no common foundation, that they are distinct products of historical development, which in effect denies any possibility of historical or social knowledge that is not particularistic.[1]

In the late twentieth century, the classic distinction between an 'objective' positivist natural science and a subjective (or, better, inter-subjective) historical and social science was narrowed by developments on the natural science side. The second law of thermodynamics and entropy, the relativity of space and time, Heisenberg's principle of uncertainty, the introduction of reflexivity recognizing that the scientist is part of the experiment and not just an external observer, complexity in cybernetic systems, and chaos theory (recognizing that there is an order in chaos) have all meant that chance gains over predictable determinism.[2]

Contemplation of the infinitely big and the infinitely small, the cosmos and the atomic particle, has made the conventional laws of physics less absolute, more relative. The gap between the natural and social sciences has been reduced. Notions of universality in the natural sciences have been weakened so that the reflexivity inherent in historical and social knowledge no longer seems so inferior as it did to the Enlightenment philosophers.

The *subjects* of knowledge, actual human beings, the concrete instances of the species *Homo sapiens*, are products of a long evolution. *Homo sapiens* has existed for somewhere between 50,000 and 100,000 years, having evolved out of species of hominids during a passage of some four million years. Some people have speculated upon a biological evolution beyond *Homo sapiens*, involving a significant increase in brain cells, which would imply trading in the 'end of history' (of *Homo sapiens*) for a 'post-human' world more like the vision of anarchism. According to some such speculations, this could lead to a self-organizing network of beings which had no need for formal institutions.

The future is open and unpredictable. This speculation does, however, under-line that our humanity is itself a product of the very *longue durée* of biological history which, having had a beginning, will by implication come to its end through either self-destruction or a further long 'post-human' biolog-ical evolution (for example, Morin, 1973).

Our capacity for reasoning is, for practical purposes, limited to the condi-tion of *Homo sapiens*. And this human reason we know is not a means of access to knowledge about Kant's noumenal world. It is a practical tool for making the best of the particular predicaments in which various specimens of *Homo sapiens* find themselves. Reason is coloured by the circumstances which give rise to our use of it. Knowledge is reflexive, it knows itself in relation to its specific historical experience.

Accordingly, several kinds of knowledge coexist as the inter-subjective truths of different groups of people. This brings us back to Vico's challenge: can a person participating inter-subjectively in one kind of truth, in one per-ception of reality, painstakingly reproduce the inter-subjective meanings of another group and its truth, its view of reality?

Carl Jung has suggested a possible answer through his theory of the arche-types that lie buried deep in the collective unconscious. These archetypes, Jung said, were common to all humanity at the origins of consciousness. As myths or forms they have acquired over time a variety of different meanings, of different contents or expressions, that are peculiar to different peoples and different eras; but, in Jung's thinking, this variety is traceable back to its origins in archetypes. This approach might be the basis for retracing the development of minds and so of penetrating into the minds of others con-stituted differently by history. Jung's method is reminiscent of Vico's in tracing myths and symbols common to the different 'nations'.[3]

As between different civilized values, active pretensions to universality are ultimately reducible to power. What E. H. Carr wrote in 1946 is still apposite:

> Theories of social morality are always the product of a dominant group which identifies itself with the community as a whole, and which pos-sesses facilities denied to subordinate groups or individuals for imposing its view of life on the community. Theories of international morality are, for the same reason, and in virtue of the same process, the product of dominant nations or groups of nations. For the past hundred years, and more especially since 1918, the English-speaking peoples have formed the dominant group in the world; and current theories of international morality have been designed to perpetuate their supremacy and expressed in the idiom peculiar to them.
>
> (Carr, 1946, pp. 79–80)

The context in which absolute values are advanced is always complex. Absolutist claims obscure real but less worthy motives of an economic, geopolitical or institutional kind. There are no absolutely pure motives as there are no just wars. This does not mean that there are no wars worth fighting. It cautions against giving a universal value to the mixed motives in an historical conflict.

In such a context of divergence or conflict in values, we are led to Max Weber's distinction between an ethic of ultimate ends and an ethic of responsibility (Weber, 1948, pp. 118–28). The ethic of ultimate ends makes absolutist claims and brooks no compromises. The ethic of responsibility looks to the likely consequences of action eschewing absolutist claims.

Human rights and universality

The affirmation of human rights poses the issue of universality. The notion of 'rights' has been defined within particular historical traditions. 'Rights' emerge from political struggles, the outcomes of which are consecrated over time as universal principles. The Universal Declaration of Human Rights was adopted by the United Nations after World War II (in 1948) and can be seen as embodying the noblest expression of the principles of the Western Enlightenment and as the product of that specific current of world history. The impetus for the Declaration came from revulsion at atrocities, especially those attributable to racial doctrines, connected with the war. That particular moment in history was propitious for the recording of world 'community standards'.

The 'community' whose standards were thus consolidated at that period was the community of victors, not all of whom, the Soviet Union in particular on the eve of the Cold War, were equally enthusiastic about the enterprise. This historical genesis has come implicitly to challenge the universality of the consensus then reached at that time in so far as the voices of other traditions of civilization were then hardly audible. This point has been argued more vociferously in recent years, for instance at the Vienna Human Rights and Development Conference in 1993, where speakers for some Asian countries argued that Western concepts of human rights contrasted with Asian values, which placed less emphasis on individual rights and more on a collective, consensual order. To the defenders of the universality of human rights the invocation of 'Asian values' appeared as an attempt to justify authoritarian and repressive regimes. Asian activists for social change took the same view. Social and political struggles in Asian countries will ultimately define what 'Asian values' are.

Behind the argument over principles, the politicization of human rights has been transparent. Western countries advanced human rights in the spirit of the Universal Declaration (and also the International Labour Organization's definition of freedom of association) as instruments of Cold War struggle. Appeal to human rights has also become a tool for advancement of political demands by indigenous people's organizations and by women's movements congregated in the Beijing Conference on Women and Development in 1995. The field of human rights remains a terrain of struggle in which the notion of human rights continually evolves. However, the struggle which was waged heretofore in the discourse of the Western Enlightenment has now become inter-civilizational.

This kindles fears of a possible retrogression from the gains made in the post-war period by undermining somewhat the universal legitimacy of rights. Are human rights as they are now recognized in the customary law of nations an emanation of one dominant civilization? The question can be posed in a different manner. Is it possible to evolve out of the different realms of inter-subjectivity expressive of different coexisting traditions of civilization a supra-inter-subjectivity that would consolidate norms consistent with all traditions of civilization without any one tradition being superimposed on others? To remove the factor of dominant power as the author of rights, these rights, to be fully legitimate, would have to be gained through struggle within each civilization or each culture.

Similar objects of struggle do arise within each civilization. The status of women is an issue that cuts across all civilizations. To take one instance of different civilizational approaches, in the struggle for self-government of the indigenous peoples of Canada, some indigenous women, while supporting native demands for sovereignty, and yet mindful of the vulnerable condition of women in some native communities, have also sought the protection of the Canadian constitution's Charter of Rights and Freedoms. Others have taken the position that self-government and control over land and resources is the primary goal and women's rights will only effectively be secured through struggle within their own communities.

This underscores the importance of understanding the historically developing nature of civilizations. This development is a dialectical process in which impacts from alien cultures play a part, but internal debate and struggle over directions of change is even more important. For change to be accepted as authentic, and in the long run legitimate, it must come from within.

Kosovo: the anatomy of a 'just war'

NATO's war against Yugoslavia was defended by its perpetrators as a 'just war' necessarily waged to enforce universal principles of morality. It is an exemplary case for examination of the relationship of power to morality in our time.

The crisis in Kosovo came about in a sequence of events in the disintegration of the former Yugoslavia, itself a consequence of the end of Cold War confrontation of Western and Soviet blocs. Kosovo was predictably the most dangerously explosive situation in a chain reaction of violence resulting from a mixture of revived ethnic nationalisms and inept foreign interventions. The cycle began with Croatia's declaration of independence and its rapid recognition by Germany and the Vatican. This activated memories among Serbs of the Nazi-sponsored wartime Croatian puppet state which had organized the massacre of its Serb population. It also prompted the Bosnian Muslims to claim their state, which in turn provoked Bosnian Serbs to respond to the idea of a merger of Serb populations in a 'Greater Serbia'.

The whole process of 'ethnic cleansing' continued in attempts to form ethnically 'pure' territories for Croatians, Muslims and Serbs, with killing on all sides and massive displacement of populations which, within the former Yugoslavia, had lived peaceably intermingled. Killings, bombardments and mass graves became the staples of the propaganda war through which the local parties sought to manipulate opinion and to secure sympathy and support from outside powers.

In this process, the Serbs were the losers. The Croatian army, in a *blitzkreig* supported by US military supplies and unofficial military advisers, drove the Serb population, some 200,000 refugees, out of the Kraijna region. The Serb leadership and people were vilified in American and western European media and in the utterances of politicians.[4]

The Kosovo crisis emerged following these setbacks for Serbia and the nationalist politics of its leader Slobodan Milosevic. The ethnic Albanian Kosovar population was experiencing, through Milosevic's policies, a revocation of the autonomy they had enjoyed under the Tito regime and a degree of repression. A civil war began in Kosovo in the form of an insurgency by radical elements of the ethnic Albanian population against Serb dominance in the province. The insurgent group, the Kosovo Liberation Army (KLA), conducted armed attacks on Serb police and assassinations of local leaders. This provoked a military response from Serb forces. In an effort to calm the potential for expanded violence the Organization for Security and Cooperation in Europe (OSCE), with the agreement of the Yugoslav government, sent a lightly armed verification mission to Kosovo, which was in place when the discussions leading up to NATO intervention were going on.

Steps leading to war

Although jurists have pointed to the undermining of international law that resulted from the NATO countries, contravening of the provisions of both the United Nations Charter and the North Atlantic Treaty, I am concerned here only with the political reasoning leading to the decision to bomb. There was insufficient consensus in the European Union to mount a credible deterrent to Yugoslavia pursuing military action to suppress the insurgency in Kosovo. The United States, urged on especially by the Blair government in Britain, provided the catalyst for an alignment of NATO governments. France and Germany were acquiescent; Italy and Greece and the new eastern European members were more apprehensive. European public opinion was divided. The US Secretary of State, Madeleine Albright, took the initiative to lead the campaign and to forge a semblance of unity in NATO.

The constraint upon her was US President Bill Clinton's decision that a war of intervention in Europe, in which no major US national interest was involved, would have to be fought by air power alone and without risk of US casualties – a doctrine partly derived from the technological hubris of the Gulf War experience, and primarily from the public memory of Vietnam and the metaphor of 'body bags'. Germany and some other NATO allies likewise excluded use of ground troops.

Ms Albright gave it to be understood that the Milosevic government would yield to NATO after a few days of bombing. This ignored the lessons of Coventry and Dresden in World War II and the US experience in Vietnam. Nor did the Gulf War support this thesis. In fact, the bombing predictably rallied public support against NATO, even among Serbs hostile to Milosevic. This military strategy was faulty at the beginning and the fault was compounded as failure to attain the purported objective of protecting the Kosovars led the USA and NATO to expand attacks from military to civilian targets, something which one US military analyst described as 'reinforcing failure'.

The diplomatic procedure leading up to the war was equally flawed. US ambassador Christopher Hill was charged with drawing up what came to be called the Rambouillet Agreement.[5] It was accepted by other NATO governments; but Russia, the party that would most likely have influence with the Serb government, rejected the military provisions of the 'Agreement' which would have given NATO forces free run of the whole of Yugoslavia (and not just Kosovo). When the text was presented to both hostile parties, the Yugoslav government and Kosovar Albanian representatives, they both initially rejected it. Ms Albright then arranged to change the composition of the Kosovar Albanian delegation by displacing the representatives of the unofficial elected Kosovar government headed by Ibrahim Rugova, and replacing them by the KLA, hitherto considered by the CIA to be 'terrorists'. Her partiality to the KLA continued by grooming the KLA leader Hachim Thaci for a leading role in shaping Kosovo's future.

The KLA leadership was persuaded to accept Rambouillet, with the *sotto voce* understandings that the KLA would have a continuing political presence in a NATO-occupied Kosovo and that NATO would not be overly rigorous about disarming the KLA.

Since the Belgrade authorities continued to reject the Rambouillet text – a text drafted in such a way that no sovereign state could accept its terms – while the Kosovar Albanian party accepted it, the way was now clear for the aerial bombardment that had been planned for some time. The fact that the Yugoslav parliament had at that moment agreed to a withdrawal of Yugoslav forces from Kosovo and to a United Nations (not a NATO) occupying force was both obfuscated in the Western media and treated by NATO as a delaying tactic.[6] Had the purpose of the negotiations been to persuade Milosevic to accept a supervised withdrawal of Yugoslav forces from Kosovo and the introduction of an international force that would pacify the civil war between the KLA insurgents and the Yugoslav police and military, the diplomatic means chosen were designed for failure. In retrospect, it seems obvious that Ms Albright's purpose was not to reach an agreement but to start a war. Diplomats, who may sometimes exhibit a professional tendency to over-personalize events that also have deeper impersonal causes, have called the NATO attack on Yugoslavia 'Madeleine Albright's war'.

But why did Ms Albright, as representative of the US government, want war? I think we can minimize the defence of human rights trumpeted by Tony Blair, and somewhat less stridently by Bill Clinton, as the activating factor. After all, the same Madeleine Albright in 1994 had intervened to prevent the United Nations Security Council from deploying sufficient military force in Rwanda to stop the genocide there.[7] Furthermore, the scale of repression prior to the bombing in Kosovo, which took place in the context of civil war and was monitored both by journalists and the verification mission of the OSCE, was much exaggerated as a justification for war preparations by NATO, something about which US decision makers would have been well aware. It is reasonable to conclude that the human rights issue was a pretext for a political decision already taken.

Why did other NATO countries acquiesce in the US decision for war? Britain's Tony Blair was concerned to maintain a US presence in Europe and US leadership in NATO; he became the most hawkish of leaders. Gerhard Schröder, with his foreign minister Joschka Fischer of the Greens, rallied to the US war plan, perhaps with a view to lifting a lingering pall over Germany's international status but definitely to manifest support for America's continuing role in Europe. Blair and Schröder were the most convinced backers of the war and the most convinced supporters of NATO and of the maintenance of a US presence in Europe.

President Chirac of France was also firmly committed to the war, while at the same time protesting his independence (he claimed to have vetoed some of the bombing targets, *Le Monde*, 12 June 1999). France acquiesced in the US initiative, perhaps in part to allay suspicion of a traditional pro-Serb stance, and in any case to avoid being isolated within NATO. The French Prime Minister, socialist Lionel Jospin, was much more doubtful about the wisdom of the war, but went along so as not to destabilize the 'cohabitation' with Gaullist party chief Chirac (Eric Rouleau, *Le Monde diplomatique*, December 1999).

In Italy, tension was higher; the life of the centre-left government led by Massimo D'Alema was at stake. Public opinion was not sympathetic to the war and was provoked to anger when US pilots at the NATO base in northern Italy severed a cable-car lift during a practice flight, killing several people (the pilots had their wrists slapped by a US military court which did little to mollify Italian public outrage), and when aircraft returning to the NATO base discarded unused bombs in Italian fishing zones of the Adriatic.

Greek opinion was hostile, generally sympathetic to the Serbs. Hungarians, bordering on Serbia, had joined NATO for protection, not to go to war with their neighbour. As the bombing went on well beyond the few days that Secretary Albright had predicted would result in Milosevic's capitulation, public questioning of the campaign grew in Europe (and in America). This was particularly threatening in Germany for the Schröder–Greens alliance.

Public support in the NATO countries weakened, and with it so did NATO solidarity.

Canada's role was perhaps the simplest to explain. The Canadian government just conformed to what the US government wanted. There was no real parliamentary debate; all the parties, including the NDP (social democrats) and the sovereignist Bloc Québecois, supported the government in following the US initiative. There was a more serious debate outside parliament. Some academics and journalists, a retired diplomat and a retired military officer, both with experience in the Balkans, resisted being drawn into the picturing of the war as a moral crusade. They saw the situation as of greater complexity. The official left which had hitherto taken a critical view of NATO, had perhaps been entranced by the Gladstonian rhetoric of Tony Blair. Among political personalities the only outspoken opposition came from a few Red Tories.[8] Solidarity with NATO justified by the human rights issue was the public face of Canadian government policy.

The course of the war

It became clear that the mass expulsion of 800,000 Kosovar refugees took place *after* the NATO bombing began. Prior to March 24, when the bombing began, the evidence is that relatively small numbers of attacks on Albanian Kosovars had occurred and that these were occasioned by the guerrilla civil war being carried on by the KLA against the Serb army and police.[9]

The expulsion required specific circumstances in order that it be put into effect. The decision to withdraw the OSCE verification mission and to begin bombing provided those circumstances; and the campaign of expulsion moved much more rapidly than NATO had expected. Mao's metaphor for a guerrilla war – the fish that swim in the sea, i.e. guerrillas supported by a sympathetic population – applied here. The Serb forces set about to drain the sea so they could dispose of the fish. The NATO decision to bomb provided the opportunity. The bombing produced what it was supposed to prevent, a logical and quite predictable military response by Yugoslav forces to clear the way for the crushing of the KLA insurgency. Since NATO intervention on the side of the KLA in the civil war was limited to air power, Yugoslav ground forces were free to clear the ground in order to suppress the insurgency in Kosovo (although the KLA also operated from bases across the border in Albania). Furthermore, the search for bodies after the Yugoslav forces withdrew and the NATO occupying force, KFOR, entered Kosovo demonstrated that however brutal the expulsion of the Kosovar population had been, the allegations of mass murder were exaggerated.[10]

When it became apparent after several weeks that the bombing campaign was not working, the initial error to rely exclusively on air power was compounded by the decision to expand the range of targets to factories, bridges, chemical and petroleum works, electrical networks, television and radio installations. Whether or not specifically targeted, the escalated bombing also hit hospitals, health clinics and schools (schools were closed throughout Yugoslavia for two months during the bombing campaign) and residential areas. Despite NATO rhetoric, these were not attacks on the Serb leadership but on the Serb people. The use of cluster bombs and depleted uranium casing on shells and missiles which leave long-term radioactivity that undermines people's health shows the nature of this war against people, killing and maiming and threatening the health of this and future generations while destroying the economic apparatus built up by the Yugoslav people during fifty years of socialist construction, something they could reasonably identify as their own rather than the property of a dominant class.

The moral issue

Moral indignation in Europe and America focused on massacre, theft, arson and rape, mainly by Serb paramilitaries given a free hand and encouragement by Milosevic in Kosovo after 24 March. Many historical cases show how situations of war and violent revolution can release psychopathic instincts otherwise repressed in more normal situations. This applies not just to Serbs but also in recent times to other participants in Balkan wars – Croats and Bosnian Muslims, and Albanian Kosovars – and, of course, we remember Mai Lai, even if we don't think back to the seizure of First Nations' lands in North America.

This horror is one aspect of an asymmetrical kind of warfare in which one side dominates the land while the other dominates the sky. The behaviour of the side with air power does not offend our refined sensibilities in the same way. The extreme case would be that of pilots of the B2 bombers, which caused the most damage in the populated areas, who took off from Missouri on a 30-hour round-trip flight to Yugoslavia where they discharged their satellite-guided missiles from 15,000 feet, from which height they could hardly see the effect of their work on the people below, returning home to mow the lawn and play with their children. A far cry from the psychopath, head hidden in a black balaclava, who murders and rapes and torches on the ground? Yes, at first appearance and in public imagery. But the psychopath here is not the pilot who releases impersonal destruction. It is the military system which has succeeded in depersonalizing warfare, in which the agent of destruction, at a safe distance from the object, is protected from any immediate knowledge of what he is really doing, a protection enhanced by the Orwellian language in which the activity is morally disguised ('assets', 'degrading', 'collateral damage', 'friendly fire', etc.), evoking no suggestion of killing and maiming and polluting the human environment. Dostoyevsky's Grand Inquisitor described well the benign dissimulation whereby political leaders reassure the general population:

> And they will all be happy, all the millions of creatures, except the hundred thousand who rule over them. For we alone, we who guard the mystery, we alone shall be unhappy. There will be thousands and millions

of happy infants and one hundred thousand sufferers who have taken upon themselves the curse of the knowledge of good and evil.

There is a moral equivalence between these two seemingly very different ways to make war. The distinction, to borrow a Marxian metaphor, might be expressed as between proletarian and bourgeois methods of warfare.

Consequences

As it turned out, Kosovo was not an unsullied success for NATO. Prolongation of the bombing without any notable prospect of victory increased pressure to resolve the issue from allied governments and peoples and also from the US Congress. In order to extricate NATO from the impasse, the G8, i.e. the G7 plus Russia, was revived as a vehicle for dealing with Belgrade and negotiations were confided to Martii Ahtisaari of Finland for the European Union and Victor Chernomyrdin of Russia. With NATO withdrawn to the diplomatic background, these two produced an agreement acceptable to Belgrade in which Kosovo was recognized to be part of Serbia, and a United Nations' administrator would be installed in a NATO-occupied Kosovo. This was not the unconditional surrender proclaimed by NATO as its goal. Yugoslav military forces withdrew from Kosovo in an orderly fashion (in contrast to the chaotic withdrawals of US forces from Vietnam and Israeli forces from south Lebanon). The bombing which wreaked havoc on the economic infrastructure of Yugoslavia and left many civilian casualties ('collateral damage') had done little to 'degrade' the Yugoslav military.

The short-term effects of NATO's 'victory' were readily apparent:

* Death and destruction in Kosovo and in the Serb territories, including a quantum leap in violations of human rights, resulted in an effective 'degrading' of the population and of the resources at its command.
* Communal hatreds were exacerbated and KFOR, the NATO occupying force, proved to be unable or unwilling to control retaliation by ethnic Albanians against Serbs and other ethnic minorities. The task of the newly appointed United Nations Commissioner, Bernard Kouchner, to bring about reconciliation among communities became virtually impossible with the minimal resources at his disposal. Animosities resulting from the civil war and foreign intervention would likely endure in some form for a generation or more.
* Because of the preferred status accorded to the KLA, NATO's *de facto* ally, no orderly legitimate rule could be established in the territory. The KLA and its various factions remained the most powerful force among the Kosovar population. They remained armed despite the UN resolution (no. 1244) calling for their disarmament. The KLA under NATO auspices, was incorporated into a Kosovo Protection Corps

(KPC), which carried out 'ethnic cleansing' of the remaining Serbs, Gypsies (Roma), Turks and Jews.[11]
- The Serbian economy, including Kosovo, was reduced to material conditions equivalent to those left by World War II, but the psychological *élan* among the population that made possible the rebuilding of a state and an economy at that time was lacking.
- Organized crime expanded throughout central and eastern Europe. The war itself had expanded the operations of the Albanian mafia which, among other activities, provided resources for the KLA. After the war, the Albanian mafia had free rein within the lawless occupied zone and extended its operations across Europe. Serbian paramilitaries, for their part, converted themselves into adjuncts of the Russian and other eastern European mafia.
- The war unleashed Albanian irridentism which became a destabilizing force in the whole Balkan region affecting, in the first instance Macedonia, and calling into question borders and the situation of minorities in all the countries.

War crimes trials

The occupation of Kosovo by NATO left unresolved the matter of trials for war crimes. The United Nations had established in the Hague a special tribunal for war crimes in the former Yugoslavia (analogous to one created for the Rwanda genocide) and indictments were issued by its prosecutors against Slobodan Milosevic and other Serb military and political leaders. The moral status of war crimes trials is fraught with ambiguity. On the one hand is the laudable goal of establishing a universal standard for conduct in war which could be applied impartially by an independent judicial authority. On the other is the reality that judgments concerning war crimes have been organized by the victors to punish the vanquished. The justification has been that the victors represent a higher standard of civilization. However, one is brought back to the awareness that the higher standard is, in the last analysis, validated by greater power.

The United States called adamantly for Slobodan Milosevic to be arrested and sent to the Hague tribunal. After Milosevic's government was overthrown by public revolt and elections and he was arrested by the new authorities on corruption charges, the US government made payment of economic rehabilitation assistance conditional on delivery of Milosevic to the Hague tribunal. Financial power succeeded where military power had reached an impasse.

Judgments rendered in the hour of victory have sometimes been revised when political power relations change. Japanese leaders who were condemned as war criminals after the capitulation and occupation of Japan in 1945 were rehabilitated during the 'reverse course', in which the United States sought to make Japan an ally against the US-perceived Soviet Communist threat. Two of these convicted war criminals became prime ministers of Japan during the 1950s (Sakamoto, 1995).

Furthermore, the powerful who call for judgment are not always ready to submit to judgment. At Rome in 1998, 150 United Nations member states negotiated a treaty for a permanent international criminal court intended to provide for trial of individuals accused of serious war crimes and crimes against humanity. Yet the United States, along with Israel and a few other countries, voted against the treaty for the establishment of the court. The United States has consistently rejected the jurisdiction of international tribunals since it was condemned by the World Court for mining Nicaraguan harbours in its covert war against the Sandinista regime; and, in its role as world policeman, does not wish to expose its officials and military to charges arising from their conduct in enforcement actions.

Memories of Vietnam were reawakened in the United States by revelations concerning an incident involving the former Senator for Nebraska and former presidential aspirant, Bob Kerry. Kerry, a decorated hero of the war who made his subsequent political career as a liberal democrat, had been responsible for the massacre of a group of women and children while he was a junior Navy officer during the early period of his war experience prior to the event for which he was decorated (*The New York Times*, 29 April 2001). Kerry, at the time of this revelation, was also a potential presidential candidate for 2004.

Then, there is the case of Ariel Sharon, who was Israeli Minister of Defence and commander in the field during the Israeli invasion of Lebanon in June 1982. He was responsible for opening the Palestinian refugee camps of Sabra and Shatila, near Beirut, to the Lebanese Phalangist forces which were supplied and armed by Israel as auxiliaries. It was predictable that a massacre would occur and the Israeli army did nothing to prevent it. The PLO fighters had been evacuated by sea, escorted by French and Italian forces and US marines under an agreement negotiated by the US envoy Philip Habib which included a guarantee of safety for the families they left behind. Hundreds of women, children and elderly people were slaughtered by the Phalangists. The massacre stimulated anti-war sentiment in Israel. Later, an Israeli Commission of Inquiry presided over by the Chief Justice of the Supreme Court noted Sharon's 'indirect' responsibility and recommended his removal from office (Fisk, 1990: 319-400; Green, 1997). In March 2001, Ariel Sharon was elected Prime Minister of Israel.

Morality demands punishment for war crimes and crimes against humanity. Power politics makes a selective and reversible approach to moral judgements. We have not come a long way from the atavistic belief that God gives the victory to the just – and therefore that victory is proof of justice.

The geopolitical significance of Kosovo

If the moral justification for the attack on Yugoslavia did not survive the *post-bellum* evidence, what other reasons led to the war? One might make a case for the arrogance of power, impatience with the recalcitrance of a dictator of a small, albeit formally sovereign, state to comply with the demands of a world superpower and its allies (the Fidel Castro syndrome). More rational, however, was the emergence of a geostrategic policy on the part of the US administration that can be seen in retrospect as taking form over several years.

Part of that strategy was to secure the subordination of the United Nations to US interests and to lessen its role as a vehicle for Third World criticism of US policies. Madeleine Albright, as US ambassador to the United Nations before she became Secretary of State, manipulated the United Nations Security Council through the threat of a veto to reject the reappointment of the sitting Secretary-General, Boutros Boutros Ghali, for a new term of office, despite the fact that he had the support of all the other Council members (Urquhart, 1999; Boutros Ghali, 1999). Boutros Ghali had been too little attentive to US requirements. In his place she secured the election of Kofi Annan, and initiated him into his new office by making him party to a deal with Senator Jesse Helms, chairman of the Senate Foreign Relations Committee. The deal was for some movement by the Senate on payment of US arrears to the United Nations in return for more United Nations compliance with US desires. The United Nations has become more aligned to the US version of a 'new world order' of capitalist globalization underwritten by the military power of the United States and its allies.[12] The United Nations, in this vision, would deal with humanitarian relief and stay out of security issues like Kosovo (Frédéric Bobin in *Le Monde*, 10 May 1999). Security would henceforth be the function of a NATO with a wider geographical sphere of action, and, in the Pacific region, of the US–Japan Security Treaty subsequently complemented by an agreement for military cooperation between the United States and the Philippines.

The fiftieth anniversary of NATO's founding was to be celebrated on 22 April 1999. There could be no question of just recognizing that NATO had done the job for which it had been created and, now that the Cold War was officially over, could be wound up. Rather, the vision of a new mission for NATO as the military support for the new world order was to be affirmed with the enthusiastic support of Britain and Germany. The war over Kosovo was a key factor in the realization of the new vision.

The long-term direction of global governance could move in one of two directions. The most apparent tendency was towards a world shaped by one hegemonic power. This hegemony is sustained by economic globalization and the homogenization of cultures through a dominant mass media, the expansion of which is protected by a unitary concentration of military-political force. The alternative was a pluralistic world in which different groups of countries pursued different paths of economic and social organization which reflected and sustained their different cultural patterns. The one defined civilization in the singular. The other allowed for the coexistence of civilizations (in the plural).

The outcome of the Kosovo War seemed to move the world markedly in the first direction. NATO, which had exhausted its original purpose with the fall of the Berlin wall, but which had created an integrated bureaucracy out of the military and intelligence facilities of its member countries, sought a new expanded role. The new role would enlarge NATO's scope beyond the geographical limitations of its founding treaty and set aside its theoretical subordination to the United Nations Security Council (under Articles 52 to 54 of the UN Charter) so as to become the military force behind economic globalization. (The intent was somewhat naively betrayed by the clause in the Rambouillet ultimatum that required the Kosovo economy to be organized on 'free market' principles.)

Any advancement of the American global hegemonic vision through the Kosovo War came, however, at the cost of a heightening of adversarial forces. In the United States public opinion was about equally divided between support and opposition to the war, and the experience might have become a deterrent to further US interventions of this kind. The total unpreparedness of western European countries and their resort to reliance on US air power stimulated a movement towards a more effective European security organization (see Maurice Bertrand in *Le Monde*, 9 June 1999). The ghost of Charles de Gaulle stood in the way of the Blair government's aspirations for Britain to lead in Europe with US backing.

Russian diplomacy had been first invoked to facilitate the entry of NATO troops into Kosovo, after which Russian troops entering Kosovo were subordinated to NATO control. The 'accidental' bombing of the Chinese embassy in Belgrade by the US air force was ill-digested by the Chinese people and government. These humiliations suffered by Russia and China could be incentives to assert their alternative conceptions of world order. Japan remained ambivalent between reliance on a US security blanket, on the one hand, and the desire to assert independent power as a 'normal' country, on the other. All of these reactions to the war, together with the hostility of other Asian countries and Africa to the spectre of NATO as the dominant world force, might have made the war in Yugoslavia a turning point away from the monolithic vision of globalization backed by military force.

The US administration's vision of world order – economic and communications globalization sustained by US and allied military power – remained predominant but not uncontested in other NATO countries. The Kosovo War tested its acceptability in Europe. The debate in the European Union over 'social Europe' and the 'democratic deficit' mobilized Left-leaning Europeans in favour of the social market or social democratic form of capitalism (on the contest between two forms of capitalism in Europe, the classic thesis is Albert, 1991, and there is now a whole literature on this theme). The projected expansion of the European Union to the east to incorporate countries of formerly 'really existing socialism' was seen by some as a potential means of strengthening 'social Europe'.

These prospects were set back by a series of defeats for the Left in western Europe. The sudden departure of Oscar Lafontaine from the German government just before the war began and the collapse of Massimo

D'Alema's centre-left government in Italy in April 2000 were among the signals of the weakening of the European Left.

The European project of integrating eastern Europe into the European Union, was pre-empted by NATO's leap-frogging into the east with tentacles reaching into Ukraine and the republics on the southern border of Russia (van der Pijl, 2000). This imperial expansion could potentially place the oil and gas resources of Central Asia and the Caucasus under Western rather than Russian control.[13] Both Russia and China saw a threat of encirclement and reacted with determination to strengthen their military forces.[14] Kosovo was the key link in this imperial vision.

Europe was a critical site for the struggle to determine whether the future world would have a place for different coexisting forms of economic and social organization. The struggle for an alternative to Anglo-American competitive market capitalism was set back by Kosovo. What emerged was a new version of the neo-liberal hegemonic project, the 'Third Way' or the 'New Middle' articulated by Blair and Schröder in their joint statement of 8 June 1999, which coincided with the conclusion of the Kosovo War. In their perspective, globalizing capital, sustained militarily by NATO, would be combined with measures to facilitate the adjustment of labour to the exigencies of the market. Their position was an extension of the Clinton administration's vision of geostrategic policy. The alignment of the Schröder and Blair governments contained the prospect of displacing the Franco–German axis which had been the political basis for a more independent European system.

* * *

President George W. Bush's 'war against terrorism' was the sequel to Kosovo. It moved the construction of the global power structure which Hardt and Negri called 'Empire' one stage further. The United States took the initiative to build an even larger coalition and was ever-more clearly the central controller of economic, diplomatic and military action. A 'hub and spoke' model with US command in Tampa, Florida, replaced the 'consensus' model for management of the Kosovo War which had provoked frustration in the Pentagon (Malone, 2001). The United Nations was brought into a closer subordinate relationship to the coalition; its reward was payment of US arrears.

Military action in the attack on Afghanistan followed the Kosovo pattern: high-level aerial bombardment by the US air force, subsidizing of Afghan opposition ground forces, and direction by US command of military components from Western allies. A great show was made to the US public, as in the Gulf and Kosovo Wars, of the technological precision of US weaponry; but civilian casualties in Afghanistan and the resulting mass movements of refugees could hardly be obscured. As US military power crushed its enemies in Afghanistan, Israeli military power set about crushing the Palestinian

Authority. The same discourse of 'terrorism' served to align the moral justifications of power in both cases.

The mobilization of public opinion behind the war aims of the coalition went beyond just maintaining support. It virtually institutionalized good and evil, right and wrong, making dissent or criticism an offence against civilized society. The enemies were personalized and demonized (Milosevic and Osama bin Laden, who succeeded Sadam Hussein and will perhaps be succeeded in turn by the same Sadam). The central power structure generated principles of law and courts for translating them into judicial judgments. Dissent in Western societies was disciplined by ostracism in intellectual, political and media milieux; and was obscured by self-censorship. Every effort was made to create a sense of unbridgeable cleavage that defied rational discussion, echoing at many levels President Bush's declaration that all who are not with the coalition are with the terrorists.

This consolidated global power structure, moreover, lost much of its *ad hoc* character. The attack on Afghanistan and on the global terrorist network headquartered there came to be represented as one phase in a continuing organization and application of power that could be directed against other 'rogue states' with Iraq at the head of the list.

As with Kosovo, in the background to the campaign against Afghanistan lay the geostrategic significance of Central Asia and its oil and gas resources. The fluidity of relations between the United States, Russia and China and the political instabilities of Central Asia and the Middle East meant that 'Empire', momentarily all-powerful, might rest on less certain foundations in the longer term.

As territorial power was being consolidated in the chancelleries, military commands, intelligence services and corporate boardrooms through war, first in Kosovo and then Afghanistan, the non-territorial (or intra-territorial) cleavage among people continued. The challenge to the unitary world of corporate and military power, after Kosovo, came most persistently from the social movements. However, the enhancement of police powers and surveillance, for which 'terrorism' was the excuse, could be used to deter or repress civil disobedience that challenged any aspect of the power structure.

Nevertheless, continuing resistance from below foreshadowed future struggle in which the morality of justice and equity would continue to challenge the morality of military security and property rights. The forces of resistance move morality away from the hegemonic imposition of a code dictated by dominant power towards the creation through struggle of moral principles consistent with a world in which power is less concentrated and more diverse.

5   Power and knowledge

Towards a new ontology of world
order

In those times when the world seems to be at a turning point, when the accustomed framework of life seems to be upset, there arises a demand for new knowledge that will better enable people to understand the changes going on about them. The assumptions upon which prevailing forms of knowledge were based are challenged. A different set of problems has to be confronted.

New thinking comes about in two ways. One way is by adapting established knowledge to new events and circumstances through incremental adjustments. The other way is by projecting thinking forward so as to attempt to understand the nature of the historical process and how to control it towards achieving desirable outcomes. This way includes normative choice along with realist assessment of possibilities. These two approaches coexist during periods of fundamental change in world order. They express different power positions struggling for control over the future. The first gives precedence to the established order and seeks to adjust it to new needs. The second opens the way for more radical change.

Since the attack on the United States of September 11, 2001, the first approach has been overwhelmed by the introduction of a vast array of controls and restrictions under the rubric of security against the terrorism which has been identified as the salient new reality. These have the cumulative effect of reinforcing established power and obstructing changes that would counter the conditions that provide recruits for violent political action against established power. They aim to protect the status quo, but they may in the longer run undermine it by substituting repression for constructive change.

The second approach lies under a cloud of suspicion in these times. It may, however, point the way towards a more secure future in a broader meaning of security that includes the material health and welfare of people and recognition of their distinctive integrity as well as the minimizing of violence. I shall pursue here this second approach.

Globalization, which is defined in a variety of ways, is the salient emerging reality around which the knowledge struggle now clusters. Old realities remain in a period of transformation. The state may retreat, to cite Susan Strange's book title (Strange, 1996), with respect to some of its erstwhile functions, but it assumes new functions. Globalization does not bring about the disappearance of the state any more than *real socialism* brought about its 'withering away'. States have made the framework for globalization, just as Karl Polanyi pointed out that states made the framework for the self-regulating market in the nineteenth century (Polanyi, 1944). However, in projecting thinking forward with normative intent, states could also become agencies for bringing the global economy under social control. The state remains a site of struggle for those who would challenge the social consequences of globalization. History does not end with globalization of the economy despite some predictions (Fukuyama, 1992). History goes on and has the potential to shape new structures of thought and of political authority. The opportunity now opens to develop the forms of knowledge conducive to such innovation and to bring them into the power struggle over the future.

The Cold War and knowledge of world affairs

For three decades and more, knowledge in the sphere of world politics was built predominantly with reference to the Cold War. What is now called neo-realism is a technology of power, a problem-solving form of knowledge applicable to the rivalry of two super powers. It was generally adequate to that purpose. Its limitation was the assumption that anything not pertaining to the superpower struggle could be ignored.

Of course, for the great mass of humankind, other considerations were paramount: physical survival in conditions of hunger, disease, violent conflicts and, at a more spiritual level, the denial of cultural identity. These were subordinated to the global power struggle, or, in so far as they became disruptive, they were linked instrumentally to the interests of the two super powers. Two competing forms of homogenization – world capitalism and world communism, respectively picturing themselves as the free world and national liberation – were the only games allowed. Once the overarching control of the Cold War was lifted, the underlying but obscured diversity of the human situation became more fully apparent. Neo-realism lost its monopoly of explaining the world and of proposing action.

In searching for an alternative basis of knowledge, it is well to begin with an understanding of how we got where we are, and then look to the problems that cluster on the threshold of the new millennium. This means finding a new *ontology* of world order.

There are two meanings of 'ontology'. The primary meaning is an affirmation of the ultimate reality of the universe – what we can call Ontology I. It probably has its roots in monotheistic religion and was taken over in secular form by the European Enlightenment. Human beings unconsciously invent the idea of God as the all-powerful creator; from that, they reverse the process of invention to assume the human mind to be God-like, i.e. to have the potential for understanding the 'truth' of the universe.[4] Ontology I can take the form of affirming the kind of truth embodied in religious revelation or in the certainties of Enlightenment philosophy. It can also, in a spurious form, apply to the universalizing of ideas that are manifestly products of a particular historical situation, but are not recognized to be such for lack of critical appraisal.

The other meaning of ontology – which we can call Ontology II (the subject of this chapter) – is the attempt to identify the factors that help towards understanding and acting upon a particular historical conjuncture. Another way of putting this would be to call it the task of perceiving the historical structures that characterize an epoch. These structures, which are mental constructions, summarize the cumulative results of collective human action in particular historical epochs. The purpose of defining them is to construct a base point for considering the problems in maintaining or transforming a particular historical order. Ontology II is a transitory snapshot of a world in perpetual motion. Such a synchronic picture cannot be a mere list of factors. To qualify as ontology, it has to show the interactive properties of a system – albeit an open system in which the homoeostatic mechanisms that maintain closure can be disrupted by forces that open the way for change.

Neo-realism had an explicit ontology – a perverse form of Ontology I – in which states, balance of power, Hobbesian-power-seeking man, and the contractual basis of polity were presumed to be eternal interrelated components of world order. The critical perspective has relativized neo-realism, perceiving it as an ideology of the Cold War. In a more positive sense, the critical perspective envisages a shift in ontology towards a more adequate depicting of the 'real world' on the threshold of the twenty-first century; but so far this alternative ontology is only a contested work in progress.

My aim here is to try to grasp the directions of ontological reconstruction that will give a proper weight to factors ignored by neo-realism, but which are relevant to understanding the power relations that affect conflict and cooperation and the prospects of human survival. Because ontological shift both reflects and anticipates structural change, it is also important that the effort focus on the forces that are capable of reshaping structures consolidated from the past.

This enquiry into structure and agency is undertaken in a spirit of realism. Realism is concerned with power; but the questions, Where does power lie? and, How is it exercised? should be asked without any prior assumptions about the answers. Neo-realism starts with the assumptions mentioned above. Its ontology forecloses a broader search. E. H. Carr, who initiated the modern study of international relations, had a much broader and more open understanding of power in world affairs. He was sensitive to economic and social structures and to culture and ideology. He saw states not as a series of like entities (*the* state), but as historically differentiated forms of political authority. Returning to Carr's realism is a first step towards escaping from the ahistorical confines of neo-realism.[2]

There has already been a good deal of work towards expanding neo-realism by adding markets to states in the conventional ontology. But even this is not a sufficient answer to the problem of where power lies in the late twentieth century. A Marxist might justifiably argue that states and markets are just two forms of alienation. The first displaces human responsibility to an artificial construction, the state. The second displaces human relations to relations between things in the market. Underlying each of these constructs are social relations, the human substance that is active in these two spheres. Really existing social power relations is the fundamental object of enquiry. We can begin by looking at how the struggle over knowledge of world affairs has evolved in recent decades as a mirror of changing power relations.

The obsolescence of IR and IPE

Perhaps the most important development in international studies in recent decades has been the emergence of international political economy (IPE) as a pendant or complement to a theory of international relations (IR) that was focused primarily on the military and political. In the world of academia, this came about as though a single organism had divided itself into two. The result has been separate funding, separate career patterns, distinct sets of journals. It is now the moment to retrace the origins of this divide and to ask whether the onward march of history does not challenge us to think beyond that phase of separation, and to envisage a more integrated form of knowledge.

Initially, IPE made its mark by giving more prominence to the economic foundations of power. But its importance was not limited to expanding the accepted subject matter of international relations. IPE gradually changed the way of thinking about world order. It put the emphasis on the frameworks or historical structures within which human activity takes place and on the slow processes of change in these frameworks. This made a sharp contrast with a politics of international relations that worked with fixed assumptions about the nature of the state system and an economics that worked with equally fixed assumptions about economic processes. The conventional methods were useful guides to problem-solving under stable conditions. They were not very useful for understanding changes in the ways people were coming to perceive their place in the world and the nature of the problems they faced. The emerging multiplicity of identities with the particular sets of problems these identities threw into prominence were an indication of the complexity of these changes.

The real achievement of IPE was not to bring in economics, but to open up a critical investigation into change in historical structures. Having done this, the emphasis on economics became merely an important incident in the movement towards a new knowledge about world order. This movement brought in many subjects other than economics in the narrow sense. It encouraged, for example, enquiry into the implications of gender, a franker look at race and colonialism, and the implications of human activity for the biosphere. And it was accompanied by a broadening of the concept of security that included many of the things that IPE had opened on to, including forms of discrimination and threats to the biosphere.

Most broadly, IPE began to look more at how historical structures – those conditions not of their own choosing within which people make history, as Marx wrote (Marx, 1969, p. 15) – are reshaped from the bottom up by slow molecular changes in societies. IPE also brought in a spirit of self-criticism, of reflexivity, the importance of becoming aware of how one's own position in time and place and social position define's one's perspective on history. Having achieved this revolution in thinking, IPE, along with IR in the earlier conventional sense, have become obsolescent, clearing the ground for a more integrated knowledge about processes of world order.

The search for this more integrated form of knowledge goes beyond the IR/IPE duality to challenge other established boundaries. In so far as we begin to see social relations as the foundation of political authorities and the origin of conflicts, the conventional separation of comparative politics from international relations makes little sense. Of course, no one can study everything and some people will know more about things that have been bracketed as comparative politics than about activities in the diplomatic and multilateral sphere. For the purpose of understanding world order or regional developments, it is necessary to draw together knowledge about power relations in society and knowledge about relations among the entities like states which are shaped by those power relations. It is also necessary to breach sacrosanct disciplinary boundaries so as to draw upon history and sociology and geography – indeed upon all the social sciences and humanities (Braudel, 1980).

We should therefore begin by examining the way social relations are being reshaped on a global scale by tendencies in the global political economy, especially since the world economic crisis of the mid-1970s.

Sources of globalization

During the Great Depression of the 1930s, the state had to become the agent of economic revival and the defender of domestic welfare and employment against disturbances from the outside world. Corporatism, the union of the state with productive forces at the national level, became, under various names, the model of economic regulation; and economic nationalism with the 'beggar-my-neighbour' practices it often involved was its counterpart in international economic relations. Following World War II, the Bretton Woods system attempted to strike a balance between the liberal world market and the domestic responsibilities of states. States became accountable to agencies of an international economic order – the International Monetary Fund (IMF), the World Bank, and the General Agreement on Tariffs and Trade (GATT) – in regard to trade liberalization and exchange rate stability and convertibility; and states were also granted facilities and time to make adjustments in their national economic practices so as not to have to sacrifice the welfare of domestic groups. This balanced compromise between defence of welfare and a liberal international economic order sustained three decades of growth and progress, but a crisis in the post-war order came about during the years 1968–75.

From then onward, the balanced compromise shifted towards a subordination of domestic economies to the perceived exigencies of the global economy, with as accompaniment growing disparity between rich and poor and gradual erosion of the social protections introduced during the post-war decades. States willy-nilly became more effectively accountable to forces inherent in the global economy, and they were constrained to mystify this accountability in the eyes and ears of their own public through the new vocabulary of globalization, interdependence and competitiveness.

How and why did this happen? The matter will be long debated. It is, however, possible to recognize this period as a real turning point in the sense of a weakening of old and the emergence of new structures. Some key elements of the transformation can be identified.

The structural power of capital

Inflation, which at a modest level had hitherto been a stimulus to growth, beneficent alike to business and organized labour, now at higher rates and with declining profit margins, became perceived by business as inhibiting investment. Business blamed unions for raising wages and governments for a cycle of excessive spending, borrowing and taxing. Governments were made to understand that a revival of economic growth depended on business confidence to invest, and that this confidence depended on 'discipline' directed at trade unions and government fiscal management. The investment strike and capital flight are powerful weapons that no government can ignore with impunity.

The restructuring of production

In so far as government policies did help to restore business confidence, new investment was by and large of a different type. The crisis of the post-war order accelerated the shift from Fordism to post-Fordism – from economies of scale to economies of flexibility. The large integrated plant employing semi-skilled workers for the mass production of standardized goods became an obsolete model of organization. The new model was based on a core–periphery structure of production, with a relatively small core of relatively permanent employees handling finance, research and development, technological organization and innovation; and a periphery consisting of dependent components of the production process – outsourcing and temporary and part-time workers. Restructuring into the core–periphery model has facilitated the use of a more precariously employed labour force segmented by ethnicity, gender, nationality, religion or geographical location. It has weakened the power of trade unions and strengthened that of capital within the production process. It has also made business less controllable by any single state authority.

The role of debt

Both governments and corporations have relied increasingly on debt financing rather than on taxation or equity investment. Furthermore, debt has to an increasing extent been *foreign debt*. As the proportion of state revenue going into debt service rises, governments have become more effectively accountable to external bond markets than to their own public. Their options in exchange rate policy, fiscal policy and trade policy have become constrained by financial interests linked to the global economy. Corporations are no more autonomous of international finance than governments. Finance has become decoupled from production to become an independent power, an autocrat over the real economy.[3]

And what drives the decision making of the financial manipulators? The short-range thinking of immediate financial gain, not the long-range thinking of industrial development. The market mentality functions synchronically (i.e. it takes account of relationships at a given point in time); development requires a diachronic mode of thought (i.e. considering planned and foreseen changes over time, the historical dimension).[4] The result of financial power's dominance over the real economy was as often as not the destruction of jobs and productive capital.

The structures of globalization

The crisis of the post-war order has expanded the breadth and depth of a global economy that exists alongside and incrementally supersedes the classical international economy (Madeuf and Michalet, 1978). The global economy is the system generated by global production and global finance. Global production is able to make use of the territorial divisions of the international economy, playing off one territorial jurisdiction against another so as to maximize reductions in costs, savings in taxes, avoidance of anti-pollution regulation, control over labour and guarantees of political stability and favour. Global finance has achieved a virtually unregulated twenty-four-hour-a-day network. The collective decision making of global finance is centred in world cities rather than states – New York, Tokyo, London, Paris, Frankfurt – and extends by computer terminals to the rest of the world.

The two components of the global economy – production and finance – are in potential contradiction. Global production requires a certain stability in politics and finance in order to expand. Global finance has the upper hand because its power over credit creation determines the future of production; but global finance is in a parlously fragile condition. A concatenation of calamitous circumstances could bring it down – a number of corporate failures combined with government debt defaults or a cessation of lending by leading creditors and international institutions like the IMF. The major crises of the world economy have been debt crises of this kind – the Mexican crises of the 1980s and early 1990s and the Asian crisis of the later 1990s. Up to now governments, even the combined governments of the Group of Seven (G7), subsequently the G8 with the addition of Russia, have not been able to devise any effectively secure scheme of regulation for global finance that could counter such a collapse.

There is, in effect, no explicit political or authority structure for the global economy. There is, nevertheless, something that remains to be deciphered, something that could be described by the French word *nébuleuse* or by the notion of 'governance without government'. There is a transnational process of consensus seeking among the official caretakers of the global economy. It aims towards generating consensual guidelines, underpinned by an ideology of globalization, that are transmitted into the policy-making channels of national governments and big corporations (see Chapter 2 and Cox, 1987, pp. 253–67). The *modus operandi* of this process of consensus seeking in the management of the global economy is a prime target for continuing analysis. Closely related to it is the private power that is effective in world financial markets. Bond rating agencies and mutual and pension funds are examples of these private forces (Sinclair, 1994 and 1997; and Harmes, 2001).

Different forms of state have facilitated this tightening of the global/local relationship in countries occupying different positions in the global system. At one time, the military-bureaucratic form of state seemed to be optimum in countries of peripheral capitalism for the enforcement of monetary discipline. Subsequently, IMF-inspired 'structural adjustment' was pursued by elected presidential regimes (in Argentina, Brazil, Mexico, Peru, South Korea) that managed to retain a degree of insulation from popular pressures. The most powerful states encourage this form of political authority as likely to be more stable in the long run than military dictatorships (Robinson, 1999a). When adherence to financial orthodoxy, i.e. the dictates of the global financial managers, result in widespread distress among the people, their pressure may overflow the bounds of authority, as happened when a popular uprising toppled the government of Argentina in December 2001.

Most countries conformed to the consensus during the last two decades of the twentieth century. India, formerly following a more auto-centric or self-reliant path, moved towards integration into the global economy. Neo-conservative ideology sustained the transformation of the state in Britain, Germany, the United States, Canada and Australasia in the direction of globalization. Socialist Party governments in France, Italy and Spain adjusted their policies to the new orthodoxy. The states of the former Soviet empire were also swept up into the globalizing trend, and in the Asian crisis of the late 1990s, the countries of southeast Asia became subject to the dictates of global finance.

In all of these processes of change, a shifting balance of social forces has been critical. It is difficult to make simple causal statements about this, as to whether the initiative has come from a strengthening of capital and weakening of labour within countries, for instance; or whether the primary influence has come from global capital which has its extensions into national societies. The forces in play are both domestic and global. Strategies to counteract them would likewise have to be both local and global. As global capital reaches into the local economy, resistance to multinational corporate globalization would build from the local to the global.

The changing social structure of the world

The globalization of production is producing a three-part social hierarchy that is world-wide in extent, cutting across state boundaries. The proportions among the three levels in society vary from one territorial unit to another, but the tendency is uniform throughout.

The top level comprises those people who are *integrated* into the global economy. This stratum runs from the global economy managers in public and private sectors to relatively privileged workers who serve global production and finance in reasonably stable employment.

A second level includes those who serve the global economy in a subordinate and more *precarious* way. This is the potentially disposable labour force, the realm of 'flexibility', 'restructuring', 'downsizing' and 'outsourcing'. It is a consequence of the phenomenon known as post-Fordism, the restructuring of production on a core–periphery basis as noted above. Employment of the peripheral and precarious kind is expanding in the industrialized countries as the proportion of stable employment in industry declines, and it characterizes most industrial jobs in poor countries.

The bottom level comprises those who are *excluded* from the global economy. Here are the permanently unemployed, superfluous labour or the underemployed and many of the people living in what one former commissioner of the European Union called the 'useless' countries,[5] i.e. those countries that have little prospect of making a go of the global economy.

The top *integrated* level are doing quite well in material terms, although they are only a small proportion of humanity.

The second *precarious* level is the one that is expanding most rapidly with the geographical extension of globalization and with the growing penetration of the social structure of globalization into the economically leading countries. Its members are placed in an ambiguous position towards the social order: supportive in their concern to find and keep a job, but potentially hostile when insecurity strikes.

The *excluded* pose a potential threat to the globalization order. But certain conditions may diffuse that threat: the fact that excluded people's energies are directed to personal and family survival rather than protest; and the proclivity of rejected people often to direct their violence against their excluded neighbours rather than against the established society.

Nevertheless, the potential for challenge to the globalization order exists among both the excluded and the precarious segments. There are also contradictions among the integrated, many of these generated from ecological concerns which affect jobs in forestry, fisheries and energy industries. The challenge to globalization, if it is to become effective, would require the formation of a common will, a vision of an alternative future, and the transcending of the manifold divisions of ethnicity, religion, gender and geography that cut across the three-level social hierarchy being created by globalization.

This restructuring of world society brought about by globalization challenges the primacy of state-oriented identities as people become aware that transnational economic organizations are determining their livelihood and populations become increasingly heterogeneous from migration. It also challenges the Marxist schema of the primacy of class-oriented identities. The nineteenth- and early twentieth-century concepts of class have been muddied by the emerging social structure. The 'working class' in its conventional meaning is now divided among the three levels of the social hierarchy and these three components can be shown to have very divergent interests. Where the sense of class remains strong today, it may be more a cultural matter than something defined by a property relationship. Yet the concept of 'class' retains vigour and calls for reformulation in late twentieth-century conditions as a means towards the formation of a common front of resistance and movement towards an alternative to the future that is being prepared by globalization. It would have to embrace comprehensively the various identities – ethnic, religious, gender, etc. – manifested by those groups that have initiated pockets of resistance.

States and the state system

After the fall of the Berlin Wall, inter-state relations became for a time more concerned with adapting state structures, policies and practices to the neo-liberal vision of a global economy than with the alliance building of the Cold War period. The 'war on terrorism' proclaimed by US President George W. Bush following the attacks of September 11, 2001, on New York and the Pentagon revived the emphasis on military alliance building. The military factor regained prominence as the guarantor of the structures that favour a neo-liberal world order, and the police and surveillance function of states was accentuated.

The emphasis on adjusting national policies and practices to a neo-liberal global economy contrasts with the post-war concept of the state as mediator between the international economy (understood as flows across national boundaries) and domestic concerns about economic growth and employment. According to the neo-liberal doctrine, domestic interests are best served by allowing free rein to the global economy, and new efforts at regulation, such as those embodied in the World Trade Organization (WTO) and the aborted Multilateral Agreement on Investment (MAI), are designed to limit the capacity of states to interfere with the working of the neo-liberal global economic order.

At the inter-state level, two main functions are performed: (1) the propagation and legitimating of neo-liberal global economic practice by international institutions, mainly the IMF, the World Bank and the WTO, but now increasingly by the United Nations itself;[6] and (2) the neutralizing of potential disruptions of the global economy that could arise from explosions among the bottom (*excluded*) segment of the world social hierarchy.

Global poor relief and riot control now tops UN priorities, displacing development assistance which had the top spot during the 1950s and 1960s. Poor relief takes the form of humanitarian assistance. Riot control takes the form of peace keeping or peace enforcement. Famine requiring humanitarian aid can often be traced to the consequence of a globalization that favours food production for world markets over local self-sufficiency. UN military intervention, intended to establish and maintain public order where local government authority has broken down, has become a back up for NATO- (i.e. US-) commanded military action against 'rogue states'. In these ways the United Nations serves as a subordinate adjunct to centralized global military power.

The emerging world order thus appears as a multilevel structure. At the base are social forces. Whether they are self-conscious and articulated into what Gramsci called a historic bloc (Gramsci, 1971, pp. 137, 366–77) or are depoliticized and manipulable is the key issue in the making of the future. The old state system is resolving itself into a complex of political-economic entities: micro-regions, traditional states and macro-regions with institutions of greater or lesser functional scope and formal authority. World cities are the keyboards of the global economy. Rival transnational processes of ideological formation aim respectively at hegemony and counter-hegemony. Institutions of concertation and coordination bridge the major states and macro-regions. Multilateral processes exist for conflict management, peace keeping, and regulation and service providing in a variety of functional areas (trade, communications, health, etc.). The whole picture resembles the multilevel order of medieval Europe more than the Westphalian model of a system of sovereign independent states that has heretofore been the paradigm of international relations.[7] With the wars in Kosovo and Afghanistan the relatively decentralized medieval model can be seen as regressing in time towards the centralized imperial model of Rome (Chapter 2, pp. 40–3).

The biosphere

Alongside social restructuring, environmental degradation is another accompaniment to economic globalization. The conventional study of international relations has heretofore recognized only human actors, but in recent years some non-human forces have appeared, threatening to constrict the realm of human action: global warming, the hole in the ozone layer, deforestation and soil erosion, the loss of biodiversity, the collapse of fish stocks, etc. These forces express the response of nature to the cumulative consequences of human activities. They are new phenomena which signal dangers to the physical environment in which human activities take place, which can lead to conflict, for example over scarce vital resources such as water, and which challenge accepted modes of understanding of humanity's place in the world.

Monotheistic religions, with their notion of a transcendent deity, encouraged a separation of human beings, the image of the divine, from nature, created by God for the use and enjoyment of humans. Scientific modernism inherited this idea in conceiving nature as something to be dominated, tamed and shaped by human beings. The irruption of forces of nature into human affairs, not as the occasional flood or earthquake, but as a deterioration of the planet's life-support system, now suggests the need to revise this notion by seeing humanity as one component of the natural world, interacting with other forms of life and life-sustaining substances. The biosphere is this larger interactive realm: an envelope circling the earth and stretching from the seabeds to the higher atmosphere.

In the modernist tradition, economics has reduced nature to land and considered land as a commodity – what Karl Polanyi (1944) called a false commodity, since land is not produced for sale on the market. Nature has been subordinated to economic logic, to the 'market mentality' which is based on the proposition that everything is for sale. The basic problem for market logic is getting the prices right. Nature, however, has a logic of its own that is not comprehended by economics and that functions independently of economics. The basic problem for nature's logic is equilibrium among the different forms of life and life-supporting substances.

So long as there is enough slack in nature, market logic is tolerated by nature; but when the effect of economic logic is to strain nature to the limit, nature responds with its veto.[8] The problem here is to rethink economics within a science of nature so that economic prescriptions are attentive to signals from non-human nature. This implies a departure from the modernist epistemology that separates human capacity for knowledge from the world of nature and conceives nature as a manipulable object. The dilemma for humans now is to think through the consequences of understanding ourselves as part of nature rather than as dominant over nature.[9]

One implication of this is to reveal a fundamental contradiction in economic globalization and perhaps also in movements of democratization. The dynamic of globalization is consumer demand. The consumption model of North America and western Europe – consumerism – is what the other peoples of the world have aspired to. To extend this model universally would likely have catastrophic consequences for the biosphere; but to suggest that relatively poor societies should drop this aspiration incurs the charge of imperialism. It seems obvious that those societies that have pioneered the quest of consumerism would have to show the way towards an alternative model that would be consistent with biosphere maintenance.

This is where the challenge to democracy arises. Former US President

George Bush anticipated it when, in preparing for the Earth Summit at Rio in 1992, he was reported as saying: 'Our life-style is not open to negotiation.' He was implicitly acknowledging that change of life-style is necessary for biospheric survival and at the same time recognizing that political survival in modern democracies makes it highly risky for politicians to advocate. If such a basic change in people's aspirations and behaviour cannot be changed by political leadership, let alone by exhortations at international conferences, then the change must come from within civil society. The issue then becomes whether the reconstruction of people's understanding of their place in nature and of what is necessary to maintain the biosphere can outpace and reverse the progress of ecological degradation.

Inter-subjectivity: civilizations and forms of political economy

Identity is important politically because it is the focus around which people can become mobilized to act to change their conditions and to pursue social goals. As already noted, the two salient forms of identity of the nineteenth and twentieth centuries, nationality and class, while remaining significant banners of mobilization, have been subsumed into a complex of other identities. The nation-state for people in the richer countries has become a less central feature of their identity (with the notable exception of the United States), while in some poorer countries nationalism has become more virulent and aggressive. Social and economic cleavages remain fundamental as economic globalization accentuates polarization between rich and poor in all parts of the world (UNRISD, 1995); but these cleavages are less frequently expressed as social class identities and more often as gender, race or ethnicity, religion, organizational affiliation, or a consciousness of historical grievance and humiliation. The multiplicity of identities underlines the significance of subjective (or rather inter-subjective) forces in world affairs.

By inter-subjectivity, I mean the prevailing sense of the nature of the world, or the common sense of 'reality' shared among a population. Inter-subjectivity can be understood as the knowledge produced in the cumulative collective response by people to their conditions of existence. Thus, inter-subjectivity is a creation of history, not something innate in the human soul, although in its unquestioned state it may appear among contemporaries to be an innate awareness of the natural order of the world.

The study of civilizations approaches this question of subjective perceptions in its largest aggregates. There was a good deal of scholarly thinking about civilizations during the first half of the twentieth century. The notion of a plurality of civilizations was put aside during World War II, which was seen (in the West) as a war to defend *civilization* in the singular. The concept of a plurality of civilizations was all but eliminated (again in the West) during the Cold War. Now thinking about civilizations has begun again, but in a state of considerable confusion.

In the world of the late twentieth century, civilizational differences were expressed through different forms of economic and social organization. This has been obscured both by dogmatic forms of Marxism and by dogmatic neo-liberalism both of which cling to an economic determinist philosophy, an oversimplified reductionist view of capitalism as a monolithic global force.

There is, of course, a sense in which capitalism is a global force: big corporate organizations based in different parts of the world compete for shares in a world market, and finance flows freely across territorial boundaries. But there is also a sense in which people in different places are organized in somewhat different ways, mainly to participate in this global capitalism, but also sometimes to exist outside of it. These differences are important for the people who live within different coexisting forms of capitalism.

Thus, we can speak in one sense of global capitalism as the dynamic force of globalization; but at the same time, it must be recognized that capitalism, the competitive drive for profits and expansion, takes different social forms shaped by different civilizational imperatives, some of which place limits upon the 'animal spirits' of unconstrained profit seeking. Concepts of society and organization can express different notions as to what is 'natural' and proper in human relations. These differences cannot be reduced just to a matter of ideology. Ideologies are conscious constructions which give general orientations to understanding and action. Inter-subjectivity is less conscious and more deeply rooted, the common sense of a people as to what is right and proper in their collective life.

Karl Polanyi's concept of 'substantive economies' is a way of seizing these differences within the more abstract notion of 'global capitalism'. Polanyi (1944, 1957) was concerned with the ways in which economies were embedded within societies. He rejected the notion that the economy can be abstracted from society in such a way as to make society subservient to the economy. Where this is attempted – he spoke of the nineteenth-century attempt to impose the rule of a self-regulating market as a utopian project – it provokes a reaction from society that will usually be expressed through political action. In Europe, the reaction began with labour legislation and later became the welfare state. Utopian projects are still current; the most obvious is the hyper-liberal attempt to construct a deregulated global market. But other distinctive forms of economic-social organization also exist; and rival forms of economic-social organization contest the terrain on which hyper-liberalism has claimed predominance (e.g. Albert, 1991).

Three salient existing forms of political economy are: (1) the Anglo-American individualistic-competitive form; (2) the European social market form; and (3) the East Asian mercantilist form. Each of these has generated ideological representations. Hyper-liberalism is the ideology of the Anglo-American form, envisaging an untrammeled open global movement of goods and money. The social market is the characteristic European form, ideologically derived from Christian democracy and social democracy. 'Asian capitalism' has been constructed, often with attribution to Confucianism, as an ideology supportive of authoritarian politics or bureaucratized paternalism. Yet the forms are more deeply rooted than these ideologies; they can be seen as constructions that find a more or less congenial base in different human attitudes and values – different forms of inter-subjectivity.

There is scope for other potential forms of political economy to emerge. What will happen in Russia? The consequence of 'shock therapy' has been erosion of public services, mass unemployment, frequent non-payment of workers, and an economy controlled by the mafia. Russia's tragedy has been its people's subjection to a sequence of alien-inspired radical reforms, first by Peter the Great, then by the Bolsheviks, and latterly by Harvard economists. Is there a possibility that even so patient a people as the Russians may ultimately reject foreign models and attempt to build their own economy drawing upon their own imagined social traditions?

In China, a new form of political economy is emerging, rather confusedly described as both communist and capitalist, yet gradually revealing its own characteristics (Ling, 1996). Is it conceivable that Islam will evolve practices that reconcile its principles of human relations with economic activity in an evolving vision of the world? (IILS, 1980). Another force lies in the Green movement which has given rise to many small, locally based economies with cooperative forms of production and their own currencies (Helleiner, 1996). These social experiments may perhaps be seen as an indication of the search for economic practices that would be consistent with biosphere maintenance.

These different forms of political economy which express civilizational differences coexist within the world economy and in some cases become rivals. They challenge the notion of a single hegemonic homogenizing global economy.

The importance of the study of civilizations lies in these basic premises concerning world order:

- There are alternatives for the human future. We are not all bound by the inexorable expansion of economic globalization, determined by competitiveness in the global market, leading to a homogenized global society on the model of contemporary America. Civilizations embodying different values and different patterns of social organization are conceivable, for good or for ill. In other words, there is still a problem of moral and social choice.
- If different civilizations do coexist, then the problem of mutual comprehension becomes paramount for the maintenance of world order. This arises in an epistemological context far different from the game theoretic notions popular during the Cold War, which assumed a single shared form of rationality.

The first problem in understanding such a plural world is to be able to enter into the mental framework of people who see the world differently from the way we do (whoever 'we' are). That is to say, different peoples may have

different perceptions of reality. 'Reality' is historically and socially constructed, and is thus different for different civilizations, not a universal given.
(This, it should be said, does not mean *adopting* other civilizational perspectives or rationalities, only *understanding* them.)

The next problem is to be able to work towards finding common ground
among these different realities as a basis for some practical degree of universality within a world of differences.

The covert world

There is a heterogeneous set of forces that can be loosely described as
involved in political corruption and clandestine activities. I group these under
the heading of the 'covert world'. It includes intelligence agencies, organized
crime and the drug trade, money-laundering banks, the arms trade, paramil-
itary bands and mercenaries, religious cults, the sex trade and terrorist
organizations. These all work in the same field, distinct both from legitimate
politics, on the one hand, and from civil society on the other. At times they
interact in cooperation as well as in conflict with each other and with political and corporate authorities. While there have been studies of some of these
components of the covert world one by one, for example of organized crime,
or of particular intelligence agencies (the CIA or the KGB), or of particular
cycles of terrorist activity, the pattern of interactions among this variety of
agents and their cumulative consequences for political systems has not
received much attention. Yet this realm of political activity has great implications for popular control. A weak civil society leaves a wide political space
for occult influences. The best way to enhance democratic accountability is to
narrow the space open to the covert world through the development of an
active civil society.

Civil society

The bottom-up forces are many and various but have rarely achieved a degree
of coherence that could plausibly be considered a basis for counter-
hegemony. The prospect for counter-hegemony is, however, the focal issue for
study of structural transformation. The French strikes of December 1996
were notable not only in rallying workers, despite the weakening over recent
decades of the labour movement, but also in gaining the sympathy and support of a public who were willing to put up with the inconveniences of a
shut-down of public transport in a big city in the cause of combating an economic policy perceived as sacrificing ordinary people in favour of dominant
global-economy interests. A comparable effort at mobilizing opposition to the
North American Free Trade Agreement (NAFTA) was initiated also by
labour movements in the United States, Canada and Mexico, with the support of women's and environmentalist organizations. It failed of its goal, but
did demonstrate a degree of political efficacy.

Working upon the hypothesis that political authority is built from the bottom up leads to a focus upon civil society. Civil society is the positive pendant to the negative weight of the covert world. More and more attention is being given by political scientists to the development of civil society. In many African countries, people have been organizing themselves on a local community basis to struggle for survival in conditions imposed upon them by governments and international organizations (Cheru, 1989). In Indonesia, the spread of organized community movements may constitute the potential basis for a new political authority to replace ultimately the corrupt and tyrannical shell of power that crumbled with the Suharto regime. A latent civil society in the Congo facilitated the collapse of the Mobutu kleptocracy, although it played no role in the immediate sequel (Braekman, 1997). In Chiapas, the Zapatista movement aimed to transcend its original condition as an ethnically based guerrilla movement to become a force for the revival of Mexican civil society and in the process, by the use of modern electronic communications, to forge transnational links as an element in a global counter-hegemonic movement (Najman, 1997).

In contrast to the covert world which by and large sustains the established power from which it parasitically extracts its gains, a dissident world can be seen as emerging through civil society movements which work towards the transformation of established power. Its components express their lack of confidence in formally constituted power by organizing themselves to express and work for an alternative world, the possibility of which hegemonic ideology denies.

Dynamics of change

So we have three realms of political activity in the world at the turn of the millennium: the hegemonic power of globalization; the covert world which grows parasitically upon it; and the dissident world groping towards the creation of a counter-hegemonic challenge.

New social movements have become the vehicles of protest and means for prospecting alternative forms of social economy. They have only partially been directed towards the state and have rarely operated through formal electoral channels. They express more a will to reconstitute civil society, and in some cases to construct a 'civic state' on the basis of a strengthened civil society – a state that would be more fully responsive to the bottom-up forces of civil society.[10]

It should not be assumed that all social movements are supportive of democratic methods and open comprehensiveness. The contemporary world is rife with racism and right-wing populism; a fascist revival is probably stronger now than at any time since the 1930s. These are as much popular movements as those usually classified as 'new social movements'. Civil society is a terrain of struggle between reactionary and transformative forces.

The context in which this struggle is taking place seems to leave the outcome indeterminate. If modernism in political terms is to be understood à la Max Weber as consisting of states that define the national identities and loyalties of people, hierarchical rational bureaucratic administrations, and classes and status groups that give people their social identities, then this modernist social structure has become weaker in all parts of the world (although more so in some parts than others). State authority has been fragmented by ethnic, linguistic and local identities, and by macro-regional institutions like the European Union and NAFTA. Bureaucracies have been experienced as alienating by those who have to deal with them. Class identities have been eroded by the growing salience of ethnic, cultural and gender identities and by the fragmenting of 'classes' in the new social structuring produced by globalization.

If we are to assume that power is grounded in human communities, and if we take a 'bottom-up' perspective on world order, then we need to ask about the condition of public affinity or comfort with the political authorities of the entities that formally constitute world order – the states and multilateral institutions and processes. That affinity seems to range from the tenuous to the hostile throughout the world. The sense of identity between people and polity is weak. Confidence in the political classes is at a low ebb.

In some parts of the world, at one extreme, people regard political rulers as predatory tyrants and seek to avoid contact with them as much as possible. But even in those countries accustomed to constitutional government and the rule of law, there is often widespread public scepticism about political leadership. The political class is held to be both corrupt and incompetent: corrupt in the sense of holding their own careers above any consideration of public interest; and incompetent in being unable to understand and deal effectively with the things that concern the public, like unemployment, erosion of public services, and social inequities. Political corruption is encouraged by the high cost of election campaigns and the importance of political decisions for corporate interests.

In part also, this lack of confidence may be attributed to the ideological hegemony of globalization. Ideology proclaims the inevitability of globalization with its categorical imperative of global competitiveness. Globalization thus appears as the ultimate form of alienation: something created by people that has come to wield absolute power over them.

Politicians no longer talk about citizens. A citizen is an autonomous individual in his or her aspect of contemplating the public good or envisaging a good future society. Since globalization abolishes choice – not choice among consumer products, but choice as to the kind of society it would be good to live in – there is really no role left for the citizen. Instead, politicians refer to taxpayers, job-seekers and stakeholders (echoes of corporatism); and government, emptied of the possibility of alternative choices about future society becomes reduced to a question of management (Guéhenno, 1993).

In these conditions, there is ample scope for forces that operate outside of the control of formal public authorities and beyond the scope of conventional political analysis – the covert world of politics. Occasional and sometimes dramatic events bring it to public consciousness: the foul-ups of intelligence operations, terrorist attacks, financial corruption and political funding scandals.

What is to be done?

The only way effectively to confront the salient issues of the late twentieth century – biospheric collapse, extreme social polarization, exclusionary politics, alienation with either apathy or violence as a response – is to reconstitute political authorities at local, national and global levels that are firmly based in public support. Only strong public authorities will be capable of dealing with these problems. Such a movement would have to come from the bottom, from a reconstitution of civil society as a support for political authorities attentive to people's needs (whereas much of the movement in civil society recently has been towards withdrawal from alienating government and corporate powers). The movement presupposes rediscovery of social solidarity and of confidence in a potential for sustained collective creativity, inspired by a commitment to social equity, to reciprocal recognition of cultural and civilizational differences, to biospheric survival and to non-violent methods of dealing with conflict. The supreme challenge is to build a counter-hegemonic formation that would embody these principles; and this task implies as a first step the working out of an ontology that focuses attention on the key elements in this struggle.

Since World War II, world political economy has gone through one major phase of structural change. The mid-1970s witnessed the transition from Keynesianism and Fordism towards neo-liberal globalization. The post-war world sought to construct an economic order that would ground economic behaviour in social responsibility, to give a priority to the goals of full employment, social security, and – in a modest but avowed way – to narrow the gap between rich and poor countries. Keynesianism and Fordism were the techniques for allowing politics to redress the inequities of the market. These policies and practices reached a crisis point in the mid-1970s. From that point on, they were gradually abandoned in favour of allowing deregulated markets free rein. The consequences have been social conflict arising from growing polarization between rich and poor, recourse to violent forms of protest, the prospect of financial collapse, and the impending threat of biospheric crisis.

If there is to be a solution, it is unlikely to be a return to post-war practices. It would more likely have to be a new concept of economy, less resource depleting and polluting, and more oriented towards the basic material needs of people which advanced technology makes possible with a smaller proportion of workers, and much greater emphasis on the more neglected labour-intensive tasks of satisfying social and human needs for health, education, child and elder care, and conviviality. This, of course, implies a radical reorienting of social values, including the way in which different kinds of work are valued. The state will most likely have to regulate and legitimate these new practices, but it seems clear that response by the state will only be triggered by bottom-up pressure of citizen activism.

6 Civil society at the turn of the millennium

Prospects for an alternative world order

Eric Hobsbawm (1994, p. 459) has written that '[t]he world at the end of the Short Twentieth Century [1914–1991] is in a state of social breakdown rather than revolutionary crisis . . . .' The conclusion is hard to avoid. 'Real socialism' has collapsed; the anti-imperialist struggle in the former colonial world has resolved itself into a series of new states seeking a *modus vivendi* in subordination to global capitalism; the left in Europe is searching uncertainly for an alternative to neoliberal globalization while in the main adapting to it; even the Islamic revolution in Iran is hesitatingly moving towards an adjustment to dominant world economic forces. There is much violence – in the Balkans, central Africa, Algeria and Ulster – but none of it could be called revolutionary in the sense of promising a transformation of society. Global finance has lurched from a Mexican peso crisis in the 1980s to an Asian crisis in the 1990s and an Argentinian crisis in the 2000s, leaving a marginalized Africa almost unnoticed; but while finance dominates and constrains all governments' policies, there is no concerted means of global financial management.

If world politics is in such a condition of turbulent stasis, with little hope of calm, but no prospect of fundamental change, the polarization of rich people and poor people is becoming increasingly accentuated throughout the world. There is also evidence that people have become disenchanted with existing forms of politics. In these circumstances, many activists and theorists have looked to civil society as the source from which alternative, more equitable forms of society might arise. Is civil society in the late twentieth century the surrogate for a revolution that seems unlikely to happen? There is a debate on the left about this and that is the question behind the revival of interest in civil society.

The concept of civil society has a long history in European and American thought. From that source, it has been exported around the world. In order to explore the transformatory potential of civil society in our time, it is useful to consult some of that history. Antonio Gramsci, drawing upon that tradition, constructed a view of civil society particularly pertinent to the present debate; and he did so at a time when revolutionary transformation still seemed a possibility. I propose to examine the changing meanings of the term 'civil society' over the years, placing these meanings in their historical and contemporary contexts, and then to reflect upon Gramsci's thought as an approach to understanding society and politics that took form in the specific historical context of Italy in the 1920s and 1930s but still has fruitful applicability in the changed world-wide context of the early twenty-first century.

Gramsci was not concerned as an abstract theorist with building a system of political analysis that would stand the test of time. He was concerned with changing his world. Any development of his thinking should keep that goal to the fore and should thus both arise from reflection on the condition of the world as it is, and serve as a guide to action designed to change the world so as to improve the lot of humanity in social equity.

Civil society, in Gramsci's thinking, is the realm in which the existing social order is grounded; and it can also be the realm in which a new social order can be founded. His concern with civil society was, first, to understand the strength of the status quo, and then to devise a strategy for its transformation. The emancipatory potential of civil society was the object of his thinking. In the *Prison Notebooks*[1] civil society is an elastic concept, having different connotations in different passages. Often civil society appears as a function of the state as in the frequently quoted equation: 'State = political society + civil society, in other words hegemony protected by the armour of coercion' (*PN*, p. 263). Gramsci honed much of his thought against the philosophy of Benedetto Croce. Croce (1945, pp. 22–32) saw the state, following Hegel, in idealistic terms as the embodiment of ethics. Gramsci, in a historical materialist perspective, understood ethics as emanating from the social and cultural practices that enable historically conditioned human communities to cope with their environment. Croce's ethical state, for Gramsci, becomes ethical through the medium of civil society. There is a dialectic inherent in civil society. In one aspect, the educational and ideological agencies that are sustained ultimately by the state's coercive apparatus shape morals and culture. Yet in another aspect, civil society appears to have autonomy and to be more fundamental than the state, indeed to be the basis upon which a state can be founded. Civil society is both shaper and shaped, an agent of stabilization and reproduction, and a potential agent of transformation.

There is little point in trying to establish a fixed definition of Gramsci's concepts from exegesis of his text. That would negate Gramsci's way of thinking. He thought historically and dialectically, that is to say, his concepts are derived from his perceptions of reality and they serve not only to seize the momentary essence of a changing reality, but also to become intellectual tools for fomenting change. Certain basic guidelines are essential in order to discern what Fernand Braudel later called the limits of the possible, the starting point from which strategic planning for social transformation has to begin. The first of these is to know accurately the prevailing relations of social forces. These have material, organizational and ideological components, together constituting the configuration of a historic bloc.

Yet Gramsci was less concerned with the historic bloc as a stable entity than he was with historical mutations and transformations, and with the emancipatory potential for human agency in history. The concept of civil society in this emancipatory sense designates the combination of forces upon which the support for a new state and a new order can be built. These forces operate in a political and social space, a terrain occupied by different conflicting forces as historical change proceeds, – a terrain which is narrowed when there is a close identity between people and their political and social institutions (in Gramsci's terms, when hegemony prevails), but which is widened when this identity is weak.

Any fixed definition of the content of the concept 'civil society' would just freeze a particular moment in history and privilege the relations of social forces then prevailing. Rather than look for clearer definitions, we should try to understand the historical variations that have altered the meanings of the concept in the ongoing dialectic of concept and reality. We should not stop with the world of the 1930s which Gramsci knew, but carry on the process into the early twenty-first century. To continue and develop Gramsci's way of thinking is more true to his purpose than to mummify his text.

The changing meanings of 'civil society'

Writing at the beginning of the twenty-first century, we must recognize that the European tradition of political thought will now be seen as that of a particular civilization coexisting with others. It can no longer make an uncontested claim to universality, even though the concepts evolved in Western discourse have penetrated into all parts of the world through the era of Western dominance. Thus, Western terms may cover realities that are different. To Westerners these terms may obscure these differences by assimilating them to familiar Western meanings. This must be borne in mind in using a term like 'civil society'. We must be alert not only to the surface appearance, but also to a non-Western meaning that may be deeply buried. Nevertheless, it is necessary to retrace the concept of civil society to its European roots in the Enlightenment.

Civil society in Enlightenment thought was understood as the realm of particular interests, which in practice then meant the realm of the bourgeoisie. The state ideally embodied universality, the rule of law. The monarch was to be the first servant of the state, bound by and applying the rule of law. An intellectual problem for the Enlightenment was how to explain the necessary compatibility of the two, of the realm of particular interests and the realm of universality. If the state were to embody universality, then civil society must generate universal principles in the ethico-juridical sphere; civil society must be seen as creating the basis of common welfare out of the pursuit of particular interests. Both Hegel and Adam Smith thought they had achieved this reconciliation by in effect refurbishing the Christian doctrine of Providence, in Smith's case as the 'invisible hand' and in Hegel's as the 'cunning of reason'

(Becker, 1932). In its European origins, civil society and the bourgeoisie were synonymous. Civil society signified the self-conscious social group whose influence, if not necessarily its executive power, was expanding.

Karl Marx was, of course, sceptical about the emergence of common good from the pursuit of individual interests. He saw rather that civil society was generating a force within itself that would ultimately destroy or change it: the proletariat. He also cast his regard beyond Europe to sketch an outline of an 'Asiatic mode of production' in which rural villages reproduced themselves *ad infinitum*; and in his analysis of French society of the mid-nineteenth century he discerned a social structure more complex than the bourgeois/proletarian dualism of his capitalist mode of production. If the bourgeoisie was the starting point for civil society, the nineteenth century opened up the concept to embrace a variety of conflicting social groups and interests.

A particularly significant nineteenth-century addition to the complexity of the concept came from Alexis de Tocqueville's (1951) work on American democracy. What impressed Tocqueville was the flourishing of associations, spontaneously formed by people for the achievement of common purposes outside of the state. In the context of American politics, Tocqueville saw this proliferation of associations as a guarantee against a tyranny of the majority that might result from an electoral sweep in an era of populist politics. He drew an analogy to the stabilizing influence he saw in European societies as arising from the existence of secondary bodies inherited from medieval times which acted as a restraint upon monarchic power.

The spirit of voluntary association thus became a significant aspect of the concept of civil society. Civil society is no longer identified with capitalism and the bourgeoisie, but now takes on the meaning of a mobilized participant citizenry juxtaposed to dominant economic and state power. For Gramsci, who was concerned with the problem of mobilizing the working class for action in combination with other potential class allies, there was never a pure spontaneity in the construction of social organization, but always a combination of leadership and movement from below. His sense of the optimum relationship was to 'stimulate the formation of homogeneous, compact social blocs, which will give birth to their own intellectuals, their own commandos, their own vanguard – who will in turn react upon those blocs in order to develop them' (*PN*, pp. 204–5). Gramsci's historical context was very different from that in which Tocqueville discovered the spirit of association in a society of farmers, artisans and merchants untrammelled by the class and status inheritance of European societies. To counter the fascist politics of the 1930s, he rejected both 'spontaneity' or 'voluntarism', on the one side, and the notion of a revolutionary elite manipulating the masses, on the other.

As counterpoint to the flourishing in America of autonomous voluntary associations outside of the state, nineteenth century Europe experienced the merger of civil society with the state in the form of corporatism. State leaders, perceiving the disruptive potential of class struggle in industrializing societies, sought to bring employers and organized workers into a consensual relationship with the state for the management of the economy and the support of state political and military goals. Corporatism left those who are relatively powerless in society out of account; but being powerless and unorganized they could hardly be considered part of civil society. The corporatist era began in mid-century with conservative leaders like Disraeli and Bismarck and extended into the post-World-War-II decades in the form of the welfare state. This era is well encapsulated in Gramsci's equation: State = political society + civil society.

The French Revolution left another legacy with implications for civil society: the rejection of anything that would intervene between the state and the citizen. Conceived as a means of liquidating medieval corporations, the principle as embodied in the Le Chapelier law of 1791 was in the early nineteenth century turned against the formation of trade unions. The same principle was reasserted by the Bolsheviks in the twentieth-century revolutionary Russian context: all allowable associations under 'real socialism' would have to be part of an all-embracing Party-state. Civil society was denied existence. Gramsci recognized the weakness inherent in this situation in his juxtaposition of the war of manoeuvre with the war of position when he referred to conditions at the onset of the Bolshevik revolution:

> In Russia the state was everything, civil society was primordial and gelatinous; in the West, there was a proper relation between State and civil society, and when the State trembled a sturdy structure of civil society was at once revealed. The State was only an outer ditch, behind which there stood a powerful system of fortresses and earthworks; more or less numerous from one State to the next, it goes without saying – but this precisely necessitated an accurate reconnaissance of each individual country.
>
> (*PN*, p. 238)

The 'proper relation between State and civil society' suggests that the State should rest upon the support of an active, self-conscious and variegated civil society and should, in turn, sustain and promote the development of the constructive forces in that society. The organic intellectual was, for Gramsci, the key link in this process.

This brief review of the use of the term 'civil society' in European and American thought yields broadly two juxtaposed meanings. One shows a 'top-down' process in which the dominant economic forces of capitalism form an intellectual and cultural hegemony which secures acquiescence in the capitalist order among the bulk of the population. The other envisages a 'bottom-up' process led by those strata of the population which are disadvantaged and deprived under the capitalist order, who build a counter-hegemony that aspires to acquire sufficient acceptance among the population so as to displace the erstwhile hegemonic order. With regard to the latter, Gramsci insisted that the revolution must occur (in civil society) prior to the revolution (in the form of the state).[2]

Civil society in the late twentieth century

Since Gramsci made his analysis, there have been significant changes affecting the relationship of state to civil society and in the development of civil society in different parts of the world. The world crisis of capitalism of the 1970s brought about a reversal of corporatism. Business persuaded governments that recovery of investment and growth from a situation of stagflation required an attack on the power of trade unions and a reduction of state expenditures on social welfare, together with deregulation of capital goods, and financial markets. As governments acquiesced in this business analysis, trade unions and social-democratic forces were weakened in most economically advanced countries. Protection for the more vulnerable elements in society was cut back; and these elements were implicitly challenged to organize independently of the state, both to protest the loss of state support and to compensate for this loss by voluntary initiative and self-help. The collapse of 'real socialism' in the late 1980s seemed to herald a possible rebirth of civil society in those countries where civil society had been eradicated by the Party-state. New independent organizations of protest grew into the political space that was opened by the disruption and uncertainty of political authority. In both cases, the political and social space in which civil society could develop was expanded. Whether or not the opportunity would be realized was a challenge to human agency.

The restructuring of society by economic globalization

The globalization of production is restructuring the world labour force in ways that challenge nineteenth- and early twentieth-century notions of class structure. Gramsci's keen sense of the strategic importance of building class alliances into a counter-hegemonic bloc which could ultimately displace the bourgeoisie – he advocated linking peasantry and petty bourgeois elements with the working class – remains pertinent in today's world. What is relevant today is the strategy of class alliance rather than Gramsci's particular form of alliance derived from his understanding of the class structure of Italy in the 1920s and 1930s. It is problematic today whether the proletariat can still be considered to be a 'fundamental' universal class. Indeed, the very notion of a proletariat as a single class juxtaposed to the bourgeoisie has lost substance in reality even if its ideological persuasiveness retains some impetus (see Chapter 5, pp. 84–5).

People who speak of civil society today do not usually have in mind the realm of economic interests as did Hegel and Adam Smith. The distinction common today is between dominant power over society shared by corporations and states on the one side, and popular forces on the other. 'Civil society' is now usually understood to refer to the realm of autonomous group action distinct from both corporate power and the state. The concept has been appropriated by those who foresee an emancipatory role for civil society.

The current widely understood usage which excludes dominant power in the state and corporations from the concept of civil society received impetus from the movements of opposition to Stalinist rule in Eastern Europe. They were characterized as a 'rebirth of civil society'(Przeworski, 1981). Similarly, movements of opposition to authoritarian rule and capitalist dominance in Asian and Latin American countries are commonly perceived as emanations of civil society. So 'civil society' has become the comprehensive term for various ways in which people express collective wills independently of (and often in opposition to) established power, both economic and political.

This current usage has more affinity to Tocqueville than to Hegel, Adam Smith or Marx. But it also has affinity to Gramsci's usage, since Gramsci regarded civil society not only as the realm of hegemony supportive of the capitalist status quo, but also as the realm in which cultural change takes place, in which the counter-hegemony of emancipatory forces can be constituted. Civil society is not just an assemblage of actors, i.e. autonomous social groups. It is also the realm of contesting ideas in which the inter-subjective meanings upon which people's sense of 'reality' are based can become transformed and new concepts of the natural order of society can emerge.

In a 'bottom-up' sense, civil society is the realm in which those who are disadvantaged by globalization of the world economy can mount their protests and seek alternatives. This can happen through local community groups that reflect diversity of cultures and evolving social practices world-wide. Looking beyond local grass roots initiatives is the project of a 'civic state', a new form of political authority based upon a participatory democracy.[3] More ambitious still is the vision of a 'global civil society' in which these social movements together constitute a basis for an alternative world order.[4]

In a 'top-down' sense, however, states and corporate interests influence the development of this current version of civil society towards making it an agency for stabilizing the social and political status quo. The dominant hegemonic forces penetrate and coopt elements of popular movements. State subsidies to non-governmental organizations (NGOs) incline the latter's objectives towards conformity with established order and thus enhance the legitimacy of prevailing order. This concords with a concern on the part of many people for survival in existing conditions rather than for transformation of the social order. For many people, clientelism may seem preferable to revolutionary commitment, especially when backed by the force of state and economic power. Moreover, the basic conflicts between rich and poor, powerful and powerless, are reproduced within the sphere of voluntary organizations, whether trade unions or the new social movements.[5]

Global governance

Gramsci's sense that national situations are specific still has validity, but now these distinct national situations are much more dependent upon the global economy.[6] The territorial distinctness of national economies and societies is penetrated by global and transnational forces. The problem of hegemony is posed at the level of the global political economy as well as at regional, national and local levels.

Global hegemony has profound consequences for the relationship of political society to civil society. As the state retreats from service to the public and social protection, the public loses confidence in the integrity and competency of the political class. Political corruption is inherent in the transformation of public goods into marketable commodities; a political favour acquires a market value. The loyalty of people to their political institutions becomes more questionable as scepticism and cynicism about the motives and abilities of politicians grow. These tendencies vary among countries. Americans honour the symbols of flag and constitution, but about half of them do not bother to vote and most seem to have low expectations of their politicians. Corruption scandals are rife in Europe and Japan; and public hopes for salvation through politics are equally low. Throughout most of the rest of the world, in Asia, Africa and Latin America, people have endured government more than they have felt themselves to be a part of it. At the end of the century, there was a world-wide problem of repairing or building political societies, of constructing a sense of identity between people and political authorities. There was a wide political space between constituted authority and the practical life of people.

Revival of civil society as a response to globalization?

Civil society would be the base upon which a new or reconstructed political authority would have to rest. This was Machiavelli's insight when he advocated the replacement of mercenaries by a citizen militia. There is some evidence of growth in civil society coming about as a reaction to the impact of globalization. In the French strikes of late 1995 and the strikes in South Korea in early 1997, reaction has come through trade union movements, in the French case with broad public support. In Japan and some other Asian countries, there has been a growth of many non-governmental organizations, often of a local self-help kind, and often actively building linkages and mutual help relationships with similar organizations in other countries. In some poor countries of Africa and southeast Asia, community organizations, often led by women, endeavour to meet basic needs on a local level, turning their backs upon states and international economic organizations that are perceived as acting against the people. In central America, the Mayan people have recovered historical initiative through armed revolt in the Mexican state of Chiapas, and the indigenous people of Guatemala have fought a civil war to the point of gaining recognition of their claims. These various instances are indicative of something moving in different societies across the globe towards a new vitality of 'bottom-up' movement in civil society as a counterweight to the hegemonic power structure and ideology. This movement is, however, still relatively weak and uncoordinated. It nevertheless contains the elements of a counter-hegemonic alliance of forces on the world scale.[7]

Exclusionary populism and the covert world

There is a gap between the retreat of the state and the development of civil society. This space, this void, attracts other forces. One is exclusionary populism: various forms of extreme right political movements and xenophobic racism. Another is the complex congeries of underground activities that constitute the covert world (Chapter 7).

The political space between constituted authority and the people is the terrain on which civil society can be built. A weak and stunted civil society allows free rein to exclusionary politics and covert powers. An expansive participant civil society makes political authority more accountable and reduces the scope for exclusionary politics and covert activity.

The question of civil society in the late twentieth century takes us back to the Machiavellian question of the sixteenth century: how to form the social basis for a new political authority. Where Machiavelli concluded reluctantly that his contemporaries were too corrupt to do it on their own and looked to the Prince to provide the initiative, Gramsci envisaged the Communist Party as the Modern Prince. At the close of the twentieth century, comes the vision of a 'post-modern' collective Prince constructed through a coordinating of popular movements. The feasibility of this project would depend upon a resurgence of civil society.

Gramsci's thought and the making of civil society

Gramsci's starting point for thinking about society, consistent with Marxism, was class structure derived from the relations of production. He referred to 'fundamental' classes (bourgeoisie and proletariat); but other non-fundamental classes, for example peasants and some elements of the petty bourgeoisie, had considerable importance as potential allies for the working class in the formation of a counter-hegemonic bloc. The consciousness of social groups and their organization for political action was built upon this basic material condition.

Consciousness was not, for Gramsci, a direct derivative of class; it was a historical construction, not an automatically determined condition. There were different levels of consciousness. The lowest form was what Gramsci called 'corporative', the collective self-interest of people in a particular material situation. Corporative consciousness did not challenge the status quo in any essential respect; it just looked out for the interest of a particular group.

The next higher level was class consciousness; it posed the question of the state. For whom was the state? Class consciousness unified various forms of corporative consciousness, for example among different groups of workers or among bourgeois whose specific material interests were in competition with one another, to focus upon the formation of political authority that would advance a concept of society based upon the leading fundamental class, in actuality the bourgeoisie but potentially the working class. Class consciousness accentuated the sense of cleavage necessary to move the dialectic forward.

Today, 'class' has become a more ambiguous notion as in common discourse it is mixed with a variety of 'identities' in the formation of consciousness: gender, ethnicity, religion, nationality. Often these identities are subjectively opposed one to another and are open to manipulation by dominant powers in state and economy so as to fragment opposition. The common sentiment among them is a sense of oppression or exclusion. Class, in its generic meaning of social divisions arising from exploitation, can be seen as the substratum of this variety of grievances. But the practical problem remains of forging the links among divergent disadvantaged groups that would bind them together in a counter-hegemonic formation.

This challenge leads to what, for Gramsci, was the highest level of consciousness. Hegemonic consciousness, according to Gramsci, would transcend class consciousness by incorporating interests of the 'non-fundamental' social groups into a vision of society based on one or other of the 'fundamental' classes; and it would make this vision appear to be the 'natural order' of society. Gramsci's particular objective in the 1930s was the formation of a bloc led by the industrial working class in alliance with peasantry and petty bourgeois intellectuals. The questions now, at the beginning of the twenty-first century, are: Who will lead? Who will follow?

This progression in consciousness from corporative through class to hegemonic can be taken as a natural history of civil society. On the basis of the material conditions of production, the potential for collective human action is built upon self-conscious human groups. It is necessary to know when production relations have created the conditions requisite for arousing consciousness and for forming a strategy for change. Not to have these basic conditions would be to fall into idealism and utopianism, leading to failure. Though the formation of class or hegemonic consciousness depends upon the existence of these material conditions, consciousness is nevertheless an autonomous force. Ideology and the organization of social forces does not flow automatically from material conditions. The critical agents in the raising of consciousness for Gramsci are the organic intellectuals; they serve to clarify the political thinking of social groups, leading the members of these groups to understand their existing situation in society and how, in combination with other social groups, they can struggle towards a higher form of society.

Two other Gramscian concepts are relevant to this process of building civil society: the war of position and passive revolution. The war of position is a strategy for the long-term construction of self-conscious social groups into a concerted emancipatory bloc within society. It is only when the war of position has built up a combination of organized social forces strong enough to challenge the dominant power in society that political authority in the state can be effectively challenged and replaced. The war of position is contrasted to the war of manoeuvre which might seize state power before this groundwork of social organization had been built up. To win a state by a war of manoeuvre would constitute a fragile victory, likely to succumb to the entrenched forces of a recalcitrant civil society. Thus, a civil society animated through popular participation is an indispensable basis for durable new political authority.

Passive revolution has a variety of meanings in Gramsci's thought. It represents an abortive or incomplete transformation of society and can take various forms. One is change induced in a society by an external force that attracts internal support from some elements, but does not overcome the opposition of other entrenched forces. This can lead to an ambivalent situation of 'revolution/restoration', where neither of the opposed bodies of forces is victorious over the other. Passive revolution can also take the form of a stalled war of position strategy which is strong enough to provoke opposition, but not strong enough to overcome it. Furthermore, a strategy on the part of the dominant power gradually to coopt elements of the opposition forces – a strategy known in Italian politics as *trasformismo* – is another form of passive revolution. Yet another form would be emancipatory strategies divorced from the material conditions of the social groups involved, inevitably incurring the illusions of utopianism and idealism. Gramsci cited Tolstoyism and Gandhism in this regard. (We might disagree that the latter has been so illusory and ineffective.) So passive revolution points to many of the inadequacies and obstacles in the attempted construction of civil society.

Variations in prospects for civil society

The restructuring of production is experienced world-wide in generating the three-fold hierarchy of social relations referred to above: integrated, precarious and excluded (Chapter 5, pp. 84–5). The proportions, however, differ from society to society. The balance between top-down and bottom-up forces in civil society, and the relative importance of right-wing populism and the covert world, result in distinct types of state/society configurations with different implications for civil society. Tentatively, four different patterns may serve to illustrate the range of conditions and prospects of civil society in the world today. These patterns or types are not intended to be exhaustive in covering the whole world, but they do illustrate some of the significantly different situations and prospects for civil society at the present time.

Evolved capitalism in Europe and America

Evolved capitalism in North America and western Europe constituted the point of impetus for economic globalization. Its influence penetrates to the rest of the world, the impact varying according to the level of material development and the resistance of persisting cultural practices in other regions. Production is being restructured in the form of post-Fordism which brings about the pattern of integrated core workers flanked by precariously linked supporting workers. Global finance exerts a continuing pressure on state budgets to reduce the social expenditures built up during the era of Fordism which gave social legitimacy to capital.

There is an implicit contradiction here between production and finance. Production and the 'real economy' that provides goods and services requires time to develop (research and development and the training of a committed labour force); finance has a synchronic space-oriented perspective directed to short-term returns which can often ignore the time dimension and undermine not only the social legitimacy of capital, but also the productive apparatus itself (for example, through predatory buy-outs and asset stripping). From the late twentieth century, it was global finance rather than production and the 'real economy' that focused people's attention on the frailties of the economic order.

Another contradiction is between the real economy and the biosphere (see Chapter 5, pp. 86–8). Expansion of consumer demand is the driving force of the global economy. World-wide emulation of the consumption model of North America and western Europe would, however, through resource depletion and environmental destruction, bring ruin to the biosphere – the ultimate feed-back mechanism. To escape this disaster would require a fundamental change in economic organization and values – a revolution in social practices and in the structure of social power.

A further contradiction is in social relations. The fragmentation of the old working class, a consequence of post-Fordism reinforced by pressures of global finance towards dismantling of the Fordist-era social safety net, has strengthened capital and weakened and divided labour.

The problem for the organic intellectuals of the Left is how to envisage a strategy that could build from this fragmented situation of subordinate social groups a coherent alternative to economic globalization that would transcend (*Aufhebung* in Hegel's meaning) the contradictions just referred to. These organic intellectuals are now themselves a fragmented lot: trade union leaders, environmentalists, social activists on behalf of the poor and homeless and the unemployed, and promoters of self-help community organizations. They compete for potential clientele with right-wing populists, anti-immigrant racists and religious cults. All of these various movements are meanwhile developing transnational linkages and organizations.

The covert world (organized crime, the drug trade and intelligence services) occupies a political space that has, if anything, been enlarged by public disillusionment with conventional politics. The high cost of electoral politics sustains hypocrisy in the political class, who ostensibly respond to public support for campaign finance reform while continuing to rely on occult financial contributions, thus remaining open to occult influences. This, in turn, further erodes public confidence in political leadership.

In Europe, evolved capitalism has two variants. One is the 'pure' hyper-liberal form which espouses removal of state intervention in the economy by deregulation and privatization and makes competitiveness in the global market its ultimate criterion. This is the dominant variant. The other is the European tradition of social market or social democratic capitalism which sees the viability and legitimacy of an economy as dependent upon its being embedded in social relations recognized as equitable by the general population (Albert, 1991). The issue between the two forms of capitalism is being fought out at the level of the European Union in the debate over 'social Europe' and the filling of the 'democratic deficit' in European institutions.

In very general terms, we can think of three constellations of forces: first, the dominant forces in states and markets (corporate management and the political class, surreptitiously sustained by the covert world); second, a heterogeneous category of groups commonly identified as constituting civil society in the emancipatory sense (trade unions and 'new social movements'); and third, right-wing and populist movements and religious cults that compete with the preceding groups for support among the unorganized mass of the people.

In attempts to construct a 'bottom-up' social force, the question arises of compatibility between trade unions and the new social movements, for example environmentalism, feminism, anti-poverty movements and peace movements. The new social movements have often been suspicious of organized labour, fearing domination by labour's tighter and more hierarchical organization which might not respect the social movements' far more loosely structured and more participatory forms of organization. Moreover, the new movements arise more frequently from problems related to consumption, for example poverty and homelessness, rather than, as for unions, from the realm of production. On the other hand, organized labour can sometimes, despite its weakened condition in evolved capitalism, be a catalyst for a more broadly based social movement to confront the established powers in state and corporations. Furthermore, a sustained concertation of social forces, i.e. one that would outlast a particular event or crisis, is hard to achieve among groups with the loose and participatory character of the new movements. Coherence and durability over time would be a necessary condition for having a sustained impact on political parties and thus on the state.

Asian capitalism and the cultural dimension

Japanese capitalism is the prototype of another form of capitalism with a different social context (Tsuru, 1993; Johnson, 1982; Fallows, 1994). In its origins, the pre-capitalist social and cultural form provided a foundation for imported Western technology and state sponsorship of industrialization. The result was a Japanese form of corporatism in which the state worked closely with business, and the firm developed on the concept of an extended, if bureaucratized, patriarchal family. Group loyalty contributed to organizational strength; but workers were divided between those integrated with the firm and others with a more casual or remote link to the central production organization (contract or out-sourcing workers). The lifetime employment of the first category corresponded to the impermanence of the second. In this manner, Japanese practice prefigured the pattern that globalization has projected on to the world scale. This initial Asian pattern coincided with authoritarian political structures. The rapid growth of economies, first in Japan during the post-World War II years, and subsequently in several of the newly industrializing Asian economies (Hong Kong, South Korea, Taiwan and Singapore, followed by the Philippines, Thailand, Indonesia and Malaysia), brought into existence both a large middle class oriented towards consumerism and a more combative working class. In some of these countries, pressures from both of these social forces has resulted in attenuation of authoritarianism.

Japan's political structures show continuity in many respects with pre-war patterns. Democratization was introduced under the auspices of the American occupation authorities. Domestic forces in Japan, reacting against the militaristic state that had brought war and ruin, supported the democratic innovations. These forces continued to urge further democratization when US policy shifted ground to bring Japan into the anti-communist Cold War alliance. Other domestic elements, including those associated with the wartime regime, rallied to the new US anti-communist line (Sakamoto, 1987 and 1995). Japan's post-war condition is a case of passive revolution in Gramsci's sense. The revolution/restoration balance remains non-catastrophic because the economic growth priority of Japanese governments during the later Cold War period achieved, at least temporarily, a high degree of depoliticization. The democratizing forces of the post-war years were to a large extent demobilized by the general preoccupation with economic growth. From the late twentieth century, however, the Japanese economy has been stalled in recession.

Japanese society has shown sufficient cohesion, sustained by the long period of economic growth, so that it has in practice made slight demands upon the state. Whether this would continue through a prolonged period of economic stagnation or recession is an open question. Moreover, some Japanese are concerned that the formerly strong cohesion of family and community may be dissolving as a consequence of modernization, leading to more emphasis on individualism as well as consumerism and to a reduced commitment to work and organizational loyalties.[8] The covert world, particularly in the forms of organized crime and political corruption, thrives in Japan as it does also in South Korea and other Asian countries.

Asian scholars point to a distinction among three spheres: state, market and civil society.[9] They see civil society in Asia as a late and still, relatively to Europe, weak development which has focused on democratization, environmentalism, human rights, the peace movement, and various mutual self-help and internationalist goals. In these respects, civil society has made gains in Japan, South Korea, Taiwan and the Philippines. Private groups (including organized crime) contributed spontaneously and effectively to relief after the Kobe earthquake disaster of 1995, when the state's response proved to be disorganized and ineffective. Indeed, the current emphasis on civil society in Asia could be seen, in its emancipatory aspect, as the transnationalizing of the democratizing and people-based forces of Japan and their effort to atone for Japan's war guilt by building cooperative arrangements with communities in other parts of Asia.

There is also a movement towards 'Asianization', or the imagining of a regional Asia-wide community of which Japan is a part, which reflects both the consumerist material values of middle-class economic success and a right-wing aesthetic rejection of 'the West'.[10] Authoritarianism has impeded the democratization movement in Singapore, Malaysia and Indonesia, although many local non-governmental organizations exist in these countries. It is difficult to speak of civil society in China so long as the authoritarianism of the Party-state limits the expression of aggrieved elements, although rapid economic growth and social polarization in coastal China is generating stresses that may be hard to contain.

Recent events in South Korea have thrown new light on the condition of civil society. The challenge here has come from the effort of the large South Korean corporations, the *chaebols*, to compete as multinational corporations in the global market. Towards this end they persuaded the government to revert to earlier authoritarian practices by restricting recently acquired labour rights so as to give the *chaebols* more flexibility in hiring and firing. At the same time, the government sought to increase the powers of the intelligence services (Korean CIA). This attempt to revert to authoritarianism and to enlarge the sphere of the covert world provoked a general strike in which the labour movement became united and gained support from students, teachers and religious organizations. The protest was a direct reaction to globalization (Pons, 1997; and Carroué, 1997).

As in the case of the French strikes of December 1995, the trade unions in South Korea provided the impetus for a response by civil society to state authoritarianism. Change in South Korea may be more authentic than passive, but it does not seem to be oriented towards radical structural transformation, rather it seems oriented towards a more liberal legitimation of political authority. In Japan, trade unions have not been identified with a 'bottom-up' transformation of civil society. They have been more aligned with corporations and the jobs they provide. During the 1970s, environmental protests that resulted in political changes at municipal and regional levels in Japan were led by citizens apart from unions. Male union members identified their jobs with corporate interests in maintaining production, while their wives felt freer to participate in the environmentalist revolt.

Thus in some Asian countries, capitalist development has generated the class basis for a development of civil society which is weaker than that of Europe in the face of state and corporate authoritarianism, but which has nevertheless made some significant progress in recent years. The social forces involved in this emergent civil society are both middle class (including students, environmentalists, peace activists and feminists) and organized workers. The coherence between middle class and worker elements is problematic. Asia gives a mixed picture of authentic and passive structural change in societies.

State breakdown and predatory capitalism

The prototype for this category is the breakdown of the Soviet Union; but instances of the phenomenon are not limited to the former Soviet bloc. Similar situations have arisen in countries of Latin America affected by the debt crisis. In broad outline, the circumstances leading to this situation are: an economic crisis generated by both internal and external causes leaves an authoritarian state unable to carry out the functions it has assumed; external pressures, welcomed by a politically aware stratum of the population, lead to the establishment of a liberal democratic regime based on electoral politics, but civil society is insufficiently developed to provide a firm basis for the new regime; external pressures then succeed in reducing state powers over the economy in favour of an expansion of market forces; the weakness of institutions to regulate the market and the collapse of state authority open the way for organized crime and political corruption to gain control in both state and market spheres; the general population, struggling for personal survival, becomes politically apathetic and non-participant, while some elements nourish a nostalgic hope for salvation by a charismatic leader. The weakness of civil society is the critical element in this catastrophic cycle.

The domestic cause of the collapse of the Soviet regime stemmed from its failure to make the transition from extensive development (i.e. the addition of more productive capacity of the same kind) to intensive development (i.e. innovating production technology with higher productivity). This was exacerbated by the external pressure to accelerate the arms race which placed an intolerable burden on the economy, preventing the state from maintaining the social services it had instituted as basic citizen rights.[11]

In the Eastern and Central European countries of the bloc, where the arms burden was less than in the Soviet Union, opposition movements developed openly. In Poland, *Solidarnošc* as a trade union became a rallying point for a broad-based opposition to the communist regime; and the Catholic Church had long stood as an alternative pole of loyalty to the state. In East Germany, *Neues Forum* mobilized people into the streets to demonstrate against the authoritarian regime. As noted above, the current scholarly interest in civil society very largely originated in observation of the popular movements in Poland, Czechoslovakia, Hungary and the German Democratic Republic, which toppled the communist regimes in these countries after the Soviet Union had signalled it would not or could not support them.

These movements crumbled later, after they had achieved their initial purpose of overthrowing established state power. In retrospect, in Gramsci's terms, they may seem more like the phenomena of a war of manoeuvre than of a war of position. Liberal democratic regimes were then established in these countries, encouraged by Western politicians and media and welcomed by local citizens. These were cases of passive revolution. In the Soviet Union, change came from the top. In Eastern and Central Europe, civil society played a bigger role. But after the collapse of the communist regimes, those who led the popular revolt did not for long remain as major political forces; and the bureaucratic elites of the former regime became the typical private market elites of post-communism. (Vaclav Havel as President of the Czech Republic is the exception who remained in a position of symbolic prominence.) The solidity and durability of civil society remains questionable.

External support for the new regimes came more in the form of exhortations and technical advice urging 'democracy and market reform' than in large-scale investment and access for trade. It was clear that market reform in the ex-communist sphere had priority in Western policy and that democracy was perceived as instrumental towards market economics.

When the erosion of state authority and the absence of effective regulation of the market led to a dramatic growth of mafia control over economic activity, corrupt penetration of the state, and the forging of international criminal links, apologists for liberal economics showed their preference for crime over state regulation. They could view it with equanimity as a probably necessary stage of primitive capital accumulation (Andor, 1996). The collapse of state authority also unleashed sub-national forces of ethnic nationalism which became vehicles for garnering the residues of economic and political power.

Several Latin American countries also fit the model – Mexico and Columbia, for example. The decline of state authority is associated with the imposition of 'structural adjustment' policies advocated with financial leverage by the International Monetary Fund and backed by US pressure. Initially, US policy looked to authoritarian solutions to introduce economic liberalism in Latin America, in the manner of the Pinochet coup in Chile. Subsequently, US policy began to advocate liberal democratic forms of state as being more able to sustain the continuity of a liberal economic regime while allowing for changes of government, making the economy less vulnerable to political coup.[12] This, again, implied passive revolution.

In these societies various forms of popular movements have taken root – trade unions, left wing political parties and the 'new social movements', as well as the episodic manifestations of 'people power' such as toppled the Marcos regime in the Philippines, or 'IMF riots' provoked by rising food and transport prices and the spontaneous uprising that toppled the government of Argentina in December 2001.

There is some evidence that, under the impact of structural adjustment, unions and social action movements have pulled together despite their mutual suspicions of earlier years and have worked to support left-wing political parties (Hellman, 1995). However, groups led by social activists have focused more on local demands, often obtained by the old patterns of clientelism, and compromise with authorities than on the broader aims of change in social and economic structures which are the concern of left-wing political parties. These left-wing parties have, in turn, been weakened nationally by the hegemony of globalization ideology. Furthermore, promotion of civil society has been coopted by forces behind the propagation of neo-liberal economics as a way of defusing and channelling potential protest (Macdonald, 1997). Consequently, civil society, in its dual form of class-based organizations and social activism, has a latent but not very fully realized potential for social and political transformation. The covert world, in the form of organized crime, drug cartels and political corruption, is rife in these countries. The decline of state authority is not yet matched by a development of civil society.

The most open challenge to the impact of globalization on social and political structures has come from a new type of revolutionary movement, the *Zapatista* rebellion of the Mayan Indians in the southern Mexican state of Chiapas that broke out on New Year's day 1994. This was the day on which the North American Free Trade Area came into effect, which symbolized the anti-globalization message of the revolt. Indigenous peoples in different parts of the world have proclaimed their distinctness as social formations demanding control of their ancestral lands. The *Zapatistas* have gone beyond this to cultivate international support and attempt to change the Mexican political system. They have sought to transcend both the hierarchical military character of the rebellion in its initial phase and its ethnic base of support in order to become a rallying force in civil society of all forces for democratic change, in other words to create the beginnings of a counter-hegemonic bloc (Najman, 1997; Marcos, 1997).

Africa: civil society versus the state

In Africa there are even more extreme cases of state breakdown and of alienation of people from the state. State structures inherited from colonial regimes had no close relationship to local populations to begin with; yet the state controlled access to any economic activity more substantial than peasant agriculture and petty trading. The political struggle for control of the state was thus a struggle for a share of the economic product of the country, a product divided between foreign investors and the power holders in the state. There has been a history of resistance to this pattern. Some social revolutionary movements and attempts at social democratic experiments have endeavoured to create political authorities that were based on African community life – movements led by Amilcar Cabral in Guinea-Bissau, Samora Machel in Mozambique, and Julius Nyerere in Tanzania, for example. However, obstacles, mainly external in origin, impeded the success of these struggles for a more participant polity.[13] The Cold War came to dominate

African politics as both the United States and the Soviet Union chose allies among the power-holders in African states and armed them. This strengthened the tendency towards military rule and towards African states taking the form of kleptocracies – dictators with armed bands that served both as praetorian guards and as gangs who pillaged the population. Mobutu's Zaire was a prime example.

In these circumstances, it is not to be wondered that African people did not readily identify with their rulers. Furthermore, foreign capital proved to be equally hostile to people's welfare. Foreign investors, with the connivance of African states, have damaged the ecology upon which local people depend for their livelihood. The international financial agencies (IMF and World Bank) impose structural adjustment policies that have placed heavy burdens on the populations of these countries. In consequence, many Africans have come to see the state and the international institutions as their enemies and have organized in a variety of self-help community groups to confront the daily problems of life, shunning any link to the state. Women have been prominent as initiators and leaders in this movement. An Ethiopian economist has called it 'the silent revolution in Africa' (Cheru, 1989). Similar movements exist in some other poor countries.

This is a form of incipient civil society that has turned its back on the state. The question remains open whether it could develop into a force that would engage with the state to alter the state's character and become the foundation for a new participant form of democracy.[14]

Conclusions

The nature and condition of civil society is very diverse, looked at on a world scale. It is, nevertheless, tempting to look at this diversity through the analytic lens of Gramsci's conceptualization of relations of forces (*PN*, pp. 180–5). Civil society is itself a field of power relations; and forces in civil society relate, in support or opposition, to powers in state and market.

The first level in Gramsci's relation of forces, is the 'relation of social forces', by which he meant objective relations independent of human will brought about by the level of development of the material forces of production. Through the effect of economic globalization and the passage from Fordism to post-Fordism in the present-day world, this has brought about a basic cleavage between, on the one hand, the beneficiaries of globalization or those people who are integrated into the world economy, and, on the other hand, those who are disadvantaged within or excluded from the world economy. The latter would include some who, in a precarious way, may become intermittent adjuncts to the world economy and whose interests may thus waver between hope for more stable affiliation and outright antagonism in despair of achieving it.

This cleavage does not yield anything so clear as the Marxian cleavage along property lines between bourgeoisie and proletariat. The proletariat is divided now between some beneficiaries of globalization and many disadvantaged. The petty bourgeoisie is also divided between some who would identify with the world economy and others who are disadvantaged or excluded in relation to it. Many people would need to be understood more in their relationship to consumption (or the inability to consume adequately) rather than to production – the more or less permanently unemployed, the inhabitants of shanty towns, welfare recipients and students. The old production-related categories are not entirely superseded; but the scheme of categories of people relevant to the problematic of social change needs to be rethought.

Gramsci's second level, which he called the relation of political forces, addresses the question of consciousness. In today's context, the challenge is to bridge the differences among the variety of groups disadvantaged by globalization so as to bring about a common understanding of the nature and consequences of globalization, and to devise a common strategy towards subordinating the world economy to a regime of social equity. This means building a counter-hegemonic historic bloc that could confront the hegemonic formation of globalization in a long-term war of position.

Gramsci's strategic concepts are pertinent here, including particularly the role of organic intellectuals. Their task now is to be able to work simultaneously on local, regional and world levels. The obstacles are considerable in that the active or potential opposition to globalization is divided on many issues. There is opposition between manual workers protecting their jobs in environmentally destructive and polluting industries and environmentalists working to stop these industrial practices. Other conflicts arise between manual workers in mature industrial countries who face downgrading through global competition and workers in recently industrializing countries or immigrant workers from poor countries who are perceived to be taking away their jobs. Still other conflicts arise from the claims by indigenous peoples for lands and control of resources that conflict with the aims of mining and forestry corporations and their workers. Also, there is the issue between the claims of women's movements for equity in employment and the fears of precariously employed male workers. Organic intellectuals linked to these various groups face a difficult task of transcending the immediate corporative instincts of these groups and the oppositions they engender to other disadvantaged or excluded groups, in order to achieve a commonly shared vision of a desirable and feasible alternative future and a strategy for joint action. They must at the same time do battle with the right-wing forces of anti-immigrant racist nationalism, neo-fascism, authoritarian populism and nihilistic religious cults, which compete for the allegiance of people where social bonds have disintegrated and apathy and alienation have become the norm.

Gramsci's third level in the relation of forces was the relation of military forces, which he divided into two parts: one, the technical military function which we may read as control of the repressive apparatus of a state; and the other, the politico-military, refers to the morale of a population, to the degree of coherence or disintegration among people. In the absence of high morale, struggle against a dominant power over people, whether foreign or domestic, would be improbable. The condition that sustains an oppressive regime, Gramsci wrote, is a 'state of social disintegration of the . . . people, and the passivity of the majority among them' (*PN*, p. 183). This, in varying degrees, is the situation characteristic of the populations engulfed by globalization today. To overcome this social disintegration and passivity will require the creation of a vibrant civil society inspired by a strong spirit of solidarity at the community level and, by linkage with other strong communities in other countries, at the transnational or global level. Upon such a basis of participatory democracy new political authorities may in the long run be constructed at national, regional and world levels.

One aspect in developing a vision and strategy is to shift from a predominantly space-oriented and synchronic mode of thinking to a predominantly time-oriented and diachronic or dialectical mode of thinking. Oppositions that are apparently objective in the immediate may be overcome through attacking the structures that ensure the persistence of these oppositions. First among these is the doctrine subscribed to by corporate capital and most governments, and propagated by the intellectuals and media of the status quo, that competitiveness in the world economy is the ultimate criterion of policy. This is the primary form of alienation in the world today – the imagining of a force created by people that stands over them proclaiming that 'there is no alternative'. This contemporary deity will have to be deconstructed to make way for an alternative vision of a world economy regulated in the interest of social equity and non-violent resolution of conflict.

The other important aspect of creating a counter-hegemonic bloc is revival of a spirit of solidarity. The crisis of capitalism in the mid-1970s and the subsequent supremacy of the globalization dynamic has not only weakened psychological bonds between people and states, but also the level of trust among people themselves and their disposition for collective action. The result is an increase in cynicism, apathy and non-participation of people in politics and social action.[15] Increasingly, politics are not about choices concerning the future of society but rather about choices among competing sets of would-be managers of the status quo, many of whom are tainted by corruption and most of whom are professedly incompetent to think of, let alone pursue, an alternative (Guéhenno, 1993). The political space abandoned by people has been readily taken up by the covert world, which has become functional to the financing of established political systems and is involved in a substantial part of world markets, most notably in the drug trade.

Civil society has become the crucial battleground for recovering citizen control of public life. It seems that very little can be accomplished towards fundamental change through the state system as it now exists. That system might be reconstructed on the basis of a reinvigorated civil society which could only come about through a long-term war of position. Meanwhile, a two-track strategy for the Left seems appropriate: first, continued participation in electoral politics and industrial action as a means of defensive resistance against the further onslaught of globalization; and secondly, but ultimately more importantly, pursuit of the primary goal of resurrecting a spirit of association in civil society, together with a continuing effort by the organic intellectuals of social forces to think through and act towards an alternative social order at local, regional and global levels.

7 The covert world

Don't be such a prude. You know very well how that game is played. It's give-and-take between poacher and gamekeeper. Everybody has to get something or there's no deal.

John Le Carré on the relationship between secret services
and organized crime in the words of a character in
Single & Single: A Novel, Viking 1999, p. 267

There are two realms of political, economic and social relationships and activities. One is the realm of overt, visible, legitimately recognized activities and institutions. It has received the bulk of scholarly attention. The other includes illegitimate and only occasionally visible activities which are often obscured or suppressed from consciousness. These constitute what I have called the covert world. Specific types or instances of covert activities have received scholarly attention, for example organized crime and the drug trade, the arms traffic, national intelligence services; and particular cycles of political violence. Much of this work has been done in the perspective of state agencies charged with combating these activities. There have been few efforts to develop a general picture of the covert world and its relationship to the better-known overt world.[1]

In the preceding chapters, I have discussed mainly the overt world of political economy in terms of the state and corporate powers on the one hand, and civil society on the other. The covert world impinges upon both. In this chapter, I propose to explore how the covert world emerges in reaction to the overt world and how it affects and is affected by both aspects of the overt world – by the political society of state and corporate power and by civil society. The relationships involving the covert world, political society and civil society are neither simple nor constant. They are complex and changing. To understand them requires historical perspective.

One such perspective which I have found helpful in approaching this problem is in an essay by Paul Vieille (1988) which examines a range of human activities produced by what he calls the 'chaos' that results from the negative effects of established institutions. Among such effects he includes the consequences of capitalism (an established institution) in recurrent economic crises, unemployment and waste; the social dislocations resulting from abandonment of the state's power of regulating the economy; the consequences of large-scale illegal immigration and urban overcrowding; 'state terrorism', for example armed attacks and retaliation by US and Israeli forces; and spontaneous popular uprisings and other forms of resistance and response to 'chaos'.

Vieille, whose work focused upon Third World societies, argued that traditional solidarities become strengthened when confronted by a unitary political structure which appears to be alien to many people. In such a circumstance the state appears to people as an external force under the control of an elite that uses it for plunder. The complex forms of response to the 'chaos' produced by the established institutions Vieille characterized as the 'social movement'. So, we have three ontological categories juxtaposed and interdependent: an alienating political authority; its consequences in 'chaos'; and a resistant response from society in 'social movement'.

Another author who has examined what Vieille calls the 'social movement', i.e. resistance and response to the 'chaos' generated by established institutions and processes, is Eric Hobsbawm (1965). In his studies of archaic forms of social movements that occurred in the nineteenth and twentieth centuries, Hobsbawm furnishes hypotheses about the conditions in which social movements have emerged and the nature of these movements. Hobsbawm's studies deal with contemporary phenomena like millenarian movements or the Mafia which are not dissimilar to movements that might well have occurred in the European Middle Ages, but which coexist now and in growing numbers with 'modernized' forms of protest like trade unions and socialist political parties in evolved capitalist societies. The response to 'chaos' in earlier times has bifurcated into, on the one hand, movements for social and political transformation which have moved out of the covert realm to become parts of the established institutional structure (e.g. trade unions), and, on the other, forces that remain covert but lose the character of agents for transformation to become parasitical upon the established order (e.g. organized crime). The seemingly archaic movements that Hobsbawm has studied cannot, he wrote:

> be simply written off as marginal or unimportant phenomena, though older historians have often tended to do so, partly out of rationalist and 'modernist' bias, partly because . . . the political allegiance and character of such movements is often undetermined, ambiguous or even ostensibly 'conservative', partly because historians, being mainly educated and townsmen, have until recently simply not made sufficient effort to understand people who are unlike themselves.
>
> (Hobsbawm, 1965, p. 2)

Hobsbawm is dealing here with phenomena that owe nothing to a theoretical revolutionary formation nor to organizational leadership by groups with a strategic plan for social and political change. The social movements he focuses upon are more or less spontaneous reactions by people alienated from established authority who rely upon their own determination and the support of those whom they influence to resist that alien authority and to establish their own.

The dynamics of these resistance movements are complex and contradictory. In one sense, they may have an eschatological, messianic character holding promise of an alternative society of harmony and equality re-established from an imagined past. In another sense, they may constitute an alternative structure of authority, and alternative hierarchy, which derives from the strength and capacity for violence of their leaders and the loyalty it inspires in the followers.

These movements are necessarily covert in nature. They are in rupture with the established society which has no recognized place for them. In their primitive form, they challenge that society by projecting an alternative authority and an alternative world view. But the initial sense of cleavage created by this challenge may provide the opportunity for dominant personalities in the social movement to accede to a *modus vivendi* with the established society in which overt and covert coexist in a symbiotic relationship, mutually understood and objectively mutually sustaining, although not acknowledged as such in polite company. Thus, erstwhile rebels can use their capacity for violence to perform some extra-legal services for the powerful in the established society by disciplining rebellious elements, thereby gaining unofficial tolerance for their own predatory accumulation of wealth and power. The two contradictory sides of the covert world are: the revolutionary potential of popular resistance; and a parasitic symbiosis with established power that enables covert elements both to prey upon society and to do some of the dirty work required to sustain established authority.

Revolutionary and the parasitic elements coexist within the covert world. In this underground quasi-invisible space they interact with each other and with the visible processes and institutions of the overt world. Their methods and actions are similar. Intelligence agencies act in the same way as criminal organizations and so-called 'terrorist' groups. Nominally, the intelligence agencies are to root out crime and terror; but sometimes they cooperate with criminals or terrorists towards the goals of their states. So, for example, the post-war French government employed the Corsican mafia to dislodge trade union and Communist Party control over shipments through the port of Marseilles; Oliver North used illegal financial circuits to provide arms for the contra insurgents in Nicaragua in furtherance of US President Reagan's unofficial war against the Sandinista government of Nicaragua; and the CIA with the Pakistan intelligence service ISI trained and supported Osama bin Laden and his armed resistance to the Soviet Union in Afghanistan.

The covert world today

It may be that the extent of the covert world is expanding at the beginning of the twenty-first century. (There are, of course, no official statistics to support this statement since official statistics belong in the overt world and do not reach effectively into the covert world.) If so, it seems likely that it is in part due to what Susan Strange called 'the retreat of the state' – the withdrawal of the state from regulation in many spheres of economic and social affairs. (This, be it noted, did not weaken the state in those areas where it wanted to act, such as in constructing the structures of economic globalization.) The extra-legal activities of the 'informal market' have been encouraged by deregulation of national economies; and informal economic activities often depend upon protection rackets.

In part, this is due to the expansion of international criminal activities which have benefited from the end of the Cold War, and from the wars in Kosovo and Afghanistan which saw the expansion of criminal networks; and from the globalization of finance which has facilitated the movement and laundering of criminal funds.

In part also, the expansion of the covert world's space can be traced to a growing alienation of people from constituted authority, a decline in the legitimacy of authority and a sense that the authorities confronting people are hostile or indifferent. The responses to alienation run from everyday forms of non-confrontational resistance to non-violent protest and disobedience, to more violent forms of direct attack upon authorities. The growth of underground resistance has prompted the conversion of national intelligence, police and military structures from Cold War preoccupations to the 'war on terrorism'.

The covert world in the early twenty-first century comprises a diverse range of activities. The international drug trade is without doubt the activity that sees the largest flow of funds and is most pervasively linked to other covert activities. Drugs, along with diamonds, finance wars. They are a common currency in intelligence operations where government budgets would be too transparent. They are thus linked to the arms trade. They are an adjunct to the sex trade which is another major covert world activity.

The US population is the world's greatest consumer of narcotic drugs. Unable to eliminate the domestic market for drugs, US governments have opted for attacking the sources of narcotics production and the suppliers' networks, with the effect of maintaining a high 'street price' for drugs and high profitability along with the high risk of the trade.[2]

The sex trade is global in scope. Organized crime controls the movement of women and children across borders from poor to rich countries and manages the development of sex tourism in specific exotic sites. Political upheaval and economic differentials have expanded the number of potential sex workers available to the criminal networks trafficking in women and children. The ex-Soviet Union and ex-Yugoslavia have become sources for the flow into western Europe; and in Asia the flow is from poorer to richer countries (Hanochi and Mushakoji, 1996).

The major income gap between Fujian province in China (as in other zones of poverty in Asia, Africa and Latin America) and North American and

European cities drives large-scale people smuggling by organized crime. Large sums are extorted from families of would-be migrants; and cheap labour is supplied to employers at the receiving end of the migration process (Kwong, 1997). Apart from the illicit traffic in human beings, there is a growing illicit trade in human organs.

The arms trade and the privatisation of security have flourished with the end of the Cold War. The United States remains a major market for small arms and the ideology of guns (linked to the Constitutional myth of the 'right to bear arms') obstructs US support for international action to regulate the trade in small arms. The plethora of arms spread about the world by Cold War protagonists continues to oversupply rebel and criminal forces and turn a profit for arms traders.

The privatization of security is on the borderline between the overt and the covert world. The affluent in societies with increasing polarization between rich and poor perceive the need to dwell in gated communities and for private security personnel.[3] Confidence in the state's 'monopoly of violence' is eroded. Mercenary forces have been widely employed by corporations operating in insecure countries for protection of their facilities and personnel. Internal warfare in various parts of the world has increased opportunities for mercenary troops and soldiers of fortune. It has even been proposed that the United Nations employ mercenary troops for peace enforcement functions.[4]

Beyond hired protection, the existence of the means of violence in private hands has led to extortion, for example as applied to expatriate Russian artists and sports people by threats to their family members at home and to Chinese businessmen in the diaspora by the triads (Shelley, 1996). Deregulation of economic activity in situations where there are no effective institutions or traditions of behaviour to ensure predictable conformity with ethical business practice leads to the use of private force. Where contracts are not observed through established institutional practice, they will be enforced by private violence. This has most notably been the case in the most recent converts to capitalism in Russia and the former Soviet sphere of influence.

The psychological condition of rootlessness and loss of identity in technologically and economically evolved societies may be linked to the spread of authoritarian doomsday religious cults like the Solar Temple, Heaven's Gate and Aum Shinrikyo amongst otherwise educated people.[5] Some of these cults have also engaged with the arms trade to acquire the means of defence and attack inherent in their situation of withdrawal from society and their visions of armageddon. Vieille saw a Third World counterpart in the 'ideology of death' that drew thousands of young people to martyrdom in Khomeini's jihad against Iraq, to which may be added the suicide bombers of Palestinian resistance and al-Qaeda.

Another phenomenon that stands at the intersection of covert and overt worlds is business corruption. One of the principal agencies of globalization, the International Monetary Fund (IMF), has been preoccupied by the extent of corruption in world business. It is aware that such corruption is prevalent in rich as well as in poor countries, in countries with liberal democratic regimes as well as in those under authoritarian rule. Consistent with their commitment to economic liberalization, IMF officials are inclined to argue that corruption will be less where there are fewer government regulations. Their concern is with bribes paid to government officials to expedite government decisions affecting business operations. In economic terms, it is a question of lowering transaction costs (IMF, *Finance and Development* March 1998). There is a rational market explanation for such corruption: it is that information, access and influence have a market value.[6]

The liberalization of global finance, including the existence of 'off-shore' banking, has become an aid to covert world transnational operations, facilitating capital flight, tax evasion and money laundering. This is another phenomenon on the borderline between overt and covert worlds. It has raised the question whether states have lost the power – or perhaps only the will – to regulate transnational financial transactions (Helleiner, 1999).

The various covert activities just discussed are all of the symbiotic type – activities that are illegal or extra-legal in established society but which, though parasitic, do not threaten or seek to transform established society. What of the other type that does challenge the existing social, economic and political order?

Resistance can take many forms which do not directly and overtly confront established authority, what James Mittelman has called 'micro-resistance' (Mittelman, 2001; see also Mittelman and Chin, 2000). These can generate a slow molecular accumulation of dissidence and withdrawal from recognized social practices. When resistance goes beyond this level to become a coordinated force with a strategy of confronting society, it will pass fully into the covert world with the leadership and capacity for mobilizing members of a secret society. Covert resistance need not take the form of a tightly hierarchical conspiracy. It may be more loosely structured as a network with a series of nodes in which initiative can pass from one segment to another in response to the repressive reactions of established power.

Developments in technology have, indeed, enhanced the possibility of coordination of such movements through the fax machine, the internet and the cell phone. The fax machine played a role in the mobilization that led to the confrontation (and massacre) in Tienanmen Square in May and June 1989. The internet gave the Zapatista rising of the Mayan people against the Mexican state an international dimension. The cell phone made it possible for Falungong to surprise the Chinese authorities by bringing together some 10,000 adherents to demonstrate in front of the headquarters of the Communist Party in Beijing on 25 April 1999.

Resistance movements provoked by the social and ecological consequences of globalization include some that are purely local and specific in character and some, like the 'battle in Seattle' and its sequels, that dramatize multiform resistance at the global level. Organization is involved in this resistance –

instruction in non-violent forms of protest, including how to confront police and military repression, and, on the positive side, the development of policy thinking for an alternative social order which would attempt to give coherence to the variety of concerns that merge into a common protest against the vision of globalization projected by state and corporate power. This movement lies within the sphere of dissidence in civil society.

Armed resistance is another matter; it falls squarely within the sphere of the covert world. The borderline between civil society movements and violent or armed resistance can be obscure. Dominant power, however, seeks to make the distinction very clear. This is where words become arms in the conflict. The word 'terrorist' is particularly important in this context. Its use was developed in the context of the Israeli–Palestinian conflict, applied by Israeli sources to Palestinian acts of resistance to Israeli occupation. Palestinian resistance challenges the legitimacy of Israeli occupation; the word 'terror' challenges the legitimacy of Palestinian resistance. In turn, Israeli acts of aerial bombardment, targeted assassination, bulldozing of houses and military and police provocation are classified by Palestinians as 'state terrorism'. The bias in the word has been taken over in President George W. Bush's proclamation of a 'war against terrorism' in the guise of a struggle of 'good' against 'evil'. Use of such language tells us only that both sides reject the other's legitimacy. The rhetorical appeal: 'all who are not with us are with the terrorists', obscured the fact that many did not see these conflicts in terms of 'good' and 'evil', but rather as problems of justice, tolerance and adjustments in power relations which cannot be resolved by absolute moral dictates. I use the term 'terrorism' without any moral judgement as equivalent to politically motivated violence.

The relationship between covert and overt worlds

How, then, can one characterize the relationship between States, the pre-eminent institutions and regulators of the overt world, and the complex of activities that compose the covert world? Conflict or symbiosis, or a bit of both?[7]

Many anecdotes relate how intelligence services have involved themselves in illegal activities. Others illustrate state tolerance of organized crime, for example the lucrative sex trade in some Asian cities, or state agencies' use of criminal 'moles', informants and unofficial agents. US covert agencies have been involved in drug trafficking, arms dealing and money laundering in pursuit of their goals. The CIA is said to have exported heroin in its aircraft from the golden triangle in northern Indochina to help finance the secret war in Cambodia. ELF-Aquitaine, the biggest French industrial group and a virtual state within the state, has been identified with French intelligence and the corruption of governments in Africa and in France (*Le Monde*, 28–29 September 1997; and 1 and 30 June 2001). Although the triads were repressed in mainland China during the Mao years (much as the mafia in Sicily under

Mussolini[8]). They reappeared in the Deng Xiaoping era. The government of the People's Republic used triad connections to ensure the personal protection of Deng during his visit to the United States in 1979 and has collaborated with the triads to facilitate the incorporation of Hong Kong into China, thereby recognizing their de facto power in the former British colony (*Le Monde*, 2 July 1997).

In the chaos following the break-up of the Soviet Union, mafia-type organizations working closely with the 'oligarchs' who had plundered state assets in the 'privatization' drive penetrated the state and key sectors of the Russian economy, notably the banking sector (Williams, 1999, pp. 1888-91, 202-3). They made use of Swiss banks to export, channel and invest their funds (*Le Nouveau Quotidien*, Geneva, 25 October 1995, citing a government report). The Russian Army in the post-Soviet era, starved for funds by a fiscally bereft state, has been reported as transporting drugs for the mafia in its aircraft from Tadjikistan on the Afghan frontier into the Russian Federation (*Le Monde*, 16 June 2001, citing an article in *Moscovski Novostni*, 29 May–4 June, 2001; see also Turbiville, 1995). There remains a question as to how far the Russian mafia now controls the Russian state – whether President Putin, whose election was secured with the support of the 'oligarchs', will be able to create a state strong enough to discipline the oligarchs and their mafia supporters.

The question of state and international financial regulation illustrates the kind of compromises that can come about between states and covert activities. Financial deregulation has not only liberalized world-economy exchanges; it has also allowed for the growth of illicit transactions that increasingly represent a parallel transnational economic sector. This sector comprises illicit capital flight, tax evasion and money laundering, much of it serviced secretly in off-shore financial markets in some minuscule state or semi-tropical island. Helleiner (1999, 2001) points out that liberals may sympathize with the ease of capital flight and tax evasion, thinking that the first is provoked by undesirable government controls and the latter by excessively high taxation. (Of course, some of the most notorious capital flight was the work of kleptocratic government leaders themselves, e.g. Marcos and Mobutu.) The US government may be influenced by these liberal sentiments and in addition by the advantage to the US economy of capital flight, including tax evading capital, flowing into the US economy. So the United States has been backward in the effort to stem capital flight, including tax evading capital, which also represents important business for US financial institutions. The US government's war on drugs, however, makes it determined to suppress money laundering which, in any case, finds no rationale in liberalism; and its 'war against terrorism' includes efforts to block transfer of money to agencies that might finance terrorists.

All of the above are instances of what Vieille called the consequences of 'chaos'. They illustrate the point that covert and overt worlds are symbiotically related. The overt world, through the 'chaos' it generates, gives rise to the covert world; and the covert world in turn reacts upon the overt world. The question here is whether the covert world's action sustains and perpetuates the 'chaos' which lies at its origin, or whether the covert world can have a transformative impact. Is the covert world the site of resistance to the 'chaos' produced by the established order – a resistance that could lead to remedial change in that order? Or is it rather a parasitical growth that profits from 'chaos' by extracting spoils from the established order?

The answer is most likely that it can be both. The kinds of activities outlined above – the 'informal market', the sex trade, the arms trade, the privatization of security, hermetic cults and organized crime – generally have a status quo supporting effect; they are parasitical on society, extracting energies from society without transforming it. But 'chaos' also generates resistance movements that aim for change in the nature of societies, change that could lead to a renewal of civil society. Resistance movements, when successful, may in time become part of the established order. Worker resistance under early capitalism became recognized in trade unionism and socialist political parties as legitimate agencies of 'institutionalized conflict' (Dahrendorf, 1959, pp. 64–7). A troubling prospect is, however, that, historically, the residues of some movements which begin as resistance have in time become parasitical upon the established order.

Enquiry into the historical origins of the covert world throws some light on its development and its relationship to the established order.

Origins and evolution

China

Chinese history provides a good illustration of the origin, evolution and transformations of the covert world and its relationship to the established order of the overt world. As in the case of European historiography on covert activities, Chinese historians long ignored or discounted the historical role of the secret societies. Secret societies have captured literary or antiquarian imaginations but have not been seen as pertinent to the understanding of general history. The French historian Jean Chesneaux (1971 and 1972) has brought Chinese secret societies into the general historical process. He argues that these occult forces have throughout Chinese history constituted an opposition better organized and more coherent than mere bandits or dissident literati.[9] The origins of the Chinese 'secret societies' goes back to the end of the seventeenth century for the Triad system which was active in the southern part of China and all the way back to the twelfth century for the White Lotus system, active in the north of China. The Triad was essentially a loosely organized political opposition to the Manchu Ch'ing dynasty which gained possession of the imperial throne in the mid-seventeenth century. The White Lotus opposed the Mongol occupation in the thirteenth and fourteenth centuries. The founder of the Ming dynasty who drove out the Mongols in 1368 was probably a member of the White Lotus or one of its affiliates (Chesneaux, 1971, p. 36).

The orthodox Confucian concept of society was that of an ordered whole: Heaven being the source of authority, and empire, clan, family, village, guild, father, husband, and elder brother each holding their proper hierarchical position. Occupations were similarly conceived hierarchically, the literati on top, followed by the peasants, then workers, with merchants at the lowest level. The secret societies were a force of total opposition: they drew membership from among individuals marginalized in the established society; they challenged the Mandate of Heaven that legitimized the power of the ruling dynasty; their rites and symbols created a different more egalitarian society with its own bonds and observances and which, for instance, accorded greater equality to women (Chesneaux, 1971, pp. 58–9); and their religious beliefs rejected Confucianism, appealing instead to the more individual path to salvation of Taoism and its rejection of the conventions of society along with some millenarian ideas derived from Buddhism (the third cosmic era or *kalpa* and the *Maitreya* or Buddhist Messiah).[10]

The Chinese concepts of *yin* and *yang* fit well with the historical relationship of established society (*yang*) and secret society opposition (*yin*), a relationship in which both are bound together, the one and the other achieving alternating pre-eminence through the movement of history in which neither the one nor the other is ever totally eliminated.

The secret societies had a popular base of support, particularly among the poor peasantry, with the prestige of centuries of struggle against imperial power. They welcomed the *déclassé* elements from rural and urban society. Their social role was manifested in mutual aid, group solidarity and utopian egalitarianism; they professed 'striking the rich and aiding the poor'. The secret societies were active in the peasant uprisings of the nineteenth century, including the Taiping Rebellion which was the greatest revolutionary movement of the nineteenth-century world.

The last third of the nineteenth century saw a marked increase in the numbers of marginal and displaced persons ejected from the accepted Confucian orders of society: migrations of peasants, urbanization, the spread of steamboat transportation which created unemployment among sailors and boatmen; and the demobilization of soldiers from the Taiping Rebellion. These consequences of modernization and social upheaval swelled membership of the secret societies.

In the late nineteenth century when the mandarin elite and the Manchu dynasty showed weakness in the face the pressure of foreign powers, the secret societies assumed the role of popular resistance to foreign domination. The first targets of popular nationalism were the Christian religious missions. The Boxer Rebellion was but one episode of many involving secret societies. The historic enmity to the Manchu dynasty was put aside by the Boxers in the anti-foreign struggle and this brought about a split with other secret societies which maintained their anti-Manchu stance. However, the whole secret society movement played a decisive role in the republican over-throw of the dynasty in the 1911 revolution. The literati and officers who led the revolution had a base of support only in the bourgeoisie. The secret societies mobilized the popular masses behind them.

The class composition of the secret societies was complex. In country areas they were sometimes controlled by rich landowners seeking a local power base. They defended the position of merchants whose activities were restricted by the Confucian authorities. This association with the merchant group whose ambitions extended beyond China to the whole Asia-Pacific world enabled the secret societies to spread abroad with the expansion of the Chinese diaspora (Chouvy, 2000). State officials also tried to penetrate secret societies so as to control them from inside. Chesneaux, while recognizing that 'the barrier between the establishment and the secret societies was far from insurmountable', concluded that 'it remains true that the secret societies were essentially forces drawn up in opposition to imperial power and established order' (Chesneaux, 1971, p. 79). In class struggle terms, the secret societies supported the peasantry against a feudal regime, and they supported the emancipation of the bourgeoisie from the restrictions of an agrarian bureaucracy. With the overthrow of the Manchu dynasty, the main political purpose of the secret societies was accomplished. Political leadership of the mass of people was henceforth assumed by mass-based political parties, the Communists and the Kuomintang (KMT). But the secret societies remained alive and active in other ways. They continued to represent the interests of the lower segments of society in regions where the political parties were not yet active. They also turned to crime, organized the recruitment of coolies, managed contraband trade in salt and other state monopolies, provided 'protection' for opium dens and bordellos, controlled public markets, and engaged in piracy and brigandage. There is some question whether they played a role in the primitive accumulation of capital (Chesneaux, 1971, p. 79; Chesneaux 1972, p. 17). Their function as criminal organizations continued into the twentieth and twenty-first centuries.

During the People's Republic after 1949, secret societies were perceived by the authorities as a hostile social force and hostile ideology. Evidence of a continued activity was extinguished other than among the Chinese diaspora. The introduction of the market and loosening of political controls on the Chinese economy in the Deng Xiaoping era, together with the growth of corruption in official circles, however, gave new impetus to this criminal activity of the secret societies on the Chinese mainland ('Shanghai's dark side' in *Asia, Inc.*, February 1994:http://members.tripod.com/~orgcrime/darkside.htm).

The question remains, however, whether a popular memory of the broader historical role of the secret societies does not survive, resurfacing in the Falungong movement at the turn of the twentieth to twenty-first centuries. There are parallels between the relationship of secret societies to the Ming dynasty and of Falungong to the Communist dynasty. The immediate forerunner of Falungong was the *qigong* movement that thrived in China from the 1980s. *Qi* is the vital force in Chinese medicine. The movement was at first supported by the government as offering improved physical and spiritual health through meditative exercises (Ownby, 2001). It quickly became a widespread social phenomenon throughout China, spread by expanding mass communications and responding to a sensed popular need for spiritual renewal in a time of crisis for orthodox Marxist ideology. Falungong was an offshoot of this movement. It seems to combine both the spiritual and the opposition features of the nineteenth-century secret societies. One can see a parallel between Falungong meditative exercises and the 'sacred gymnastics' of the nineteenth-century Boxers. Given the lessons of Chinese history, it is not surprising that the political authorities – the new Confucians – would come to perceive Falungong as a threat to social and political order (Zong Heiren, 2001). It is also not surprising that American authorities, nourished in the tradition of the Pilgrim Fathers, would read the government's attempt to suppress Falungong as a case of religious persecution.

Sicily

On Easter Monday of the year 1282, by the Church of the Holy Spirit outside the old wall of Palermo, an incident occurred portentous for the future of Sicily and the whole Mediterranean world. Sicily was under the unpopular rule of the French occupying forces of Charles of Anjou. As Sicilians gathered convivially to celebrate Vespers, a group of French officials mingled with them and began drunkenly to harrass the young women. The husband of one of these women stabbed her French molester to death. The other Frenchmen, coming to the aid of their colleague were slaughtered by the Sicilian crowd. Revolt spread quickly. By morning 2000 French men and women lay dead and the rebels controlled Palermo. In a fortnight most of the island of Sicily was in rebel control. The French fleet at Messina, the military means to control the Mediterranean, was set on fire and destroyed. Charles of Anjou, then the most powerful potentate in Europe, had been planning, with the support of the Pope, to conquer the Byzantine Empire and unite the Mediterranean world under his imperial rule. The Sicilian Vespers put an end to that dream.

To explain how all this happened so suddenly, we have to understand the event in terms of covert and overt worlds. Sicily for centuries past had been subject to a series of occupations – Greek, Phoenician, Gothic, Roman, Muslim and Norman – prior to the Angevin. The Sicilian people absorbed something from all these elements, the main lesson being to maintain a measure of local autonomy under successive imposed authorities. The Norman rule of the twelfth century – the Normans considered themselves kings of Sicily with their court in Palermo – was the golden age for Sicilians during which multicultural fusion evolved into a nascent sense of nationality. The Angevin rule was by contrast an offence to Sicilian pride. A people accustomed to rule by invaders had created their own self-defence system. Historians infer the existence of secret societies as a continuous phenomenon of Sicilian history. It is hard to explain the extent and rapidity of the uprising of 1282 without the hypothesis of the mobilizing force of secret societies that effectively influenced large segments of the population. This was the covert world component of the Vespers. In addition, there was a conspiracy linking King Peter of Aragon, whose ambition rivalled that of Charles of Anjou, with the Emperor in Constantinople and Sicilian notables in opposition to the Angevin rule, to the Pope and to the King of France. Historians debate which was the determining factor: the popular rebellion or the conspiracy. The answer is probably that both were determining, in concert (Runciman, 1958).[11] The conspiracy was the connection between the covert world of clandestine popular rebellion and a new emerging political authority.

One is tempted to read the origins of the Mafia into the secret societies that provided self-protection for Sicilian peasants in medieval times. The term *Mafia* belongs to the nineteenth century, particularly from the 1860s (Hobsbawm, 1965, p. 36). But the conditions which gave rise to this modern phenomenon go back for centuries. Hobsbawm writes:

> No doubt Sicilian peasants have lived under the double regime of a remote and generally foreign central government and a local regime of slave or feudal lords; since theirs was *par excellence* the country of the *latifundium*. No doubt they were never, and could never be, in the habit of regarding the central government as a real State, but merely as a special form of brigand, whose soldiers, tax-gatherers, policemen and courts fell upon them from time to time. Their illiterate and isolated life was lived between the lord with his strong-arm men and parasites and their own defensive customs and institutions. In a sense, therefore, something like the 'parallel system' must always have existed, as it exists in all backward peasant societies.
>
> (p. 36)

Both Hobsbawm and the sociologist Pino Arlacchi, who is foremost among present-day researchers into the Mafia phenomenon, stress that the Mafia is not a large centralized organization (Arlacchi, 1986, pp. 44–7; Hobsbawm, 1965, pp. 33–4).[12] Primarily, Mafia is a cultural phenomenon, an attitude towards the State and law on the part of the mafioso who relies only on his own toughness and courage to deal with problems, recognizing no obligation other than the sense of honour or *omertà* which excludes giving information to the public authorities. Mafiosi are individuals who, through their own strength and violence, are able to secure the respect of their community and, with that respect, to raise themselves out of the lower ranks of society from which they usually come. Respect carried with it for the traditional mafioso the obligation to help others in the community to deal with their problems.

Wealth came along with respect but was by no means equivalent to respect. The traditional mafioso blended outward commitment to the traditional social order with the man of honour's quest for personal wealth and power. As Hobsbawm writes: 'So long as Sicily was no more than a static feudal society subject to outside rule, *Mafia's* character as a national conspiracy of non-cooperation gave it a genuinely popular basis' (1965, p. 41).

The individual mafioso was linked to a group of blood relatives and friends who together constituted a *cosca*, a group bound to a specific territorial place of origin. The imperative of secrecy and trustworthiness inherent in *omertà* imposed a limit on the numbers who could be included in a *cosca*. One of the main functions of the traditional mafioso was to mediate in local disputes among members of the community and between the community and external forces (Arlacchi, 1986, p. 31). Mafia of this kind might also act in the service of powerful men, for example landowners who required toughs to enforce their claims. Mafia also acted to control the life of their community as a system of enforcement parallel to, or substituting for, the law of the State. After the unification of Italy in 1861, the Mafia mediated the impact of the national market on the society of southern Italy. *Clientelismo*, managed by the Mafia, filled the space between the new alien administrative state and the existing community, taking the place of any modern political activity and preventing the emergence of mass parties (Arlacchi, 1986, p. 22).[13]

The State, over time, has worked out various forms of *modus vivendi* with Mafia groups. The Bourbon monarchy in the late eighteenth and early nineteenth centuries began to incorporate local offenders into its police system. This became more systematic under the government of Italy in the first four decades after 1861. The new Piedmontese Italian state left law enforcement in the south to the local elites which meant in practice to the Mafia. Between 1943 and 1945, the Allied occupation government appointed mafiosi as mayors in many communes of western Sicily and Regio Calabria. The parallel system became the real system, a recognition of local autonomy which in some measure seemed to serve all local interests.

World War II effectively destroyed the pre-existing social order in both northern and southern Italy. In the south the forces for change were emigration from south to north and public intervention in the economy, accompanied by the growth of mass-based political parties, the Communists and the Christian Democrats. The mass parties, particularly the Communists, became rivals of the mafia for popular allegiance. In 1945–59 Mafia reacted by murdering trade unionists. The Christian Democrats, particularly the Fanfani faction, incorporated Mafia into their political machine. The Mafia became an important means of securing votes in elections; and political party control over the new State investment in infrastructure and in the allocation of credit allowed the Mafia access to economic activity. Construction entrepreneurs sought assistance from the Mafia, which gave the Mafia an *entrée* to that industry.

Arlacchi traces the evolution of the Mafia during the post-war decades from being dependent on the political party, to becoming managers of autonomous business enterprises. The spate of kidnapping after 1970 was, he suggests, the method of primitive capital accumulation employed by the Mafia in its transition to becoming a business – archaic methods of primitive capitalism made possible the transition to investment in the style of contemporary capitalism (Arlacchi, 1986, p. 115). Control of the heroin trade gave the Mafia a transnational dimension. Management of the State-aided economy in the *Mezzogiorno* – subsidies, pensions, public sector jobs – fell increasingly into the hands of the Mafia. With this evolution towards running modern capitalist enterprises and battening parasitically on the state, the nature of the Mafia became transformed: the traditional culture disappeared; wealth and conspicuous consumption now became the source of respect; the modern mafioso was more likely a man of some education and more complex background (no longer the tough son of a peasant); the size of Mafia organizations grew larger; and the *cosche*'s connection with the community of origin became more tenuous.

Japan

Philippe Pons, long-time correspondent of *Le Monde* in Japan has written about poverty and crime in Japan from the seventeenth century to the present in a study much inspired by Michel Foucault's approach to history (Pons, 1999). Like other pre-industrial societies, Japan in the seventeenth and early eighteenth centuries manifested a symbiotic dualism between a social order consisting of recognized social classes – warriors, farmers, artisans and merchants in descending order – in which people knew their place in the social hierarchy, and a 'counter-world' or 'floating society' of marginalized people who lived outside the established order. The counter-society was nevertheless tolerated and used by established society for activities like prostitution and gambling that lay outside its bounds. A grey zone linked established society to the counter-society. Individuals who were or became marginal to the social order (masterless warriors or *ronin*, for instance) could, by their personal force and virtuosity, achieve power in this grey zone.

During the seventeenth century there was a vast movement of people towards the cities, people who, being uprooted, lost their membership in any of the four recognized social classes or status groups. New forms of solidarity formed among this uprooted population in the cities. A popular esoteric Buddhism appeared in this milieu, preached by itinerant 'holy men' who appealed to archaic traditions and the egalitarian elements of Taoism. The dominant personalities who emerged in the grey zone as leaders among these people could both give them a sense of security and also become intermediaries with the established order. There developed an articulation of power whereby the leadership of the floating population maintained order within it.

Social change in Japan during the late seventeenth and early eighteenth centuries saw the creation of an urban proletariat and the rise of the merchant class. These social transformations accelerated during the Meiji period in the late nineteenth century. The state needed immigration into the cities to build the economy, but it lacked the means of integrating and controlling this new population. The social controls inherent in the established social order could not do the job. So the state had recourse to the criminal element – the *ronin* who had achieved authority through their personal prowess – to supervise these 'masterless' people. The criminal element acquired a social function. Japan became a place where the crime rate was among the lowest in the world while there were proportionally more criminal organizations and gangsters (*yakuza*) than, for example, in Sicily or the United States. Japanese cities contained open spaces in which a criminal subculture was tolerated – a space in which night life, prostitution and gambling could flourish and in which the rebel who rejected the norms of established order could exist and even become a kind of folk hero. The *yakuza*, drawing upon the cult of personal honour from the feudal era, could penetrate through occult processes into the political and business worlds.

Social banditry of the kind described by Hobsbawm, in which the bandit defends the poor and the victims of discrimination and attacks established power and wealth in a millenarian appeal to re-establish an imagined ancient order of equality and justice, had only momentary periods of existence in Japan. There was some evidence of it during the time of troubles that preceded the unification of the country under the Tokugawa shogunate, and again at the end of the shogunate and before the consolidation of power in the Meiji period, in other words at those times when there was no effective central power. During these times, the criminal element lost temporarily its function of regulating the floating population. Even in such times, outlaw bands did not play the same role of social mobilization as did Chinese secret societies. Alliance with the poor was an opportunistic move to enhance pressure on the powerful who controlled the wealth the criminal elements wanted access to.

During the twentieth century, Japanese gangsters worked alongside the Japanese imperialist forces in China and Korea, linking up there with local gangs, entering the opium trade and supplying 'comfort women' to the Japanese occupying forces. The same gangsters subsequently benefited from the US occupation of Japan. The Americans found allies among convicted war criminals and gangsters in the anti-communist struggle. *Yakuza* leaders became supporters of the Liberal Democratic Party and other conservative groups that formed the succession of post-war Japanese governments.

In the 1990s, the new generation of yakuza, like the Mafia in Sicily, became modern businessmen. The old ethic of honour and loyalty (*omertà* in Italian) remained. *Yakuza* saw themselves as the last people in Japan to have a sense of honour. The patriarchal relationship of leader and follower prevailed, but no one cared about a person's social origin. As in Sicily – and by extension in the United States – wealth now became the mark of status, superseding power through personal virtuosity. The *yakuza* extracts his fortune from the powerful without calling into question the system of power. Crime is but the reverse side of the economic and social functioning of a normal society.

Dynamic forces

The Sicilian history of the relationship of covert to overt worlds over some seven centuries bears some similarity to the Chinese over the same stretch of time and Japanese history shares in this similarity. There is clearly something common in the relationship. But similarity is complicated by cultural differences. The modes of expression, the styles, of covert activity are different. In all three cases the covert world took shape out of the chaos generated by established systems of social and political authority which were perceived to be alien and hostile by large segments of the population. In China the sense of cleavage may have been more clear-cut – an ordered, hierarchical Confucian concept of society confronted by the individual path to salvation of Taoism with egalitarian and messianic utopian visions of the future. The Sicilian imagination was perhaps more pessimistic, in which strong and ruthless individuals might assure survival for themselves and their communities in a hostile world. In the Japanese case, a symbiosis between the two worlds was the predominant feature; the revolutionary potential, so important in the Chinese case, was minimal.

In all three cases the covert world became peopled by the poor, the marginals and the outcasts. The most dominant personalities could acquire both fortune and prestige through the violence they were capable of and could play the role of leaders and benefactors to their communities, thereby constituting a counter-society. This phenomenon has been replicated elsewhere. The struggle against the apartheid regime in South Africa mobilized a broad resistance, some members of which assumed responsibilities in the post-apartheid state or in licit economic activity, while others who could not be absorbed in the overt world carried on their personal struggle as gangsters, perpetuating the psychology of violence with the abundance of arms available in a site of long-standing conflict (Mittelman and Johnston, 1999, p. 116; *Le Monde*, 15 June 2001).

The evolution of the covert world has been influenced by economic issues arising in the overt world. The restrictions placed upon trade by the Chinese Confucian bureaucracy gave merchants, as the lowest ranking status group, a natural affinity to the secret societies. Triads helped the merchants of the coastal regions to overcome official impediments to foreign trade. The expanding Chinese commercial diaspora was accompanied abroad by the triads. In Italy, the Mafia mediated the impact on the traditional communities in the south of the national market that came about with the unification of Italy in the late nineteenth century. Later, as the social disintegration of traditional communities proceeded with the advance of capitalism in those areas, the Mafia joined in the capitalist drive transforming itself by means of a 'primitive accumulation' through violent methods into a modern efficiently managed capitalist enterprise, a transformation carried out also by the Japanese *yakuza*. The covert world has marched in lock step with changes in the nature of the overt economy using violence and the threat of violence at each stage.

The covert world has also been shaped by political conflict in the overt world. The Cold War was an accelerator of covert world activity and organization. The Cold War explains the expansion of intelligence services which, once in place, find new justifications for their continued existence (Williams, 1999, pp. 179, 199). Anti-communist politics favoured the revival of Mafia influence in Italy after World War II and of *yakuza* influence in Japanese politics. Anti-communism was the rationale for the CIA's venture into drug trading to raise extra-budgetary funds for the 'secret war' in Cambodia. It was the rationale for Oliver North's arms trading and money laundering to finance a civil war in Nicaragua.

Globalization and the covert world

The covert world is today an aspect of globalization; it both builds upon the social consequences of globalization and has become globalized in its own practices. Organized crime has become transnational. Combinations are negotiated among crime syndicates based in different countries – between a Colombian cocaine cartel and Sicilian Mafia, for example, and between Russian and Italian mafia. Transnational ethnic networks, for example the recent Nigerian diaspora[14] as well as the long-standing Chinese diaspora, have served as major channels for organized crime. Deregulation of national and international finance and technological developments in finance have facilitated covert activities both for organized crime and for the covert operations of national intelligence services. Both criminal and intelligence services are involved (on opposite sides) in the proliferation of weapons of mass destruction (nuclear, chemical and biological). With new computer technologies, intelligence services, as in Europe and North America, cooperate across borders. The activities that go on in the covert world range from the archaic to the modern and the post-modern, often combining all of these features. The Sicilian Mafia's cohesion is maintained by a pre-modern ethic; it operates with the most modern technology; and it is structured in a decentred post-modern manner. The Aum Shinrikyo authoritarian doomsday cult, whose membership included highly trained scientific personnel, attacked the Tokyo subway system in 1995 with deadly sarin gas killing and injuring some 5,000 people (Iido, 1997). The categories pre-modern, modern and post-modern are distinctly blurred in describing it.

The post-modern aspect of the contemporary covert world is, however, its salient characteristic. It is decentred, although containing organizations with tight hierarchical authority. It has no overall scheme of organization: organized nodules form *ad hoc* networks of relations – being able to combine, dissolve and recombine – for particular purposes (Williams, 1999, pp. 181–3).

Agents in the covert world exhibit a primarily synchronic consciousness, a fixation on immediate results. In these respects, the covert world has analogies with the latest tendencies in the corporate sector of the overt world where tight hierarchical command structures give way to more flexible combinations.

The inter-subjective meanings that constitute the sense of reality for the dominant world elites are consistent with behaviour in the covert world. These inter-subjective meanings frame a mentality in which market behaviour expresses the essence of reality. There are, however, residues of other kinds of inter-subjectivity that serve to strengthen covert world organizations. Familial and lineage loyalties have been much weakened among the 'modernized' elites of the overt world, but these, together with artificially constructed group loyalties, shore up and discipline behaviour in the covert world. Where the state uses the force of law and public administration (in Weberian terms rational-bureaucratic legitimacy) to enforce its rules, the covert world employs manipulated group loyalties and violence.

The inter-subjectivity of the covert world is the dark side of *laissez-faire* in the overt market. It is a world of total commodification, with no limit or restraint other than that of the unregulated force available to those active within it. Everything – human beings, alive or dead, human body organs, narcotics, nuclear fuel, state and industrial secrets – is available for a certain quid pro quo.

Forces for transformation

Globalization is generating a global resistance movement. In this we can see a recurrence of the phenomenon that gave rise to the secret societies of China and Sicily – the alienation of people from the established institutions of authority. Vieille's 'chaos' is sensed as a global condition by those who are marginalized in, or excluded from, the material benefits of globalization or who fear for the future of the planet as a result of globalization's fixation on immediate profit at the expense of longer term survivability.

Resistance becomes overt in the demonstrations that take place whenever the leaders of governments and institutions of the world economy meet to coordinate policies. This resistance is mobilized through networks loosely connected through the internet. A heterogeneous group of non-governmental organizations interact to plan resistance and to train their members in non-violent means of protest. In moments of confrontation they are joined by a few self-styled 'anarchists', who are quite ready for acts of symbolic violence. Participants in the anti-globalization movement are at work devising policies and practices as alternatives to those which are advocated by neo-liberalism and are backed by a consensus of governments and international economic institutions. The juxtaposition of the two creates a sense of cleavage, displacing the sense of inevitability that has been associated with globalization – Margaret Thatcher's 'there is no alternative'.

The extent of the protest measures the degree to which people have become alienated from the electoral processes and political party systems of liberal democracies or what Robert Dahl called polyarchies (Dahl, 1971). Polyarchy, for Dahl, refers to a system in which a small group actually rules, and mass participation in decision making is confined to leadership choice in elections carefully managed by competing elites. In the context of globalization, polyarchy has become the favoured type of political regime promoted by US foreign policy and by the dominant forces of the world economy. The authoritarian regimes once favoured to maintain a good investment climate in less developed countries are now considered by the world economy's leaders to be less stable than polyarchic regimes and less reliable as supports for the neoliberal world economic order (Robinson, 1999).

This type of electoral politics requires increasing infusions of money. Furthermore, established economic interests, not only domestic but also foreign, have a major stake in outcomes of the political process. The electoral process is dependent upon corporate funding. Illicit political fund raising scandals have focused public attention recently in France, Belgium, Japan and the United States. American funds and organizational assistance were crucial to Boris Yeltsin's electoral victory in the Russian presidential campaign. Campaign finance reform is often a popular public issue but when it comes to decisions, politicians are reluctant to legislate prohibition of the means to seek office; and a sceptical public ultimately does not seem to care.[15] Awareness of the extent to which political parties are beholden to corporate funding generates cynicism; and the obscurity in which politics are financed gives scope for the influence of criminal elements. Polyarchy provides opportunity for the covert world to participate clandestinely in overt political processes.

A constant factor in the merger of covert and overt worlds is a psychological dualism or innate hypocrisy whereby consciousness is focused on the legitimate realm of action, what is 'normal' or expected in behaviour, while at the same time a corner of the mind acquiesces in its antithesis: business respectability and shady dealing; political integrity and occult influences; mature sexuality and prostitution.

The current world situation bears comparison in one respect with the origins of secret societies in medieval China and Sicily, that is to say, a situation in which a significant portion of the public perceives existing political authorities and the *idées reçues* of social and economic order to be alien, in total opposition to their own sense of justice and well being. That is why reformist solutions have no appeal to this segment of humanity, since reforms seem to be merely manipulative schemes for adjusting people's behaviour to the dominant consensus.[16] The recurrent collisions of demonstrators and police at economic summits – from Seattle through Genoa and beyond – portray an image of total cleavage, a psychodrama in which imagined forces face one another in a catastrophic confrontation.[17]

Opposition does not take the form of a secret society, but rather of a loose network envisaging an alternative society, or perhaps several different alternative societies, united in a rejection of the future proffered by globalization. This loose network contains the germ of a counter-society.

Alienation and the sense of a total cleavage obliterates the legitimacy of constituted authorities. The grounds upon which the legitimacy of authority rests, that it ultimately provides security for all people, are negated. All forms of opposition generate their own legitimacy and there is no argument other than superior force to affirm that one claim outweighs another.

The violence of the weaker party is called 'terrorism' by the stronger, in a vain attempt to reaffirm its own legitimacy. This violence is often a response – 'blowback' in the vocabulary of the CIA (Johnson, 2000) – to what the weaker party perceives as 'state terrorism'. It is fed by the anonymous violence of bombing from 15,000 feet and by missiles launched from submarines by people who never see the death and destruction they have wreaked. It is sustained by the slower death and debility brought about by economic blockade. It is aggravated by the arrogant behaviour of foreign military occupation – by the people killed in Italy when a US air-force pilot doing 'cowboy' tricks with his plane cut the lines of their cable lift, or the rape of a 12-year-old Okinawa girl by three US soldiers 'for fun'.

The sense of cleavage, together with the polarization of rich and poor produced by globalization creates conditions propitious for appeals to an imagined primitive purity that confronts the dissolute and aggressive materialism of the enemy. Fundamentalism, Islamic most notably but also the 'born again' Christianity that has become the unofficial creed of American leadership, thrives in this context. These are conditions ripe for expansion of the covert world.

The grey zone that fills the space between the established order and the counter-society is cleft in two. One part is committed to revolutionary violence that directly attacks the powerful. The other part consists of parasitical elements that objectively sustain the established order from which they benefit. At times the two components of this covert world clash – as when criminal elements serve as *agents provocateurs* to expose resistance movements to police repression.

8 Civilizations
Encounters and transformations

During the first half of the twentieth century, the notion of a world formed by historical and coexisting civilizations was explored in the work of Oswald Spengler (1939) and Arnold Toynbee (1946), among others; but this initiative fell under criticism from professional historians and became marginalized in scholarship. Although many of the criticisms of these earlier works on civilizations were well founded, the real reason why the study of civilizations ceased to attract scholarly attention in Europe and America was political. The Cold War of the second half of the twentieth century came to define the objectives and limits of international studies. During the late twentieth century, civilizations once again became an object of interest in international relations; but this revival was still circumscribed by the residues of Cold War mentality. Meanwhile, during the early 1950s, a Canadian political economist, Harold Adams Innis, had undertaken an approach of his own to the study of civilizations that gave promise for a new beginning free from prevailing ideological baggage. In this chapter, following some critical comments on the current revival of interest in civilizations, I shall explore the promise that lies within Innis's approach.

The refocusing of international studies

From the 1950s through the 1980s, when the Cold War was the central organizing principle of the academic study of international relations, a whole system of knowledge was built up with that principle as its foundation – studies of military-political conflict, of the rivalry of economic systems, of ideological constructions of the meaning of the world, all built around a fundamental manichaean cleavage of we and they, self and other, good and evil.

This system of knowledge survived the supposed end of the Cold War and the search for a new central set of preoccupations began. Three scenarios have been proposed from American sources. The first of these is the 'end of history' thesis of Francis Fukuyama (1989), a senior official of the US State Department. Fukuyama, basing himself on a reading of Hegel, argued that the collapse of the communist project of society meant that the dialect of history had come to an end with the triumph of capitalism and liberal-pluralist politics. This, according to Fukuyama, was the ultimate synthesis. Some more or less technical adjustments remained to be made to fit some backward polities into this mould, but there were no fundamental new challenges to social, economic, or political organization that could be foreseen. Thenceforth, attention should focus on the process of liberal economic globalization, which would be the means of expanding prosperity and dealing with those residual adjustments necessary to complete the integration of some societies into the global system.

The second scenario offered a less benign prospect. This was the thesis of 'the coming anarchy'. It was vividly articulated in an article by one of the editors of *The Atlantic Monthly* (February 1994), Robert D. Kaplan. Kaplan envisaged a general collapse of political authority that would accompany massive movements of populations, environmental crises and epidemics. A non-compatible intermingling of peoples with very different experiences of social existence would lead to a total breakdown of the norms of sociability and mechanisms of government. Legitimate governmental authority was already being usurped by mafias, drug cartels and warlords exploiting the Cold War legacy of arms and technologies. Fukuyama's 'post-historical' people, a privileged minority of the world's population, would be living a defensive garrison existence surrounded by this anarchic threat.

The third scenario was presented in a well-known article by Samuel Huntington in *Foreign Affairs* (1993) entitled 'The clash of civilizations?', the thesis of which was expressed in the line: 'The next world war, if there is one, will be a war between civilizations.'[1] Huntington argued that ideological cleavages were now being replaced by the 'fault lines of civilizations', reinforced by a revival of religion and culture as the identities that distinguish friend from foe. These cleavages are ultimately reducible to that between 'the West and the Rest'; and the threat to the West was primarily from a putative alliance of Islamic and Confucian civilizations.

It must be underlined that these three scenarios are of *American* origin. In the way they are presented they tell us something about the American psyche and its hopes and fears. But they do not attract universal acceptance.[2]

'Globalization', which has attained through constant repetition the status of inevitability as well as beneficence in the discourse of Western media and politicians, is regarded among intellectuals from the Third World as the current ideology of Western dominance. Globalization has also evoked scepticism and pessimism among some Europeans. A senior French public servant and scholar, Jean-Marie Guéhenno, has written a little book, called *La fin de la démocratie* (1993), that in some ways parallels the argument of Fukuyama, but gives it a very different meaning. Guéhenno maintains that the state has become obsolescent as it has been unable to deal with many current problems and as the credibility of the political class has faded. Decision making is now the realm of bureaucrats and lobbyists and is fragmented into innumerable confrontations between specific interest groups. Politics has become a game of management, in which there are no conflicts of values, only adjustments of interests. Politics in the sense of choice by political subjects among different social projects is disappearing. The death of politics is the death of the citizen, which is the death of democracy. What for Fukuyama seemed the apotheosis of the West, for this author is the end of the dream of active citizenship that the European Enlightenment inspired – the end is post-modern non-politics.[3]

In its crude form, the coming anarchy thesis offers an opening to the exponents of counter-insurgency warfare and the globalization of police operations. At a more reflective level, it dramatizes the loss of social solidarity that incapacitates collective action. It focuses attention on the circumstances detrimental to solidarity: growing polarization of rich and poor, ecological degradation, and epidemic disease.

The focus on civilizations in Huntington's formulation remains tied to his intellectual milieu's Cold War past. Some European responses, and not just those from the left, have introduced the social dimension which Huntington explicitly excludes from his argument. The *Neue Zürcher Zeitung*, one of Europe's quality newspapers, whose editorial opinion is in the mould of von Hayek, and whose target reader would be a Zurich banker, ran several articles on Islamism (or what the North American media call Islamic fundamentalism). These argued: that the real problem of the Arab world was a lop-sided distribution of wealth between the poor overpopulated countries and sparsely populated oil-producing states;[4] that Islamism articulates deep-seated resentments prevalent throughout the Third World today and among Muslims suffering a marginalized existence in European countries;[5] and that the Gulf wars were about regional attempts to secure control of a vital resource for local purposes which were blocked by Western determination to prevent any one Gulf nation acquiring an energy monopoly with which they could blackmail the West.[6] To put this all down to the mentality of an alien civilization, say these writers for the Zurich gazette, would be to suppress harsh economic and social facts that are uncomfortable to contemplate.

A special 'Survey of Islam' in *The Economist* (6 August, 1994), a journal whose editorial pages celebrate neo-liberal globalization, underlines that Islam is not an unchanging monolithic entity, but one which has its own internal dialectic of change. The survey concludes by suggesting that there may be a potential for mutual understanding between western post-Marxist left and Islamic radicals. The basis for such an understanding – a narrowing of distance, not a convergence – would be that both are concerned with placing the market within a moral order of some kind that would put limits on possessive individualism.[7]

What are civilizations?

The question of civilizations has thus re-emerged in the discourse of international affairs, but as a source of conflict. Moreover, civilizations have been represented as territorially based, geopolitical entities. The 'clash of civilizations' in this thinking would reassert the priority of the military-political in relation to the issues of global economy, ecology and social disparities, and would impute an underlying nefarious coherence to the apparent anarchy threatening the relatively rich. This residual Cold War focus on civilizations distracts attention from the socially polarizing consequences of globalizing market economics, the true generator of chaos. It could also open the way towards examining how the effects of economic globalization might be counteracted among different peoples so as to arrive at a mutual and pacific recognition of different directions of development, different civilizations.

'Civilization' is a very fluid and imprecise concept. It refers both to a process of becoming civilized and to a condition of being civilized. Used in the singular, it contains an implicit exclusive, hierarchical meaning distinguishing the civilized from the uncivilized or barbaric. Used in the plural, it acquires a pluralistic, inclusive meaning – that there are different ways of becoming civilized.

Thus states and civilizations are not equivalent entities. States are characterized by territory and authority structures. Within a state more than one civilization may coexist. This can arouse uncomfortable, apprehensive and repressive feelings among some inhabitants. It has been evident, for example, in debates about education in France and in the United States. In France, should girls be allowed to wear the *foulard islamique* (the *chador*) in school? In the United States, should the curriculum make space for African-American and Hispanic studies?[8] In these cases, the existence of dominant and subordinate civilizations becomes manifest.

It also happens that more than one civilization can coexist within an individual. Susan Strange (1990) spoke of a 'business civilization' which defines the way of being and thinking of the agents of economic globalization – from the sameness of the business-class compartments of aircraft and the international chains of hotels in which they spend some of their time, to the mental frameworks through which they interpret global economic and political events. CNN and *The Financial Times* provide information geared to the discourse of globalization and are available world-wide (in the preferred hotels and aircraft compartments). Yet the 'business civilization' may be only one segment of reality for some of these people. They may adopt different dress and distinct family and social customs in another segment of their lives. For such people there can be continuing tension between two visions of reality and two sets of values. While acting as an accepted participant in each civilization, they may feel as a stranger in both.

Edward Said (1979 and 1993) has explored this ambivalent relationship between civilizations. He writes of 'orientalism' as the Western study of Eastern civilizations and sees it as an instrument of power and domination. The characteristics of the dominated have been defined by the dominant: the dominant purport to know the subordinate peoples better than they know themselves, which can imply, at least for the elites of the subordinate peoples, that the form of knowledge possessed by the dominant civilization in all its manifestations is both superior and universal.

But the self-knowledge of subordinate civilizations is not, for all that, wiped out. It continues to survive in hidden form, ready to reappear when activated by a certain set of circumstances (Mushakoji, 1997). These circumstances include perceptions of economic and social injustice, inequality, and exploitation.

There are two conflicting ways of thinking about civilizations. One represents a civilization as a fixed essence or spirit – Western, or Islamic, or Chinese, or so forth. The other thinks of a civilization as a product of collective human action, an amalgam of social forces and ideas that has achieved a certain coherence, but is continually changing and developing in response to challenges both from within and from without. Orientalism puts that fixed essential quality upon non-Western civilizations, while allowing the West to be the dynamic, expansive exception.

Oswald Spengler, in *Decline of the West* (1939), more logically made no exception for the West. He considered each civilization to be the expression of a unique spirit. Each was totally independent of the others; and all went through a cycle of birth, maturity and death. His study, written just before World War I, was intended to show that the West had entered irrevocably upon its concluding phase.

Yet this notion of a civilization as the expression of the manifold manifestations of a single ideal essence does not really stand up to serious historical examination. Fernand Braudel (1994, p. 8), in his study of civilizations, wrote: 'the history of civilizations . . . is the history of continual mutual borrowings over many centuries, despite which each civilization has kept its own original character.'

Islam is an example. Its idea, the Koran which the faithful acknowledge as dictated by God to Muhammad, came about at a specific time and place, the Arabian peninsula in the seventh century. We cannot, however, speak of Islamic *civilization* until a century later when the Caliphate was established in Baghdad. Nomadic Arab warriors, unified and energized by the new faith, rekindled the spirit of the ancient civilizations of the Middle East. It was not the nomadic life of Arabia, but the urban life of the conquered areas that became characteristic of Islamic civilization – towns, roads, ships and caravans.[9]

This is a salient example of a process encountered in the creation of other civilizations. The initial impetus comes from marginal peoples who reinvigorate and amalgamate pre-existing somnolent civilizations.

The fourteenth-century Islamic diplomat and historian, Ibn Khaldun, built his theory of historical change around an oscillation between two cultures: the nomadic and the urban (Chapter 3). He was reflecting upon North African society in the decline of a hitherto brilliant and powerful Islamic civilization (Ibn Khaldun, 1967; Lacoste, 1984; Cox, 1992). The stimulus to the creation or revival of a vibrant culture, in his reading of history, came from the conquering nomadic military-political formation. The nomadic culture generated the *'asabiya*, the disciplined solidarity of a group sharing an austere lifestyle in relative equality, which enabled it to dominate settled populations. In time, however, the conquerors became corrupted by the affluence of urban life from which they extracted their tribute. *'Asabiya* provided a stimulus to the development of a prosperous urban culture, but this culture eroded that very stimulus. The flourishing of civilization can be traced to this extra-civilization force.

Critical theorists of the Frankfurt School trace a similar dialectic in capitalism. Max Weber's religiously ascetic primitive accumulators built a new capitalist civilization by their work ethic and postponement of gratification; but the very success of capitalism changed its nature as affluence engendered desire for immediate gratification, encouraged corruption and undermined legitimacy (Habermas, 1973).[10]

There are a number of historical instances of stimuli to civilizational development coming from external forces. The nomadic movements across the steppes of Central Asia brought Mongol conquerors to revivify the empire in China and also to challenge and reinvigorate political structures in Europe.[11] These nomads brought little of the artefacts of civilization; they took over the culture of the conquered and served as its bulwark. Similarly, the Arabian tribesmen, united by the religious zeal of Islam, restimulated the old centres of Middle Eastern civilization which they overran. We can see these instances as illustrating a dialectic of military power and culture, generating renewed energies and strengthening political structures in a people.

Other stimuli come from marginalized people within a civilization and from mass migration. Both groups differ markedly from nomadic invaders. Their influence is not that of the direct shock of conquest, but the slow accumulation of pressure upon an established order. These are people, by and large, who seek survival and a place within civilization rather than the overthrow of civilization, though their frustrations may erupt on occasion in anomic or more coherent revolutionary violence.

Toynbee proposed the concepts of external and internal proletariats to embrace these forces (Toynbee, 1946, pp. 375–428). What we have listed here are situations in which: (a) an external nomadic force revives a somnolent civilization; (b) a new moral force, for example the ethic of Protestantism, builds its own material base and transforms civilization, but is in turn undermined by its very success; and (c) there is a slow build-up of pressure within a civilization, both by marginalization of part of its population and by immigration of outsiders.

At present, while nomadic populations are no longer of great historical significance, marginal people and migrants are. Both categories are not confined to poor survival seekers. There are also rich immigrants and marginalized intellectuals who have greater potential for transformative influence in the societies where they are to be found. Transnational social movements may arouse among their participants some of the ascetic commitment of Max Weber's early capitalists – a commitment to different goals like peace, human rights, social equity and ecology. Conceivably, their commitment could mobilize marginal people. One can look to the margins to sustain a movement for change. The carriers of interpenetrating influences among contemporary civilizations may also be found there.

There is both a rupture and a continuity in the birth of a civilization. It has to be explained in complex terms as the product of geography, economic organization, social conflict and the appropriation of practices of other conquered peoples, as well as religious innovation. All of these factors, moreover, are in constant movement, so that a civilization is never completed, never has a final definitive form.

While exogenous influences most readily attract attention, it is perhaps even more important to be aware of the internal dialectics of civilizations which continually reshape their differences (Senghaas, 2002). The status of women is an issue within every form of civilization at the present time and one in regard to which the world-wide women's movement has had to confront the issue of uniformity or separate paths. Recognition of difference, which looks to women in different cultural contexts to define their own goals and methods of action, has gained in acceptance. This does not preclude mutual support across the lines of civilizations, but it does preclude the imposition of one particular concept of emancipation, framed by women of one particular cultural background, upon all the others (Goetz, 1991; Mohanty, 1991).

Ethnic conflict also is not susceptible to a hegemonic type of solution. It may seem to sustain Huntington's 'clash of civilizations' thesis. Yet there exists reserves of good will within all civilizations, a readiness to live in tolerant coexistence with people of other civilizations provided there be a minimum of mutual recognition. Beyond nationalisms, there is also a consistent intellectual trend favouring a larger, more generous notion of community *among* cultures and civilizations (Said, 1993; Chatterjee, 1986). The most encouraging recent case has been the developments in South Africa, which tended to be obscured in media prominence by events in Yugoslavia and Rwanda. The prospects of compatibility in world order depend very largely upon the strengthening of this recognition and acceptance of difference through internal developments in each civilization.

What are some of the basic grounds of difference? To accept difference is to allow that others may be activated by different sentiments and see the world in a different way. There is a difference between societies that are conceived in terms of individualism and those conceived in terms of group solidarity. These are, of course, tendencies rather than exclusive opposites. They affect ways of thinking (methodological individualism versus holism) as well as behaviour patterns. Each has its strengths. The capacity for innovation of the one is balanced by the capacity for building effective organization of the other.

Religious traditions define differences which shape mental processes among individuals who profess no religious faith. The difference between transcendent and immanent deities is fundamental. Transcendent monotheism has created a sense of unity that has been capable of merging the particularism of ethnicity and social class into a larger community. But monotheism separates the City of God from the worldly city. Its vocation for inclusiveness becomes ultimately exclusionary; and the emphasis on transcendence separates the spiritual end of humanity from nature. The immanence of pantheism and polytheism leaves humanity fragmented; but at the same time, it leaves open space for religious pluralism and a fusion of humanity with nature. Immanent conceptions of religion are more compatible with thought geared to the biosphere. Ecologists have discovered an affinity with the indigenous nations of the Americas. The manifold deities of Japanese tradition provide the Japanese with a sense of uniqueness, while they are also an obstacle to Japan embracing a universalist ideology that might become an incentive to found a Japan-centred world order. Polytheism can admit of the addition of new religious (or, in modern instances, more likely secular) faiths, and also that people may embrace more than one faith in different aspects of their lives.

Such abiding differences will influence the way different traditions of civilization respond to both internal and external pressures. Today, the principal pressure, both internal and external, is economic globalization. Neo-liberal enthusiasts of globalization have embraced one aspect of vulgar Marxism: the notion that economic relations determine the superstructures of thought and institutions. I think that what we can see is that the powerful pressure of globalization is met and refracted through the prisms of different civilizations. These abiding differences shape the way economic forces become institutionalized in different societies; and the encounter with globalization provokes a conflict of internal social forces within civilizations.

Thus, despite the rhetoric of globalization, there is no uniform global capitalism. There are distinct and rival forms of capitalism in the process of being reshaped by the internal struggles within different traditions of civilization. This is becoming evident with the rise of China as a major economic power, and in the example of Japan and the Asian 'tigers'. It is also evident now in Europe: while an Anglo-Saxon form of capitalism has become implanted within Europe, it has encountered the European tradition of social democratic or social market capitalism (Albert, 1991). The outcome of the struggle between these different traditions is now uncertain. It has generated a deep unease among European peoples, who have in the past subordinated rampant individualism to practices of collective solidarity. Whether or not the European left will be able to conceive and build consensus around a stable alternative to American-type capitalism is more a matter of civilization than it is of economics.

The relevance of Harold Innis

In his last years, Innis wrote in *Empire and Communication* (1986) and *The Bias of Communication* (1991) and in the scattered notes collected in *The Idea File* (1980), a series of thoughts about civilizations, and particularly about the contrasting characteristics among civilizations and the developmental movements within them. He sought to understand change in civilizations – and did not look upon them as distinct immutable essences. These latter works read as an attempt to jot down rapidly the sketch of a vast research project he never had time to complete. What he gave us is a method and an approach, not a worked out theory. It stands as a challenge to others to develop from his beginnings.

An obvious question follows: why hasn't this happened? Innis's work did stimulate theorizing about communications, but there was no follow-up to his interest in civilizations, which was what led him to study communications in the first place. He himself put the question: What is it that makes the condition of civilization a compelling preoccupation?

Innis's concern with civilization is evident from his early writings on Canadian economic history. They were enquiries into the kind of civilization that came about in Canada, in the encounter of European with indigenous peoples, and in the subsequent tension between the European form of civilization and its American offshoot.[12] His interest was not just, or perhaps even primarily, in economic linkages *per se*, but in how these became embedded in social and political structures and in mental habits. He saw Canada as shaped by rivalry between European and American forms of civilization, and there was no doubt about his personal affiliation with the European.

In his late years, Innis's sympathies lay with the aborted concept of a Third Force based in Europe standing between America and the Soviet Union; but any such notion was suppressed by the prolonged rigidities of the Cold War which came to dominate social science, as well as other facets of life, with its own exclusive dualism. Innis's thinking was one of many intellectual casualties of the Cold War. Only now, as the curtain of Cold War obscurantism may be partially lifting, is it more feasible and more necessary to take up again his reflections on civilizations.

I see two strands of thought that Innis has left us to work with. One is most evident in his writing on Canadian economic history with its stress on physical geography, technology and staple exports. His focus here is on the material conditions that circumscribe the potential for human activities. One can read into it an implication of positivism and a hint of technological determinism. I think this is a misreading.

Innis's work on furs and fish examined the link with Europe and how these staple exports shaped Canadian political institutions and mental processes. In the 1920s and 1930s, he saw this West–East orientation being displaced by a North–South reorientation, towards North American continentalism in which the newer staples of minerals and forest products and hydroelectric power became salient. The West–East orientation underpinned Canadian unity, but the North–South orientation had more fragmenting implications, subordinating the different regions of the Canadian economy separately to the southern market (Innis, 1956).

Newsprint, commanded by the insatiable demand of the American press, was a case in which to examine this reorientation. This led Innis to reflect upon the growth and power of the popular press, the role of advertising in shaping the content of this medium, the challenge to the press from radio and with it a different kind of politics, and thence more broadly to the history of communications and its formative influence on the development of civilizations.

Cochrane and historical method

The other strand in Innis's thinking about civilizations is more directly concerned with the development of mind. His concern lay in the thought processes through which people of different civilizations define their vision of reality. This preoccupation followed from his earlier work, except that it now extended to the world of history as a whole. An important influence upon Innis's thinking at this time – constituting what I see as the second strand – came from his encounter with Charles Norris Cochrane, his contemporary at the University of Toronto and author of *Christianity and Classical Culture* (1944), a book which Innis praised as 'the first major Canadian contribution to the intellectual history of the West'(Innis, 1946).

Cochrane worked in the manner of R. G. Collingwood, his mentor at Oxford. Collingwood was both a philosopher and a practising historian. The historian's task, as he defined it, was to rethink critically the thought of the past (Collingwood, 1946). For Collingwood this meant not the passive assimilation of that thought, but the attempt to reproduce it in an awareness of all the circumstances in which it was formed. This was not an injunction to a simplistic idealism which would see history as shaped by the ideas in people's minds, but rather a method in which mind becomes the point of access to the historical process, the point at which the material conditions of existence bear upon human consciousness, leading to action or to inaction. This way of understanding history dispelled whatever hint of positivism may have appeared in Innis's economic writings.[13]

Innis's writings on civilizations indicate directions for thinking and present some hypotheses. They are often apparently contradictory. They address the inter-subjective content of civilizations – though Innis never used that term – how habits of thought define the real world in different ways for different peoples. He suggested some distinctions that can help us to grasp these differences in habits of thought: principal among them are the distinction between the oral tradition and the written, and the distinction between space and time.

Oral and written: Is the medium the message?

Innis was himself devoted to the oral tradition which he identified with the Socratic dialogue, the common law and the university seminar. These he saw as having decentralizing, egalitarian and democratic connotations. There is, however, nothing essentially democratic about the oral tradition. In classical Greece, it was sustained by a slave society. In Innis's own world, oral communication by Mussolini and Hitler forged the bond between leader and mass. Radio, in the 1930s, gave influence through oral communication to William Aberhart and Father Coughlin on the populist fringes of the North American right,[14] but it was also used effectively by Franklin Roosevelt, through his fireside chats, to counter the hostility of the written medium of the American press. The oral tradition Innis admired might better be described as dialogue among equals seeking truth. It stood in antithesis to the oral communication that bound followers to their charismatic leaders.

Writing, in Innis's analysis, had equally contradictory implications. He thought the alphabet and writing had strengthened democracy, individual expression, decentralization and rational science in ancient Greece. But he wrote also that it facilitated bureaucratic centralization and control in the ancient empires.

There is nothing in either the oral or the written that can be linked to specific outcomes – democratic or authoritarian, centralizing or decentralizing. Yet in specific instances, a shift in preponderance as between oral and written communication may have been significant in shaping such outcomes. The significance lies in the circumstances of struggle, in which the introduction of one or the other mode of communication becomes an instrument of political and social change.

Innis saw a tendency for each medium of communication to create a monopoly of knowledge in the hands of some privileged group – the oral in preserving the esoteric knowledge of the Spartan oligarchy, writing on papyrus in sustaining an ancient imperial bureaucracy, on parchment the medieval clergy, and in print the modern press lords. These monopolies of knowledge are in turn challenged from the margins of society as the human spirit breaks through established monopolies using a new mode of expression which in turn, if successful, creates a new monopoly of knowledge.

I think that for Innis the medium was *not* the message.[15] The message derives from the realm of values and values are what social struggle is about. The medium is a weapon in the struggle of values and has no inherent value in itself. Innis's fundamental concern was with values, and with the material conditions conducive to the expression of the human spirit. He was interested in technologies of intellectual and moral struggle, just as he was interested, perhaps to a lesser degree, in military technology – as instruments, not finalities.

It is possible to pick sentences from Innis that suggest technological determinism. Take this one for example: 'The monarchies of Egypt and Persia, the Roman Empire, and the city states were essentially the products of writing' (Innis, 1986, p. 8). This can be set alongside an often cited passage from Marx: 'The hand-mill gives you society with the feudal lord; the steam-mill society with the industrial capitalist.' Surely neither statement is to be taken literally. Both are devices to set you thinking. Stephen Marglin (1974) reversed Marx's formula: 'The steam mill didn't give us the capitalist; the capitalist gave us the steam mill.' The reversal is both more credible and more consistent with the whole body of Marx's thought, in which social power relations are determining, and the powerful select from available technologies those that are consistent with the maintenance of their power.

Rather than attribute predictable political and social outcomes, whether democratic or authoritarian, to different forms of communication, Innis's insight is on firmer ground in positing a connection between a shift in the predominant form of communication and in the nature of power. That is to say that the development and transformations in civilizations are associated with (though not caused by) changes in the media of communication.

To this proposition can be added Innis's view that new communications media tend to be associated with monopolies of knowledge. The techniques of communication are the means of expression of such monopolies. The paramount influence of television in mass communication, combined with an opening of markets across the world, has led to competition among big concentrations of capital for the power to disseminate throughout the world an essentially American pop culture which will shape popular ideas of the nature of the world. CNN, in complementary fashion, serves the business civilization by providing a view of events with a similar bias.

In contrast to the passive receptivity of the television viewer, communication through computers was heralded as putting the individual in control; but apart from the fact that those with access to such communication are a small minority, the increasing use of e-mail and the internet challenges capital and political authorities to attempt to control these channels of communication for commercial and political purposes.

How far do the communications media bias thought in specific directions? Do they lead towards a globalized, homogenized Disney World and CNN culture? Or are there media opportunities, perhaps yet to be discovered, for alternative world views? The long-term success of transnational social movements depends upon finding a means of getting around the dominant media in order to be able to articulate their alternative perspectives.

Space, time and the struggle for the future

The space/time duality in Innis is crucial for determining the quality of civilization. The spatial dimension he associated with the state and with military power. The time dimension he associated with religion and the institution of the church.[16] The distinction, I suggest, does not relate to two institutions – state and church – so much as to two orientations of the human mind. One orientation is towards extension and interaction of existing structures at a given moment in time. The other is towards duration and development over time. Braudel and the *Annales* school of historians use the terms synchronic and diachronic to convey this duality. The synchronic dimension covers the interactions of an existing social system, a prevailing set of structures. It is the realm of what Braudel called *l'histoire événementielle* – events history. It is the realm of problem-solving within the prevailing order of things. The diachronic is the dimension of structural durability and structural change, what Braudel called the *longue durée*. We are confronted here by the questions of how the existing order came into being, what are its internal contradictions, and how may it be changed.

Innis was much concerned by what he called 'present-mindedness'. He saw this reflected in and propagated by the popular press in its emphasis on sensationalism and the ephemeral. He thought the balance between space and time had been seriously upset in favour of the spatial dimension 'with disastrous consequences to Western civilization' (Innis, 1991, p. 76). His ideal was a more equal balance between space and time. Curiously, despite his commitment to the oral tradition of Greek antiquity, he identified that situation of balance with Byzantium and some of the ancient empires. This raises an important, but unanswered question about Innis: was his real commitment to an ordered, prolonged Byzantine-type stability, that could almost be qualified as totalitarian because of its fusion of church and state; or was it to conditions that would make possible a new breakthrough of the human spirit from the margins of civilization? You can find quotes to support both positions. This may be at the heart of Innis's own ambiguity – his own internal dialectic.

To focus on the space/time struggle for pre-eminence in the mind is particularly apposite to the present. The seemingly unstoppable globalization of economic relations is perhaps the ultimate form of synchronic organization in which political authorities and social and cultural practices become subordinated to a disembedded global financial network. This prospect is too recent to have been addressed in Innis's writings but can be considered as latent within them. Consummated globalization, with its implication of the death of politics and the homogenization of culture, would indeed mean the 'end of history'. It would mean the final suppression of the time dimension and with it the sense of a capacity for choice in the form of society and in the hierarchy of values.

The time dimension brings with it the challenge to change. Put in abstract language, the struggle between the diachronic and the synchronic is perhaps the basic issue of our time. It is being fought out in Europe today in the contest between the concepts of financial Europe and social Europe at the level of the European Union.

Italy is an interesting case in point. Following the elections of March 1994, a new government, led by Silvio Berlusconi, took power in Italy. It registered the disillusionment of the electorate with political parties from the centre to the right, compromised by corruption, and the left, bereft of a convincing alternative. Berlusconi, who controlled private television, offered himself as the entrepreneur-saviour of a state verging on bankruptcy. His government was an artificial combination of entrepreneurial liberals, northern autonomists, and fascists anxious to regain entry to political power after fifty years of exclusion. It was sustained by a mainly petty bourgeois constituency fed up with corruption and mismanagement. Berlusconi set about gaining control over public as well as private television as an instrument for consolidating power around his movement and for enforcing a financial market logic in public policy. More than three million Italians took to the streets in protest. There was obviously no consensual basis of legitimacy for this regime; and Berlusconi gave place to a transitory government of technicians, the basic question of power remaining unresolved.[17] There also proved to be no effective alternative. The patched together centre-left government that followed had neither coherence nor a vision that could mobilize popular support. Berlusconi came back as the dominant leader of a right wing coalition in March 2001 and proceeded to use his majority to pass legislation that would immunize him against legal challenges of fraudulent business practices and conflict of interest in his control of both public and private television. This time no one took to the streets.

The doubt that hangs over this confrontation is whether the protest movement that challenges the supposed 'inevitability' of economic globalization will have sufficient creativity to generate both the bonds of solidarity and the innovation in institutions and practices that could become the harbinger of an alternative vision of society. And there is much pessimism about this. Writ large, it is the predicament of the left in the Western world. The strength of resistance is there, but is the vision of a real creative alternative still missing? And if present, where lies the capacity to communicate it?

Italy is in this a paradigm for European civilization. Italy illustrates the extremes of current tendencies: the merger of nostalgic fascism with economic liberalism, together with the existence of a profound, instinctive popular rejection of that merged force, which still lacks coherent leadership and a clear vision of its road ahead. Italy epitomizes the doubt hanging over the future.

Virtù *and* fortuna: *the problem of creativity*

Innis's fundamental concern was, as I said, with values and with creativity. One of his commentators, Robin Neill (1972), in a book that is helpful in constructing a reading of Innis, said Innis's ultimate faith was in creative individualism. I think this may be a one-sided statement. It is true in the sense that creativity comes from individuals. But if you read Innis through the mind of Charles Cochrane, his focus is less on the individual than on the character of the society that produces individuals and either releases or suppresses their creative potential.[18]

The problem of origins, development and decline has been the central preoccupation of those who in the past have made the study of civilizations their special concern. Spengler adopted a biological metaphor which led him to see a deterministic cycle of birth, creative development, mature consolidation, decline and ultimate death. Others have sought to escape from such determinism while trying to probe the factors making for creativity and decline. Those writing from a Western background have been stimulated by the sense of a loss of creativity in Western civilization (except, perhaps, in the realm of technology) and are questioning how a new phase of creativity might be able to reverse the process of decline (Toynbee, 1946, 1955; Sorokin, 1957).

This problem, be it noted in passing, can exist only for a historicist mentality. The historicist seeks an understanding of what makes historical change, whereas the positivist can merely observe that changes happen and may recur in certain patterns. The historicist search for reality behind events may find answers in Divine Providence, in the laws of motion of capital, or in some less deterministic knowledge of the structures of material life and mentalities, for example the *longue durée*, that shape events. The positivist can see only events and is sure about them, though incapable of giving them meaning. The historicist is concerned with what lies behind events and can never be quite so sure. However, events are a reliable check upon the explanatory hypotheses that suggest meanings.

We can introduce here a third duality to add to oral/written and space/time. This is the duality which Cochrane saw as the predicament of late Roman civilization between virtue and fortune – two words that have become transformed and trivialized in meaning from their Latin origins and are better understood through Machiavelli's use of *virtù* and *fortuna*. In a more modern idiom, we could render these ideas as creative collective energy, on the one hand, and the objective limits of the possible, on the other.

Cochrane saw the failure of the classical world in its final stage as a waning confidence in the creative capacity of politics when confronted with the despair engendered by the sheer degradation of the material conditions of existence. The balance in the classical mind had shifted from virtue to fortune, from creativity to fate (Cochrane, 1944, esp. pp. 157-61). Was this caused by the invasion of oriental mystery religions, or were these religions merely filling a mental void opened by material decay, and rigified social and political structures? Today, there is some analogy in the proliferation of cults obsessed with death and the apocalypse.

A millennium later, Machiavelli made a similar analysis of his own society: too corrupt to restore within itself the spirit of civic competency, or *virtù*. He looked to a Prince who would be capable of arousing once again the civic spirit that in earlier times had sustained a Republic (Machiavelli, 1961; Chabod, 1958). Four centuries later, Antonio Gramsci looked to the Party as the modern prince, to perform the same function (Gramsci, 1971 esp. pp. 123–205). What is common is the awareness of a moral and intellectual failure and a search for a means of moral and intellectual regeneration.

This may be the answer to Innis's question: why do people at certain historical junctures concern themselves with the problem of civilization? The answer would be, as I think it was with Innis himself, because of a deep unease about the continuing vitality of their own civilization.[19]

This is not a peculiarity of Western civilization. The fourteenth-century

North African Islamic diplomat and historian Ibn Khaldun confronted the same predicament. Though by all accounts a devout Muslim, he wrote history with an accent of historical materialism. He was attentive in the first place to the geographical and ecological constraints upon human action, and to the life styles of people rooted in their economic conditions. But in the last analysis, he attributed the creation or decay of political authority to the presence or absence of a moral quality he called *'asabiya*, the sense of group solidarity capable of founding and sustaining a state (Ibn Khaldun, 1967; Cox, 1992).

Virtù and *'asabiya* are words that apply to something missing, something required to trigger a response to a failure of civilization. They give a diagnosis, not a prescription for recovery. What it would take to generate a sufficient collective response remains unidentified. Neither Harold Innis nor Ibn Khaldun give us a simple answer.[20] The answer lies within our own collective existence, but where can the effective stimulus come from?

These thinkers concur in identifying a moral quality of social energy, solidarity or collective spirit that is an essential condition for creative political authority reposing upon the social basis of a coherent community. The absence or weakness of this quality made them aware of its importance. Reflecting on history, they see those periods when it is present as creative phases in the springtime of civilizations, and its decline and disappearance as characteristic of stiffening and increasingly fragile and corrupt social and political structures.

Knowledge is suspended, however, at the point where we enquire how this quality can be called forth from within a human group. Some have offered hypotheses, for example Toynbee's list of stimuli: hard physical environment, new ground, blows, pressures and penalisation (Toynbee, 1946, I, Part VII). A great challenge is required to evoke a creative response; but too great a challenge may overwhelm and extinguish this possibility. The challenge and response dialectic may be a good model for exploring the potential for change. In the contemporary world context, as globalization and the business civilization coast on the myth of the 'end of history', some evidence of responses do seem to have the germ of *'asabiya* or *virtù*. They have mobilized people outside of the conventional channels of politics, both in street demonstrations and in the development of alternative thinking. These manifestations of resistance may not yet have attained sufficient force to sustain an alternative society; and the capacity of the dominant forces to fragment and isolate such protests is powerful. But these uprisings are indicative that the promise of new life is present, sometimes active, sometimes latent.

Those who have reflected on the question of the revival of creative collective initiative have taught us where to look: first to a critical analysis of the material conditions of existence and the mental and institutional structures that delineate the condition of civilization; and then to the marginal social forces whence contestation and innovation may come. Those marginal forces today, as in earlier times, are both internal and external and they are contradictory. They include: those groups of people who are being adversely affected by the dominant trend of globalization; the mass migrations that are mixing traditions of civilization at the most popular levels; and transformations taking place in contiguous civilizations, a primary example being the struggle within Islam. The challenge is to distil some coherence and common purpose out of these contradictory elements – and this challenge is directed in the first instance to marginal intellectuals, those who work outside the mainstream.

* * *

To return to one of the scenarios with which I began, Samuel Huntington's picture of the world is of a clash of civilizations, each with its own territorial domain and each having its own essential quality. A more adequate construction of reality, I suggest, would show a world of civilizations overlapping in space, each beset by grave problems of change, some apparently blocked in their capacity for creative development – Western civilization not least among these – and some experiencing deep internal conflict which is also often transformed into external aggression. Rather than to prepare for war – hot or cold – and to sharpen the negations between the West and the Rest, it makes more sense to enquire into the processes of transformation in our civilization and in others, to address the problems of economic polarization and ecological degradation, and to seek out ways of assisting parallel efforts within other civilizations.

To frame the question this way implies recognition that there may be different ways of approaching these problems. We may be a useful stimulus as somebody else's marginal, if we can rid ourselves of the habit of thinking of ourselves as the holders of universal truth. Previous world orders have derived their universals from a dominant society, British or American, itself the product of a dominant civilization. A post-hegemonic world order would have to derive its normative content in a search for common ground among its constituent traditions of civilization.

What common ground is conceivable? A first condition would be mutual recognition of distinct traditions of civilization. This is a difficult step for those who have shared a hegemonic perspective. It is perhaps even more difficult for those who have suffered subordination to an alien but dominant view of the world, who have experienced denial of their own identity. A second condition would be to move beyond the point of recognition of difference towards some elements of shared consciousness that would provide a bridge among the distinct and separate subjectivities of the different coexisting traditions of civilization. The grounds for this common element of consciousness might be:

- recognition that all forms of life are interdependent in the biosphere and that therefore all forms of civilization share a common concern for survival and sustained equilibrium in global ecology;
- mutual support in achieving and sustaining social solidarity and equity,

thus avoiding a situation where internal class cleavages become a stimulus to aggression towards other civilizations;

- mutual restraint in the use of violence to decide conflicts – not that this would remove conflict, but it could involve a recognition that the propensity to use force (because, as we sometimes hear, 'force is the only language they understand') is evidence of a failure of communication;

- a building of consensus on human rights that would not be seen as the imposition of one civilization's values over those of another.

These reflections lead finally to several propositions. The theme of civilizations is again ripe for study in the human sciences. It has become important as an aid to understanding the conflicts and predicaments of the contemporary world. The wrong approach is to think of civilizations as having fixed essences inherently in conflict one with another. A better approach is to study the transformations and encounters of civilizations and encourage compatibility in development while avoiding the illusion of convergence and homogenization on a Western model. Blockages in the development of civilizations arise from material conditions, with causes both internal and external. A growing polarization of wealth and poverty, increasing ecological degradation, and a rise in the level of violence indicate that civilization has reached an impasse. Development beyond the blockage point depends upon a moral and intellectual response, a revival of creativity. This, in turn, depends upon social conditions conducive to creativity and an openness to developments in other civilizations.

Finally, Canada may not be a bad place to pursue this effort because the multiculturalism that has emerged in Canada makes it possible for Canadians to think of themselves as on the margins of several civilizations; and because there is a somewhat neglected, but still resilient Canadian tradition of political thought deriving from Harold Innis and some of those who have been influenced by him upon which to build.

9 Conceptual guidelines for a plural world

Civilizations represent continuities in human thought and practices through which different human groups attempt to grapple with their consciousness of present problems. At some times, these continuities appear to be vigorous, reaffirmed, even redefined. At other times, they are obscured, subordinated to other dominant modes of thought and practices. At such times and for such groups talk of civilizations is absent, suppressed or seemingly irrelevant. When and why do civilizations become a significant object of knowledge?

For three decades and more, knowledge about world affairs in the West and in the Soviet sphere was constructed predominantly with reference to the Cold War. Its pre-eminent form in international relations theory, particularly in its American expression, was neo-realism, a problem-solving form of knowledge applicable to super power rivalry. Neo-realism was a technology of power based upon the premise of a common rationality shared by both sides in the US–Soviet conflict in which game theoretic exercises and rational choice hypotheses could be taken as guides for policy understandable in the same way by both sides.

Once the overarching control of the Cold War was lifted, the underlying but obscured diversity of the human situation became more fully apparent and neo-realism lost its monopoly of explaining the world and proposing action. But the salience of the Cold War was succeeded by the salience of globalization: the vision of the inevitable homogenization of economic and cultural practices, driven by competitiveness in a global market and by new technologies of communication.

There is, however, a historical dialectical resistance to this vision of global homogenization – an affirmation of diversity through many forms of identity: gender, ethnic, religious, linguistic, attachment to the land, and a sense of historical grievance and humiliation. The two most prevalent forms of identity of the earlier twentieth century – nationality and class – are submerged, though not eliminated, in these other forms. The largest aggregate of identity is the civilization. Globalization is countered by the affirmation of civilizations in this dialectic of homogenization and diversification. This is the basic reason for a revival of concern about civilizations.

How should we theorize civilizations and their role in this future world?

What are the implications for international studies? In approaching an answer to these questions it is necessary to determine a conceptual framework. Since the problem is historical, this framework has to be adapted to the movement of history. Concepts that are fixed and timeless freeze movement into an eternal present. Historical concepts must, as E. P. Thompson (1978, pp. 229–42) affirmed, be elastic. They must give a clear direction to thinking while allowing for the continuing transformations of the historical process. Historically relevant concepts arise from a dialogue between social being and social consciousness, between the empirical evidence of what exists and the manner in which people become aware of its existence. In this vein, I discuss three themes in this chapter:

1   The changing awareness of civilizations in Western thought. (For someone born into the Western tradition, this is a necessary reflexive exercise in self-awareness as a precondition to awareness of other civilizations.)
2   A workable definition of the entity 'civilization'. What is a civilization?
3   The dimensions of the concept of 'civilization' which can be a means of analysing the dynamics of civilizational change.

The changing awareness of civilizations in Western thought

The origin of the word 'civilization' is traceable to eighteenth-century France (Braudel, 1994; Elias, 1994). In German, the word *Kultur* assumed comparable significance about the same time. Both had the connotation of a process of increasing civility, the antithesis of barbarity. The context was the emergence of the bourgeoisie as a strong social force – in France more closely linked into state power as the *noblesse de robe*, in Germany more separate and having its stronghold in the universities. The civilizing process was conceived as a universal phenomenon characterizing the Enlightenment of eighteenth-century Europe, at one with universal reason and natural laws applicable in the physical sciences, economics, law and morality. The finality of the process was civilization in the singular.

The Enlightenment perspective of civility was soon challenged by the romantic movement which rejected the notion of an objective world governed by universal laws and striving towards the attainment of universal norms of law and morals. The romantic thinkers gave more place to subjectivity and uniqueness. Each distinctive national culture had its own aim and destiny in world history. Herder in Germany, Michelet in France, Burke in England voiced this counter-perspective to the universalism of the Enlightenment. The theme was developed later during the nineteenth century by German historicism (e.g. by Wilhelm Dilthey). The European expansionism of the nineteenth century gave substance to these philosophical leanings. *Les bourgeois conquérants* – to borrow the phrase of Charles Morazé (1957) – encountered other civilizations. Civilization in the singular gave way to civilizations in the plural. But imperialism and its accompanying scholarship now defined the non-European civilizations as objects of knowledge. European civilization (and its American offshoot) was to be thought of as dynamic, an active agent inspired by the doctrine of Progress. Non-European civilizations were thought of as passive and fixed.

Conditions during the later nineteenth century – the long depression of the last three decades, the social conflicts arising from urbanization and industrialization, the social transformations that Tönnies described as from *Gemeinschaft* to *Gesellschaft* and Durkheim as from mechanical to organic solidarity, and ultimately the imperialist rivalries that led to World War I – encouraged scepticism about the doctrine of Progress. Oswald Spengler's *The Decline of the West* (1939), the first major European work of the twentieth century on the theme of civilizations, reflected this more pessimistic mood. The manuscript was substantially completed just before the outbreak of World War I and was worked over and published in 1918 in the context of German defeat. The English translation was published in 1926 and 1928. Its pessimism resonated to the era of the Great Depression and the rise of fascism.[1]

Spengler saw history as recording the birth, maturity and decline of a number of civilizations, each with a distinct spirit. This he called his 'Copernican revolution'. Europe and the West was not the centre around which other societies revolved; it was one among other civilizations, each of which followed a predetermined sequence of stages; and European civilization was entering into its final phase. His approach elaborated upon the visions of Giambattista Vico (1970) and the romantics of the earlier nineteenth century. Spengler's thoughts for his own time focused on what remained possible for Western civilization to achieve during its inexorable decline.

The other great work on civilizations of the first half of the twentieth century, Arnold J. Toynbee's *A Study of History* (1946, 1957), was more optimistic in tone since it envisaged the possibility of rebirth of civilization through a religious revival. This monumental work was published in a series of volumes through the 1930s. Its major impact came after World War II and was quite important especially in the United States. A major promoter of Toynbee's work in America was Henry Luce, the publisher of *Time, Life,* and *Fortune* magazines. Luce seized upon Toynbee's concept of the 'universal state' as the ultimate stage of a civilization and put the United States in the role of creator of a new universal state for the world. He signed an editorial in *Life,* entitled 'The American Century', which reflected the internationalist and interventionist views of the Eastern Establishment against American isolationism. *Time* published an influential summary of Toynbee's work by Whittaker Chambers, the ex-communist soon to attain renown as the principal witness in the trial and conviction of Alger Hiss. Luce undoubtedly enhanced Toynbee's reputation, but his use of the work deviated from Toynbee's own preoccupation with religion as the road to salvation for civilizations as well as individual souls.[2]

Luce's appropriation of Toynbee placed emphasis once again upon civilization in the singular – the creation of a single all-embracing American-inspired world order. As the Cold War came to dominate thinking about the future of the world, the choice seemed to be between two forms of universalism, capitalism and communism, both derived from the European Enlightenment. The sense of coexistence of a plurality of civilizations was obscured. Whatever was not pertinent to the Cold War did not matter in the top levels of world politics. Of course, at the lower levels, the Cold War was less a matter of concern than the daily struggle for survival in conditions of poverty and deprivation, the subordination of peoples to imperialism, and various forms of discrimination. But such sentiments were obscured in the top-down view of the Cold War.

Voices from what came to be called the Third World were indeed heard in the West (for example, Panikkar, 1953). Even in the West, the dominant manichean vision was challenged, though not much weakened, by sources outside mainstream thought. In the immediate post-war period, the most innovative journal of history in France, the *Annales*, dropped the word *histoire* from its title and substituted *Économies, Sociétés, Civilisations* (Daix, 1995, p. 214). The use of the plural for civilizations was significant, but this brand of historical study was not fully accepted by the university elite and only began to make an impact in the English-speaking world in the 1980s, particularly through the influence of Fernand Braudel.[3] These negations of the bipolar Cold War paradigm remained an undercurrent. The fall of the Berlin Wall in 1989 is now seen as the psychological threshold to a post-Cold War era. What we can call the formal Cold War, the stalemate between capitalism and communism, between the United States and the Soviet Union, came to an end with the disintegration of the latter. But there was no significant change in the structural Cold War – in the institutions that had been built up to carry on the Cold War, particularly the intelligence services, and the mental frameworks and bodies of knowledge linked to that conflict. These continued, in search of new applications: deterrence of new perceptions of threat like Islamism; counter-insurgency warfare techniques to suppress popular movements disruptive of the global economy; combating terrorism and controlling the drug trade.

With the formal end of the Cold War, the aspirations of people at the lower levels of world power began to be more clearly articulated as affirmations of identity. However, these new burgeoning identities were contradicted by the triumphant universalism of the Cold War victor: by the ideology of economic globalization.

Western consciousness has been split between a dominant universalistic perspective that sees civilization as a *Western* civilization encompassing the whole world, and a pluralistic perspective that sees Western civilization (variously defined) as coexisting with and interacting with other civilizations. In the Western historical trajectory, the pluralistic conception is recurrent as counterpoint to major historical upheavals: the affirmation of national cultures in response to the conquest and containment of the French Revolution, the *fin de siècle* pessimism of the late nineteenth century, and the loss of certainty in the exhaustion of the certainties of World War II and the Cold War in the late twentieth century. The universalistic notion of civilization has, however, remained a characteristic of Western consciousness and an intellectual obstacle to recognition of the ontological equality of other civilizations.

What is a civilization?

Archeologists who have studied ancient civilizations have defined them in material terms (e.g. Childe, 1942). The process of civilization is associated with urban life, state structures and technological innovation, from neolithic through copper to bronze eras, including invention of the wheel, ox-cart and sailing ship. Such material civilizations are recorded *c.*2500 BCE in the Nile Valley, Fertile Crescent, and the environs of Mohenjo Daro in the Indus valley. Gradually, these separated points became linked into a contiguous expanse of material civilization extending from the western Mediterranean through to the northern Indian subcontinent by about 100 BCE – and this does not include other sites of autonomous civilizations being found in China, Africa and Central and South America.

These material, technological, economically organized and class-structured entities were unified by religion. It is common nowadays to call civilizations by the names of religions – Judeo-Christian, Islamic, Confucian and so forth. Religion enabled people encompassed within a civilization to develop a shared consciousness and symbols through which they could communicate meaningfully with one another. Myth, religion and language were all the same thing until language became secularized and rationalized. Those sets of symbols which made meaningful communication possible among the participants in a material civilization can be called sets of inter-subjective meanings. The material world provided a common ground of experience; religion provided a common ground of subjectivity. *So a working definition of a civilization can be a fit or correspondence between material conditions of existence and inter-subjective meanings.*

The notion of a 'fit' does not imply a base–superstructure relationship in the sense that common material conditions automatically generate similar ideological superstructures in a 'vulgar Marxist' sense. One can attribute more autonomy to the realm of inter-subjectivity while at the same time positing a necessary correspondence, or what Max Weber called 'elective affinity' (Weber, 1948), between thought and the material conditions of existence. The challenge of material conditions may be confronted in different ways in different forms of consciousness. Different sets of inter-subjective meanings may correspond to the same material conditions of existence. The requirement is that they make sense of these material conditions for the people concerned and make it possible for them to conceive their future and to concert their activities towards certain ends. The material limits of the possible are constraining, but there is always some scope for ethical choice.

The nature of inter-subjectivity has become particularly important in the current condition of civilizations. Ideologies born of the European Enlightenment and propagated throughout the world under European dominance, notably liberalism and Marxism, have been losing their hold in popular imagination and the field is open to competing world views.

Other terms have been used alongside 'civilizations' with analogous or related meanings: 'empires', 'cultures', even 'societies'. Spengler (1939) used 'culture' to refer to the initial creative, poetic phases of a single organic process in which 'civilization' represented the mature, rationalized and declining phases. Toynbee (1946) used 'society' and 'civilization' interchangeably; he was concerned with the 'intelligible field of study', i.e. the unit (or we could also say 'social system') which is adequate to explain what happens in its various parts, and he argued that the civilization is that unit. 'Empire' has both territorial and political implications; as referring to ancient empires it may connote the political structure of a civilization in a particular historical phase and thus represent a concept of unity comparable to religion in its inter-subjectivity (Eisenstadt, 1993). For Spengler, empire or imperialism is the last stage of decline in the organic life of a culture-civilization.

I would like to suggest another distinction between culture and civilization. This is the distinction between the synchronic and the diachronic (Piaget, 1965; Braudel, 1980). 'Culture' has been appropriated by structural-functional anthropology and takes the form of synchronic analysis concerned with how the composite of practices and norms in a given social system interact in maintaining the whole. Culture is an anthropologist's word and civilization is a historian's. 'Civilization', especially as relevant to the understanding of global change today, can be thought of as the diachronic or historical dimension of culture. Of course, 'culture' is also commonly used in discussing relatively small human groups, for example a tribal community, or a segment of society, for example 'culture of poverty', or an ethnic or religious group within a broader society. 'Multicultural' refers to a society composed of a number of such groups, all of which may belong to the same civilization.

The synchronic dimension is uppermost in all of these usages. It evokes the notion of homoeostasis as a natural restorer of equilibrium. The idea of equilibrium is alien to the notion of civilization. The focus is rather on origins, encounters and transformations of civilizations. Stability and equilibrium give place to development and responses to internal and external challenges. Civilizations are the media through which people have come to organize themselves materially and mentally to cope with their material contexts and to imagine a collective future.

Civilizations do not remain static. In the movement of history, there are recurrent struggles to reshape consciousness into a new fit with a changed material context. In these contests, religious zeal confronts secularism and rationalized individualism confronts compassion and community. To begin an enquiry into the developments in civilizations and their impact on world political economy today, it is useful to set out a brief inventory of the principal arenas within which these struggles over the mental orientations of civilizations are taking place.

Another word has recently come to prominence in any discussion of perspectives on the world. Post-modernism has given wide currency to the notion of 'identity' as the self-consciousness of collective subjects of history, especially those whose existence has been obscured in the dominant discourses. Feminism and post-colonial literature have given particular prominence to such identities. One might think of a civilization as a very large realm of identity, and often it seems to be so in the rhetoric of appeals to defend the principles of Western civilization, or of some other definition of civilization.

I prefer to leave the notion of identity to refer to self-consciousness. In so far as it may relate to civilization, it refers only to a conscious affirmation of belonging to a civilization. It does not refer to the 'common sense' or perceptions of 'reality' that characterize particular civilizations and which are to be found at a deeper level of consciousness – a level at which something that has been shaped by the historical development of a people comes to be understood by them as universal and natural. It is only through deep critical reflection that the formation of such 'common sense' through time and the perceptions of 'reality' that corresponds to it can be revealed.

Some implications flow from the definition of civilization as a fit between material conditions of existence and inter-subjective meanings:

1 *Epistemology*   The emphasis on inter-subjectivity implies that there are different perspectives on the world, different understandings about the nature of the world, different perceptions of 'reality'. Accordingly, the 'real world' is not a given, external to thought. 'Reality' is socially and historically constructed as part of thought interacting with its material environment. Different civilizational perspectives perceive different 'realities'; and these different realities are constantly changing and developing. One inference from this is the need for reflexivity, for self-awareness of the social and historical conditioning of our own thought. Another inference is the need to be able to enter into the mental frameworks or inter-subjective meanings of others.[4] It leads to the post-modern dilemma: if there are no absolute foundations for social knowledge, where is truth?

2 *Theories of history*   Various theories of the development of civilizations may yield heuristic hypotheses, but must be rejected as laws of history. Giambattista Vico (Chapter 3, pp. 46–7) posited that each civilization[5] had a distinct origin and a history independent of other civilizations. These separate histories, however, followed a common pattern, the 'ideal eternal history'

which, from heroic creative origins out of the barbarism of the senses evolved a rationalized society under universal laws, which in time descended into the 'barbarism of reflection' in which pursuit of self-interest was unconstrained – a condition more depraved than the original barbarism of the senses. Vico minimized the importance of contacts and borrowing among civilizations, placing all the emphasis on the internal dynamics of development activated primarily by class struggle. He formulated the classical statement of the cyclical concept of the history of civilizations.

Oswald Spengler's view of the distinctness of civilizations was similar to Vico's. Each civilization had its distinct spirit, but each also went through the same phases of birth, creativity, rationalization and decline. The characteristics of these phases were somewhat different from Vico's but the pattern was the same. Toynbee introduced more interaction and borrowing among civilizations. He was interested in the process of succession linking one declining civilization to another emerging civilization; but he retained the essentials of the cyclical hypothesis. A triadic view of the history of civilization preceded and coexisted with the cyclical hypothesis. The fascination with the number three in Western consciousness as a key to history can be traced to the twelfth-century Calabrian monk Joachim of Floris and was derived from the Christian doctrine of the Trinity. Joachim of Floris divided history (for him there was only one history, i.e. the history of Christianity) into three periods: the reign of the Father, the rule of the un-incarnate God, an authoritarian pre-Christian era; the reign of the Son or the Christian era, in which political institutions were necessary to constrain people's behaviour in conformity with the revelations of religion; and the reign of the Holy Spirit, which he imagined as a communitarian future in which harmony would naturally prevail without the need for political or institutional constraints. This triadic form, entrenched in Western consciousness, lent itself to the dialectical theories of Hegel and Marx. In simplified form, it became a linear, progressive doctrine of history. Triadic and linear forms conceive of only *one* civilizational trajectory.

In non-Western perspectives, a dyadic picture of history has been more common. Its foremost expression is in the Chinese conception of a fundamental rhythm of the universe alternating between *yin*, a quiescent phase of unity and harmony, and *yang*, a phase of activity, conflict and fragmentation. The fourteenth-century Islamic diplomat and philosopher Ibn Khaldun posited a recurrent swing between two forms of social and political life, *'umran badawi* and *'umran hadari* (Ibn Khaldun, 1967; see also Lacoste, 1984, pp. 92-117). The first derived from rural life and the second from urban life, but the meanings go far beyond those terms. *'Umran badawi* is the origin of social organization and is conceived of as an ascetic form of life in which a spirit of solidarity (*'asabiya*) may arise, through which people become capable of creating a state. The aim of the state will be enjoyment of sedentary, urban civilization or *'umran hadari*; but urban life and the affluence it generates is corrupting and ultimately erodes the spirit of solidarity which created it. Thus history, in both Chinese and Ibn Khaldun's conceptions, is cyclical rather than progressive. Both conceptions refer to the dynamics of one civilization and say nothing about the coexistence of civilizations.

3 *Boundaries in time and space*   Spengler and Toynbee do not agree about the number or the boundaries of civilizations, which suggests this is not a matter about which any categorical statements can be made. Fernand Braudel (1994, pp. 9-10) insists that each civilization develops from a specific geographical zone:

> To discuss civilization is to discuss space, land and its contours, climate, vegetation, animal species and natural or other advantages. It is also to discuss what humanity has made of these basic conditions: agriculture, stockbreeding, food, shelter, clothing, communications, industry and so on.

Historically, civilizations have evolved upon specific geographical sites and have, as Braudel remarks, been coloured by these origins. Today, however, with demographic expansion, migratory movements, the diffusion of ideas, and the proliferation of diasporas, geographical definitions become more problematic. Susan Strange has referred plausibly to a non-territorial 'business civilization' (Strange, 1990). Different civilizations coexist within the geographical space of one country, even within the personal space of one individual. Nowadays, it makes more sense to think of a civilization as a community of thought, taking up the inter-subjectivity side of my proposed definition, while acknowledging that inter-subjective meanings evolve in relation to material conditions in which geography continues to play a role alongside transnational economic networks and world-spanning communications technologies.

Braudel also wrote: 'The history of civilizations . . . is the history of mutual borrowings over many centuries, despite which each civilization has kept its own original character' (Braudel, 1994, p. 8). One can agree with this statement and at the same time acknowledge that it leaves unresolved problems. If civilizations are continually borrowing and changing, how do we recognize the core identity? How do we know the boundaries?

Thinking of a civilization as a community of thought allows for the physical intermingling of civilizations. It loosens the analogy of civilizations to nation states and the notion that one can plot the 'fault lines' between civilizations on a map. I would therefore rather focus on inter-subjectivity and the dynamics shaping different forms of inter-subjectivity.

Dimensions of civilizations: what are the factors that shape inter-subjectivity?

What follows has no pretensions to completeness. I signal here some of the factors that influence the ways in which peoples understand the world in which they live. These are factors which seem to be at work within all civilizations. They may differentiate civilizations that coexist, but they also account for changes within each civilization. There may well be other factors that the following itemization overlooks.

Social economy (or social relations of production)

The way people are organized to satisfy their material needs is a basic aspect of civilization. Both liberalism and Marxism see capitalism as an economic system functioning according to inherent laws, although they differ, of course, in their evaluation of that system. Karl Polanyi's view was different. As a social anthropologist, he studied 'substantive economies', i.e. the various historically created forms through which people had become organized to satisfy their material needs. In these different substantive economies, economic processes were embedded in social relations. They served the social goals or conformed to the social norms of the community. In consequence, different substantive economies, different modes of social organization of production and distribution, have come into existence throughout history, each conforming to a particular form of society.

Polanyi's concern centred upon the attempt initiated in England in the early nineteenth century to sever that historically prevalent connection between economy and society: the attempt to create a self-regulating market over and above society. This 'utopian' venture, according to Polanyi, tore at the fabric of society, reducing whole classes to the condition of isolated and helpless individuals. It provoked a reaction from society that later in that century began to re-establish social protection against the destructive effects of economic processes: factory acts, organized industrial relations, social security, ultimately the welfare state (Polanyi, 1957). Another effort to introduce the self-regulating market on a world scale is now happening through economic globalization. There is an implicit conflict between the dominance over society of abstract economic laws and the construction of substantive economies that organize economic activity in compatibility with the norms of existing societies. That conflict is expressed in practical policy issues in different parts of the world today. In that conflict, civilizational perspectives challenge the dominance of the global self-regulating market.

Globalization is in practice challenged by resistance from below, from the aroused consciousness of people hurt by globalization; and also by the affirmation of different forms of capitalism rooted in different cultural traditions or different and conflicting views of the future. Capitalism is global to the extent that it seems to function according to certain general laws, specifically the behaviour of markets in respect of supply and demand. This common nature of capitalism is reinforced as governments have lost the will, and with it the power, to intervene in market behaviour. But capitalism remains culturally specific in so far as its institutional structure in different parts of the world has been shaped by different historical experiences and different conceptions of social purpose. Herein lies the conflict between globalization and civilizations, for civilizational forces work towards the social embedding of different forms of capitalism.

This conflict is most salient today in Europe as the European Union (EU) is confronted on a variety of issues by the choice between hyperliberal and social market (or social democratic) conceptions of capitalism (e.g. Albert, 1991). The debate in the institutions of the EU over 'social Europe' and the 'democratic deficit' is propelled by social and political forces in the different countries. Lionel Jospin seized the point when he qualified the unexpected Socialist Party victory in the June 1997 elections as 'un choix de civilisation' *Le Monde*, 7 June 1997). Varieties of capitalism are the object of struggles in Russia, China and other countries of Asia as conflicting social forces seek to construct the social and political context in which economic processes will operate (Chapter 10, pp. 181–3).

A conventional Marxist would say it is all capitalism, and in one sense that is probably a fair statement; but it obscures the fact that the differences in social organization and in widely accepted values and norms of behaviour and expectations may be very significant for people living and working under these different forms of society. Civilizations confront the economic imperatives of capitalism and move social economies in different directions.

Dominance and subordination

Civilizations have often been superimposed one upon another in a dominant and subordinate relationship. At a time when people are affirming their identities in terms of civilizations, consciousness of this kind of relationship becomes central to politics.

Edward Said described the Western approach to Eastern civilizations as 'orientalism' (Said, 1978; see also Said, 1993) by which he meant a form of knowledge through which Eastern civilizations were seen as subordinate to the West. Western scholarship, assuming a position of universalist objectivity, defined the characteristics of dominated civilizations and had the power to transmit to the dominated this knowledge of themselves. The elites of the dominated could thus become absorbed into an alien universalism. Kinhide Mushakoji has used the term 'occultation' to describe the manner in which the thought processes of one civilization have been displaced by those of another dominant one. Yet the thought processes of the dominated civilization are not totally suppressed, but remain latent, ready to be aroused by some crisis (Mushakoji, 1997).

Antonio Gramsci's concept of 'passive revolution' has some relevance here, although Gramsci was not discussing civilizations (Gramsci, 1971, pp. 105–20). Gramsci took the term from Vincenzo Cuocuo, the historian of Naples under Napoleonic rule, for whom passive revolution was the introduction of ideas from an alien society which were embraced by a local elite, though they did not resonate with the common people. The result was a situation Gramsci called revolution/restoration in which the newly adopted ideas and modes of behaviour were never securely entrenched since they never penetrated thoroughly to the mass of the people. One might draw a parallel with British intellectual and institutional influence in India, seemingly secure in the Nehru era but subsequently contested by the Hindu nationalists when they gained power.

Oswald Spengler, despite his thesis that civilizations were separate and did not impinge upon one another, put forward an interesting concept that suggests how an impetus from one civilization penetrating into another can partially transform that other, but be constrained by the persisting structures of the other. Spengler explored this relationship in developing his concept of a Magian civilization. This is the name he gave to the amalgam of Middle Eastern mystery religion and Graeco-Roman rational politics that shaped what European conventional history calls the late Roman and early mediaeval period, from the time of Augustus to the tenth century CE. Borrowing a term from mineralogy, he called the process 'pseudomorphosis' (Spengler, 1939, II, p. 189).[6] A nascent Arabian spiritual energy became configured by a fixed and persistent Graeco-Roman political form. Spengler discerned a similar phenomenon in the way Westernization imported into Russia by Peter the Great framed and shackled the Russian spirit.[7]

All of these concepts – orientalism, occultation, passive revolution and pseudomorphosis – evoke the phenomenon of dominance of one civilization over another, but also of the continuing latency of the dominated culture and the potential for reaffirmation of its authenticity. A most important object of enquiry is thus to trace the evidence of linguistic and conceptual superposition, to try to assess the different meanings given these superimposed concepts in the discourse of subordinate groups, and to identify the kinds of crisis likely to precipitate a rejection of the superimposed discourse by subordinate groups.

Spiritual consciousness

The sociologist Pitrim Sorokin contrasted two types of culture: the sensate and the ideational (Sorokin, 1957). The sensate culture admits only observation of external phenomena. The observer achieves 'objectivity' by classifying and plotting the relationships among the data observed. The ideational culture posits the existence of a spiritual world behind the observable phenomenal world – the thing-in-itself or noumenal world of Kant. For Sorokin, these two cultures were ideal types neither of which has ever existed in a pure form, but always in combinations stressing the one tendency or the other.

The notion 'spiritual' here need not mean mystical; it can just as well mean a world animated by thought both at an individual and a collective level. Nor need 'ideational' imply 'idealism' in the sense that the world is the concrete expression of ideas alone. Recognition of a spiritual element behind observable phenomena is consistent with a recognition that the specific form the spiritual may take in different times and places responds to the material conditions of existence that people have experienced and the social practices they have devised to cope with these material conditions. Max Weber recognized this in his sociology of religions (Weber, 1948, Part iii, pp. 267–359; also Bendix, 1960, pp. 49–281). It is the common feature of historicist thought in the West from Giambattista Vico, through the German historicism of Wilhelm Dilthey and the English of R. G. Collingwood, to the Italian of Croce and Gramsci. The common theme is that thought is the point of access to an understanding of the continuing interaction of mind and material conditions in the making of history. As method, the ideational hypothesis is the obvious key to an understanding of civilizations, since civilizations represent the ways large aggregates of people interpret the world, respond to it, and shape projects for acting in it.

Pitrim Sorokin had in mind something more than a method for understanding, however. He saw an alternation between a predominance of the ideational culture and that of the sensate as marking changes of era. All the main components of a culture: science and philosophy, law and ethics, forms of social and political organization – all he saw as changing synchronously and in the same direction (Sorokin, 1957, p. 223). The ideational was characteristic of a creative, poetic initial phase of a culture (Sorokin always speaks of culture rather than civilization). The sensate emerged in a mature phase and fully characterizes a post-mature culture. This reading of the process of civilization is similar to that of Vico and Spengler. Spengler, we saw, used the term 'culture' (which has that special connotation of creativity in German) for the initial phase of the historical entity which, in its mature and declining phases, he called a civilization. Sorokin, writing in the 1930s, like Spengler writing somewhat earlier, predicted a crisis of the prevailing sensate culture of the West (Sorokin, 1957, p. 622).[8] In his thinking, as in the *yin* and *yang* of Chinese culture or in the alternations of rural and urban in Ibn Khaldun's thought, the demise of the sensate culture should make way for a revival of the ideational.

Such notions of the alternation of attitudes towards the world, as suggested above, may be taken as heuristic hypotheses though perhaps not accorded the status of laws of history. Whatever value may be placed upon a notion of historical sequence or alternation of cultural perspectives, it is useful in the study of the dynamics of inter-subjectivity to reflect upon the implications for human understanding and action of different types of spiritual consciousness. Theology, over the centuries, has given us three types that have contemporary applicability: monotheism, polytheism and pantheism.

The monotheistic idea may have been derived from the centralized power of ancient hydraulic empires where everything appeared to flow from a single source. The idea took root in the eastern Mediterranean and spread worldwide through the three monotheistic religions: Judaism, Christianity and Islam (Armstrong, 1993). The monotheistic mentality, however, is not limited to adherence to one of these three religions. Its most important aspect is belief in absolute truth which may be retained by people who have severed any formal religious affiliation.[9] The absolutist cast of mind not only affirms with certainty; it also excludes and anathematizes heresy. This cast of mind impresses an indelible character upon the civilization it shapes.

Polytheism admits of multiple truths and accepts the coexistence of non-exclusive religions. Polytheism is relative where monotheism is absolutist; and it has been more characteristic of Eastern civilizations. The point is not to stereotype civilizations with the monotheistic or polytheistic mode of thought, but rather to examine the way such tendencies may be indicators of change in the evolution of civilizations. Post-modernism in Western civilization may be seen as a polytheistic development to the extent that post-modernists accept that different individuals and different groups have their own 'truths', that 'truth' is socially and historically constructed. David L. Miller (1974) has described it thus:

> Polytheism is not only a social reality; it is also a philosophical condition. It is that reality experienced by men and women when Truth with a capital 'T' cannot be articulated reflectively according to a single grammar, a single logic, or a single symbol-system. It is a situation that exists when metaphors, stories, anecdotes, puns, dramas, movies, with all their mysterious ambiguity, seem more compelling than the rhetoric of political, religious, and philosophical systems. They seem more compelling than tightly argued and logically coherent explanations of self and society because they allow for multiple meanings to exist simultaneously, as if Truth, Goodness, and Beauty can never be contained in a logic that allows for only one of the following: good versus evil, light versus dark, truth versus fiction, reality versus illusion, being versus becoming. In a philosophically polytheistic situation the 'new science' of the time will break forth with principles of relativism, indeterminacy, plural logic systems, irrational numbers; substances that do not have substance, such as quarks; double explanations for light; and black holes in the middle of actual realities.
>
> (p. 5)

Pantheism sees a spiritual unity to the cosmos which is manifested through the manifold variety of forms of existence. Everything is linked to, and dependent upon, the whole. This has been a common feature in the religious consciousness of indigenous peoples. It is also present in the Hindu Upanishads which posit a single Reality or Unity that manifests itself in multiple ways (Chandra, 1997). Pantheism has arisen within contemporary Western civilization in deep ecology or the sense of unity and interdependence of all forms of life and life sustaining substances within the biosphere (e.g. Lovelock, 1979; Capra, 1996).

Modern societies have also known an extreme form of spiritual consciousness that takes the form of doomsday cults. These cults mix science or science fiction with doctrines of salvation under the supreme authority of their leaders. They have attracted technically sophisticated people, which suggests that some formally educated people do not find sufficient meaning in their lives within the contemporary world. Some, like the Solar Temple and Heaven's Gate, have led to mass suicide of their members. Others, like the Aum Shinrikyo have actively sought to make their doomsday prophesy self-fulfilling (Iida, 1997).

No civilization is ever reducible to a single form of spiritual consciousness. Civilizations are shaped through a mingling of different forms and a shifting predominance of one or other of these forms; and this mingling and shifting consciousness is related to the development of the material world. Monotheism is not powerful through a resurgence of church going, but through the absolute certainty of the ideological exponents of global capitalism (see Soros, 1997, for a critique of this certainty).[10] The strengthening of alternative forms of social economy could encourage an acceptance of diversity reminiscent of polytheism. The advancement of Green economics gives substance to pantheism; and the alienation from society of the cultist is not unrelated to anomie produced by modern economies.

Time and space

Harold Innis, from his study of civilizations (Chapter 8), inferred that the relative emphasis on time and space gave a bias affecting broad aspects of a culture. A stable society, he concluded, had a proper balance between a time orientation and a space orientation (Innis, 1986, 1991).[11]

Time is a most complex idea. The more one reflects upon it, the less certainty there is about it. According to Henri Bergson, whose philosophical work is of the late nineteenth century, there were two contrasting conceptions of time (see Bergson, 1945). One was the common-sense notion of time, what we can call 'clock time', the notion of a universal homogeneous medium measuring from outside whatever is happening. This was, as Bergson thought about it, time reduced to space, the space travelled by the hands of the clock. The other kind of time, which interested Bergson more, he called *durée*. The term is not very adequately rendered into English as 'duration', since duration may also have the spacial meaning of an externally observed trajectory between two points, a beginning and an end. *Durée*, for Bergson, signified rather lived time, experienced time, the subjective feeling of acting and choosing, and of pressures limiting action and choice.

Modern physics since Einstein has destroyed the common-sense absoluteness of clock time. Time and space, since Einstein, are seen as interrelated and relative to each other. Time, with the universe, has a beginning, and so will have an end. There are different times depending on the relative motion of bodies in space. Time is not an absolute in the mind of God but a construct of the minds of human beings. The post-Einsteinian physicist John Wheeler has said: 'The word Time came not from heaven but from the mouth of man' and he reduced the concept to the rather modest definition that 'Time is nature's way to keep everything from happening at once' (quoted in Davies, 1996, pp. 236, 267). For modern physics there is no absolute standard against which happenings in the physical world, let alone the human and social worlds, can be plotted.

In the history of time, the European Middle Ages held time to be an organic, subjective thing, a part of nature. The Enlightenment, with Newton, initiated the idea of time as an abstract independent standard of measurement, divorced from nature. Einstein put time back into nature and at the same time deprived it of the common-sense certainty inherited from the eighteenth century.

The subjective notion of *durée* has also undergone development. Bergson's work was related to the individual's consciousness of time. Fernand Braudel expanded it to cover historical time (Braudel, 1980; see also Braudel, 1979, III, esp. ch. 1 and conclusions). For Braudel, different aspects of human and social life have different tempos. Economic change moves at a different pace from art and architecture or from change in law and mores. In this he differs from the vision of Vico or Spengler in which all aspects of society change simultaneously from a single impetus. For Braudel, changes in these different departments of life are not unrelated, but they are not synchronous. So there is a history of mentalities moving at a different pace from a history of material life, but nevertheless interacting with it.

In all these different histories – these different 'times' – there are three levels of time according to Braudel. The level of immediacy is the time of events (*l'histoire événementielle*). Events can be recorded, but they do not explain themselves. To be explained, they must be understood within their context in time and space. The first level of explanation is what Braudel called *conjonctures*, an intermediate time-frame such as that of a long economic cycle, a persisting configuration of social forces, for example Fordism or social democracy, or the duration of a scientific paradigm. The *conjoncture* in turn is explainable within the framework of the *longue durée*, a historical structure created by collective human activity over long periods of time which comes to be regarded in common sense as the natural order of things. Language, the moral code, property relations, the state and the interstate system are all constructions of human collective activity in the *longue durée*, though they come to be regarded as enduring foundations of human life. They are all, however, subject to slow change through collective human activity and that change can, often in retrospect, reach points of radical transformation into new historical structures.

A historical structure of the *longue durée* is to be understood in both synchronic and diachronic dimensions – both in terms of the interactions and interdependencies of its different component elements, and in terms of its development over time. Braudel's *magnum opus* on the world economy of capitalism seemed to privilege the synchronic, the understanding of this economy as a world-system; but one can read into it that the purpose of understanding the synchronic dimension is to be able to see the contradictions out of which structural transformation could come. Braudel's theorizing of history bridges the gulf between the homeostasis of structural-functional sociology and the change through conflict of Vichian and Marxian dialectic. It brings us back to Harold Innis's problematic of balance between a space orientation and a time orientation.

Structural change, for Braudel, results from a 'dialectic of duration'. Events are conditioned and shaped by the structures of the *longue durée*, but events may also cumulatively challenge, undermine and transform these structures. The explanation of historical structural change involves the interaction of all three levels of time. Well-grounded strategies for making a better future – for a realistic application of collective free will – involve as a starting point an understanding of the limits of the possible through an awareness of the *longue durée*.

In our own world, the time/space balance is having a profound effect on economic behaviour and, through the economy, on all other aspects of life. Money is a symbol of economic power. The real economy is the actual production of goods and services. Money is fungible and mobile at the speed of electronic communication. Production is fixed in specific enterprises and it takes a long time to develop – technological innovation and building of producer goods, training of workers. The symbolic economy of finance operates in a synchronic dimension; it is space oriented. The development of production takes place in a diachronic dimension; it is time oriented. As the world economy has become global in extent, global finance has come to dominate production. Globalization means the triumph of space over time, the victory of the transitory and the ephemeral. The economic basis for the subordination of the time orientation is reinforced by the globalization of the media which propagate a consciousness of an eternal present. This is the psychological meaning of 'the end of history'.

Time in the Braudelian sense is the medium in which the collective creative powers of human society continually invent the future within the limits of the possible. Space (and spatially conceived time) orients the mind towards the present complex of relationships. The present seems fixed, determined. Within the spatial orientation of mind, the future is imaginable only as the further development of tendencies apparent in the present. The ideology of globalization is sustained by space-oriented thinking. The possibility of transcending this ideology, and with it the notion of a one-civilization world, will depend on recovering the time dimension in thought that will enable human action to use the contradictions of globalization to envisage a possible alternative future. The time dimension is the remaining medium of freedom.

Revival of civilizations would shift emphasis from space to time. Civilizations are entities of the *longue durée*. In part, this involves a sense of continuity and development from past origins; but primarily, it implies the construction of alternative visions of a future – an escape from the inevitability of the eternal homogenized present of globalization into an active collective construction of future economies re-embedded in self-conscious societies.

* * *

If different civilizations do coexist, the problem of mutual comprehension becomes paramount for the maintenance of world order. This arises in an epistemological context far different from the game theoretic and rational choice notions popular during the Cold War, which assumed a single shared rationality. An ability to enter into the mental framework of the Other becomes an essential ingredient in peaceful coexistence.

Collingwood's *New Leviathan* (1942) put forward a relevant thought. The book bears the marks of its conception during World War II in its insistence on the struggle between civilization (in the singular) and barbarism. But it contains a thought about the process of civilization – the process of generating civility – that is relevant to a coexistence of civilizations (in the plural). Collingwood refers to the distinction made by Plato between two kinds of discussions: eristical and dialectical. In an eristic discussion each party tries to prove itself to be right and the other wrong. In a dialectic discussion each party hopes to find that initial disagreement will, through the process of discussion, lead to a perception by both parties that they are both right (Collingwood, 1942, pp. 181–3). Each sees one aspect of a truth that both, through the process of dialectic may ultimately share. To Collingwood, dialectic discussion was especially appropriate in a Heraclitan world, i.e. a world of change in which reality, the object of discussion, was in constant transformation. Dialectic was, he argued, the means of absorbing non-social elements into a larger society; but it might also, extrapolating now from Collingwood, become a means of understanding among coexisting civilizations each of which had a different perspective on a world common to both.

Mikhail Bakhtin, using a different vocabulary, took a not dissimilar but perhaps more fully applicable approach to the problem of coexistence (Bakhtin, 1984). Bakhtin rejected the term dialectic in so far as it had been appropriated by Hegelian and Marxist theories of history in which the dialectic is determined by a single central impulse, whether ideal or material. He uses the term 'dialogue' which derives from the Socratic dialogues of Plato (Collingwood's source for the term 'dialectic'). For Bakhtin, the Hegelian and Marxian dialectics are monologues, the expression of a single thought interpreting and explaining the world. Bakhtin's world is peopled by self-conscious beings each with its own perspective on the whole. In his reflections on Dostoevsky, these beings were the characters of the novels, each of which brings a distinctive perspective to the action; and there is no overarching 'author's' interpretation. But we may also think of civilizations as beings each with its own inter-subjectivity, together engaged in an interaction in which there is no authoritative overarching theory of historical change. These civilizational perspectives evolve in time; and the world of coexisting perspectives is open-ended. There is no closure, no end of history. No one being (individual or civilization) may legitimately reify the Other, i.e. treat it as an object (as in orientalism). The condition of dialogue is mutual recognition of self-conscious beings. Referring to Dostoevsky's novels, Bakhtin writes: 'there stands in place of a single cognizant and judging "I" to the world, the problems of the interrelationship of all these cognizant and judging "I's" to one another' (Bakhtin, 1984, p. 100).

10 Civilizations and world order

The word 'civilization' – in the singular but also in the plural – has become common of late in the mouths of politicians and in the writings of international relations academics. Samuel Huntington (1993 and 1996) stirred up a storm in political studies by his vision of the future world as a 'clash' of civilizations (in the plural); and the war in Yugoslavia, followed by the war in Afghanistan, generated an increased frequency in political rhetoric of the word 'civilization' (in the singular). Indeed, as I shall argue later, conflict in the Balkans revealed more clearly than before the meaning of civilizations and of civilization (in both plural and singular) for our time.

Most people do not think of themselves in the course of a normal day's activities as belonging to a civilization. Civilization is for most people pretty far down on the scale of self-conscious identities. And when politicians evoke civilization, it is usually when they want to arouse their constituents against some demonized enemy. The everyday manifestation of civilization is not in a feeling of belonging. It is in the almost unconscious, taken for granted, *common sense* that expresses a people's shared idea of reality. This idea of reality also includes the sense of what is right and proper in ordinary behaviour. Common sense includes a normative guide to action as well as a perception of 'objectivity' (or what is really out there). This common sense, which is different for people in different times and places, is shaped by a people's collective practical responses to their material conditions of existence.

Context and meaning

During the nineteenth century, as European dominance embraced the world, 'civilization' became, in European thinking, joined to 'imperialism'. The civilizing process had emerged through a European history conceived as Progress, whether in the Hegelian or the Marxian form, which Europe was spreading to the rest of the world. *La mission civilisatrice* was the more sophisticated and universalistic way of expressing this movement; 'the white man's burden', was the more openly racist.

The imperial movement, however, encountered *Others*, human

communities constituted very differently from the European by their respective histories. These other communities, during the nineteenth century, were overlaid by and subordinated to European norms and institutions. Their own norms and institutions were not obliterated. They were occulted, obscured from view, awaiting some stimulus that would arouse once again the native energy that remained with them (Mushakoji, 1997). The encounter obliged Europeans to recognize the existence of other civilizations while maintaining the conviction that these others would ultimately become included within the embrace of the one civilization – their own – which had a universal vocation.

Change in civilizations comes about both from internal contradictions and from encounters with other civilizations. Geography has been at the foundation of civilizations – the ground upon which the material structure of civilization was erected and the site of the myth and poetry that gave it meaning. But historical development loosens the determining influence of geography. As civilizations encounter one another and as peoples migrate, meanings mingle and are discordant. Different peoples in the same geographical site come to perceive reality differently. First nations people in Canada do not see the same reality as middle-class urban Canadians. The same goes in France for Islamic North African inhabitants of the urban *banlieux* and graduates of the *Grandes Ecoles*. Civilization is something we carry in our heads which guides our understanding of the world; and for different peoples this understanding is different.

The common sense of one people is different from that of another and their notions of reality differ. It may even be that a single individual has to reconcile within him or herself the perspectives and the claims of two different civilizations – the Indian or the Japanese executive of a multinational corporation, for example, or the Central American immigrant in Los Angeles. This is what has made the drawing of geographical boundaries around civilizations in our own times an exercise in futility. We need to know more about the modes of thought characteristic of different civilizations, how these modes of thought came about, and how they may be changing.

Three dimensions of thought can help distinguish among civilizations: first, the notions they have of time and space and the relative emphasis on the one or the other; second, the tension between individual and community; and third, what one can loosely call spirituality or cosmology, the common notion of the relationship of humanity to nature and the cosmos.

A focus on time imagines a common past and projects a common future – myths of origin that shape a people's character and vocation, and an eschatology of destiny. A time orientation is protected by the continuity of institutions like churches and states. It is nourished by literary traditions and intellectual dialogue. It is expressed in a concern for planning and development, activities that take place in time and require time for fulfilment.

Shifts in emphasis between time and space can mark transformations within civilizations. European civilization began with a strong time orientation centred in the Church and its sense of historical progression from the Old Testament rule of God's law to the moment of revelation in time through Christ and an eschatological anticipation of the Kingdom of Heaven; eighteenth-century Enlightenment modernity marked a transition point which gave more emphasis to space through a science based upon universal laws; and contemporary post-modernism undervalues both time and space in a sense of the immediacy of events and their proximity in a world in which everyone is involved with everyone else.[1] This is, of course, a very broad generalization, but it suggests that a shift in time and space orientations can be a clue to civilizational change.

Individualism is a product of European civilization, reaching its most extreme development in America. The civilizations of the East are perceived as stressing solidarity and the obligations of individuals to a range of communities, from the family to the clan and the nation as a whole. Furthermore, individualism is not confined to human behaviour. It also arises in forms of thought. Methodological individualism recognizes only discrete entities and ignores collective wholes. It obscures those phenomena that bind societies together, and which merge the individual into the whole. In the extreme form it denies the existence of society. Only individuals exist.

Individual and community are not, however, mutually exclusive categories. The nature of a civilization depends upon the mix; and the mix can change. Individualistic behaviour may increase among people who still maintain a belief in communal norms; and the disintegration of a society beset by excessive individualism may stimulate a reaction to rekindle a sense of common welfare. This shifting mix is another indicator of civilizational change.

The spirituality dimension touches people's sense of the fundamental nature of the world and of humanity's place in it. Much human conflict is overtly justified as defence of absolute truth, even when covertly less lofty motivations are at work. The absolutist residue of monotheism remains resilient despite the decline of formal religion. No one preaches polytheism as such to the world today, but an openness to a plurality of values and to recognition of difference challenges absolutism in public discourse.[2] Pantheism is an emerging force in public concern for maintenance of the biosphere in which humanity shares the fate of other forms of life. In pantheism the cosmologies of aboriginal peoples meet with a new cosmology derived from deep ecology.[3]

These different and conflicting forms of spirituality are also shaping changes in civilizations. They find expression in conflicts concerning material life – in the connection of race, gender, ethnicity and religion with economic oppression, and in the common fate of humanity in a fragile biosphere.

Beyond these internal dimensions of civilizations is the sense of relationship to other civilizations. Awareness of the Other may be the catalyst for arousing a self-consciousness of one's own civilizational identity. For the European Middle Ages, Islam was the significant Other. At that time, Islam was the higher of the two in terms of philosophy, medicine, trade and urban development; and it aroused in Christendom a fanaticism manifested in the Crusades. In twentieth-century Europe, Islam reappears as Europe's Other but now, as a consequence of the imperial expansion of Europe during the nineteenth century and the technological and economic supremacy of Europe and America, in a relationship of subordination and resentment which is perceived as a latent threat to a dominant Euro-American civilization.

The material foundations of this dominance and subordination have been echoed in modes of thought among both dominant and subordinate civilizations. Euro-American dominance in scholarship and media have defined the identity of subordinate civilizations in what Edward Said (1978) called 'orientalism'. The elites of subordinate civilizations confront the choice of imitating the dominant civilization while trying to preserve something of their own or of reviving their myths of origin in order to reject the dominant civilization and to claim the intellectual space to create something different.

Present day issues in the development of civilizations

Development and change in civilizations today has to be approached from two aspects: first, the contradictions within civilizations that pose choices among visions of the future; and second, the external influences coming from coexisting civilizations that have an impact on those choices. This puts the emphasis upon the dynamics of civilizational development. It differs from attempts to draw the boundaries of civilizations which is the more usual approach. To attempt to define the essence of a civilization reifies it in a non-historical way and reinforces exclusionary defensive tendencies. I would aim rather for a global perspective on the processes of change in a full range of contemporary civilizations, avoiding so far as possible a perspective rooted in any one of them.

Taking as a guideline the definition of a civilization as a fit between material conditions of existence and inter-subjective meanings, political economy or *social economy* is, I suggest, the most promising field in which to seek the potential for change and development. Social economy is precisely the area in which different forms of human organization, including the language and the concepts that make human organization intelligible, mesh with technologies and material resources to create viable human communities.[4]

One form of civilization, which Susan Strange (1990) called the 'business civilization', is clearly pre-eminent in discourse about world affairs. It is the vehicle for economic globalization. Its ideology is nourished in business schools around the world and in economic journalism and political rhetoric in the economically powerful countries. The business civilization has no formal organization. It is informally structured by the *nébuleuse* of interrelated bodies which generate policy – international agencies like the World Trade Organization, the IMF, the Bank for International Settlements, the World Bank and the OECD and unofficial bodies like the annual World

Economic Forum at Davos (Cox, 1996: 27). This civilization cuts across pre-existing historical civilizations in different parts of the world, although it is an offshoot and transformation of Euro-American civilization rooted mainly in the United States. Members of the business civilization who are drawn from other civilizations – Indian, Japanese, Islamic, African, for example – must confront the personal dilemma of dual civilizationship.

The transformation of the Euro-American tradition into the business civilization privileges space over time. The 'end of history' idea (Fukuyama, 1993) springs from it: the notion that with globalization the ultimate in human society has been achieved and nothing further is possible except more of the same. The spatial orientation is implicit in the synchronic concept of the market. The absolutism of monotheism is rendered into a universalistic economic theory with its social correlates – what in French has been called *la pensée unique*. Individualism and competitiveness are its basic assumptions regarding human conduct; and society, the real existence of which is moot, is just their by-product, an illusion created by the invisible hand.

The business civilization is, however, something of an abstraction or ideal type – a projection into the future of some powerful tendencies in the present. There are other forces at work which are rooted in the gradual transformation of the social organization and practices of coexisting civilizations. The interaction of these forces shape social economies which are the different ways in which people are organized to satisfy their material needs. Karl Polanyi (1957) called these 'substantive economies' by contrast to the formal economics of theory. There is a growing literature on comparative capitalism which demonstrates the substantive variety of forms of social economy that constitute the different realities of peoples who all experience in some measure the impact of globalization.[5] These different social economies are all beset by issues, contradictions and open or potential conflicts, the resolution of which will orient their future course. Globalization says: There is no alternative. In the thinking of globalization, societies will inevitably be shaped to conform to the requirements of economic competition, which means they will become more and more alike. Those who contest globalization affirm the possibility of alternatives that embody values both derived from their past and imagined as more desirable futures.

In America, which is the model for globalization, a thriving economy has in recent years generated both a high level of employment, much of it in low-paid and precarious jobs, and a growing polarization of incomes. There are signs that rampant individualism may have passed the point at which it serves as a dynamic of economic competition to become a threat to social cohesion.[6] The vitality of civil society – those voluntary associations which de Tocqueville once saw as the strength of the American polity – is reportedly in decline. But so anchored in public consciousness is the 'American way' that there, in America, it becomes hard to imagine an alternative future.

In Europe, the emulators of America hold the preponderance of economic power and political influence; but popular opinion is more sceptical regarding the social consequences of economic globalization.[7] This critical response has become divided as some social democratic leaders, won over by neo-liberal arguments of the need to strive for global market competitiveness, now propose to moderate the social consequences of globalization by policies to enhance the competitive opportunity of individuals, and to strengthen a form of 'competitive corporatism' that would offer more security to established workers.[8] At the same time, those who remain suspicious of this social liberalism have so far failed to present a compelling alternative. European societies show signs of following the American course – with growing income gaps, and culturally and ethnically distinct pockets of urban squalor and violence. The difference from America is the residual survival of a stronger social base for an imagined alternative.

The conflict in Europe, which is social and economic at bottom, opposes two modes of thought, two sets of inter-subjective meanings – one is spatially oriented towards competition in the world market, individualist in its ontology, absolutist in certainty as to the principles on which it is founded, and dominant in its relationship with 'backward' and less efficient societies; the other is time oriented towards building a future which embodies social as well as economic goals, with more emphasis on community as a basis for human security, and open to the acceptance of difference without domination among peoples.

Asia has been the site of a variety of forms of capitalism, much influenced by that in Japan. Japanese capitalism grew within the framework of a continuous social tradition which gave loyalty to institutions – state and corporation – precedence over individualism.[9] However, many of the features considered characteristic of Japanese society have been strained in the decades since World War II by the nature and rapidity of economic growth and the impact of American-inspired popular culture. The identity of state and corporation, symbolized by the notion of Japan Incorporated, has weakened as corporations have gained more operational autonomy; and the formerly strong cohesion of family and community may be dissolving, leading to more emphasis on consumerism and individualism and to a lesser commitment to work and organizational loyalties.[10] A by-product of these disruptive tendencies has been an outbreak of radical forms of alienation.[11] Contending social forces in Japan which might foreshadow a transformation of the 'common sense' of Japanese people, and which are rooted in the economic and social changes of recent decades, are reflected in the choice Japan faces between remaining within the American security blanket and asserting its independence as a geopolitical entity; and the option of independence opposes those who would revive an imagined imperial past to those who would pursue the post-war hopes for a new form of non-aggressive democratic and internationalist future. The factors of individualism versus community and of dominance versus sharing are inherent in this predicament.

Other societies in southeast Asia, devastated by global finance in the crisis of 1998, must either succumb to external direction in their economic development or else devise means of regulating international financial flows so as to gain room for pursuit of internally determined social and economic goals. The crisis created conditions for Western firms to gain financial control over Asian productive resources (Richardson, 1998). Resentment against global finance, perceived as Western controlled, was also a stimulus to construct more indigenous forms of social and political economy. Change might move in the direction of state-directed capitalism, evoking traditions of community and authority; but a more radical alternative could emerge from the development of a civil society able to mobilize people in a common social project and to gain acceptance of sacrifice with equity in its pursuit.[12]

Russia and China are both old civilizations that have in different degrees been subordinated to concepts of civilization derived from Europe – in the form both of socialism and capitalism. Russia has experienced three successive waves of Westernization: under Peter the Great, the Bolsheviks, and the attempt through 'shock therapy' to introduce Western capitalism. The last has produced a predatory, corrupt, mafia-dominated, version of capitalism. The weakness of civil society has left people passively vulnerable to the kleptocracy, and has left government without a secure base in the people. It has also, together with the preponderance of foreign financial and political influences, obstructed the emergence of an alternative social and political project.[13] Yet a sense of the uniqueness of Russian history remains latent as rejection of the West and as an alternative vision of society. The 'Russian idea' appeals to an imagined past of communal values and the hope of a future good society guided by belief in the absolute truth inherent in the Russian soul.[14]

In China, elements of the old Confucian tradition survived into the Communist era and remain a stabilizing force in society. The Confucian inheritance combines sentiments of social responsibility with an open attitude towards truth. Capitalist processes have been introduced under Party-state control with less sense of cleavage than in Russia. The regime's effort to retain socialism within capitalism has combined economic decentralization and high growth with movement towards integration into the global economy. Chinese capitalism, like neo-liberalism elsewhere, has produced a polarization of rich and poor, massive unemployment and the decline of public services for health and welfare, moderated only slightly by socialist ethics. The Party has monopolized the functions of civil society and remains suspicious of any autonomous grouping of people which inhibits the articulation of any alternative social project.[15]

Up to now, international studies have been concerned primarily with states, the interstate system and markets. The tendencies I have been discussing suggest that civilizations and civil societies be brought into the picture in order to explain the historical transformations of the late twentieth and early twenty-first centuries. Civilizations explain the potential of societies to espouse new directions of development. Civil societies shape common sense and collective purposes. A strong civil society can be the inner strength of a civilization and the creative force for its development; its absence, the explanation of subordination to an expansive Other.

If the challenge to established ways of understanding the world is everywhere rather weak compared to the form of 'common sense' propagated by global media, it is nevertheless true that popular movements stimulated by material inequities and grievances have articulated alternative projects of society.

These latent new directions are very diverse: the perhaps utopian goal of an Islamic social economy (Choudry, 2000; IILS, 1980), movements towards self-sufficiency and internally determined development by indigenous peoples; and the activity of 'Green' dissenters in more affluent areas of the world towards a social economy subordinated to maintenance of the biosphere. Some of these movements appeal to alternative absolute values, while others are more open to recognition of a diversity of truths; some are grounded in a sense of time and continuity, in contrast to the space orientation of modernism; most emphasize community over individualism; and the pantheist notion of humanity in union with nature is now more prominent in reactions to the hegemony of globalization. The 'battle in Seattle' gave some evidence of this diversity of protest.[16]

World order: the options for the future

Civilizations, I have argued, are to be thought of as processes or tendencies rather than as fixed and bounded essences. The historical dialectic moves ever onward. Each apparent culmination engenders the contradictions that lead to a further movement. The problem for political analysis is to spot these contradictions and to assess the possible directions of change.

The bias implicit in enquiring into the development of civilizations is an acknowledgement that there *is* collective choice about the future of societies. By 'collective choice' I mean the gradual emergence through civil society of a common understanding of the nature of the world and a vision of the future of society. It is conceivable, but unlikely that one single vision could emerge common to all people. More likely, there will be several collective visions.

The war in Yugoslavia has been a catalyst of issues in the contemporary development of civilizations (Chapter 4). The war solved nothing, but it did illustrate options and potential directions of change. Broadly, for the world as a whole and not just the NATO countries, it underlined the choice between a single concept of civilization and recognition of a plurality of civilizations. NATO military force, which was primarily a projection of American air power, represented and was perceived, both by its proponents and by its opponents, to be an expression of the one civilization option. NATO power became a potentially global force foreshadowing similar interventions, the next being the 'war against terrorism' that struck first against Afghanistan and promises to continue against other targets.

These interventions directed by the United States and joined by different combinations of other states have demonstrated a mode of warfare that is lethal for enemy populations and economies, while minimizing loss to its perpetrators. As such, it was a warning to forces resisting the one-civilization vision of the future. American and NATO military-political power are a support for economic globalization, which is the material basis for the one civilization perspective. These interventions are represented as the pursuit of a doctrine of human rights derived from Euro-American historical experience and grounded in individualism which has been universalized as the one-civilization's core moral value.

The air campaign against Serbia also mobilized public opposition as well as government opposition to NATO in Russia and China, while opinion in other countries of Asia and in Africa was apprehensive about Euro-American global dominance. A prospect of global hegemony that had hitherto moved with stealth in economic globalization and cultural penetration now appeared as an overt military-political challenge. Non-European civilizations were challenged by the attack on Serbia to affirmations of self-conscious difference and rejection of the universal claims of NATO-backed Euro-American power.

A major factor in the apparent dominance of globalization ideology and the one-civilization perspective has been the weakness of civil society in both West and non-West. Indicators are a weakening of public support for political institutions as shown by low voting turnouts at elections and a sense of the futility of party politics; the erosion of public services held hostage to budgetary constraints imposed by global finance; the progression of organized crime and its corrupting influence on politics and economy; and the atrophy of social solidarity with the progress of individualistic consumerism. The weakness of civil society is the greatest factor of uncertainty in the strengthening of social forces that could sustain the development of civilizations.

There are, however, signs of a renaissance of civil society out of people's alienation from formal politics and economic power (Chapter 6). The component elements of a multi-civilization world are perceptible in the resistance to the negative effects of globalization among states and within civil societies; but these reactions are fragmented and still lack a coherent doctrine and institutional support such as NATO and the *nébuleuse* of economic governance provide for the one civilization project.

The United Nations might be thought of as the obvious institutional framework for a multi-civilizational world were it not for the fact that the United Nations has become a hostage to American power – either used as an instrument of American policy where this is possible or, where this seems impractical, substantially set aside as in the case of the war against Yugoslavia.[17]

In a multi-civilizational world order, the role of a world organization would be to seek out principles acceptable in the 'common sense' or inter-subjectivity of each of the different civilizations – to distill a kind of supra-inter-subjectivity from the distinct inter-subjectivities of its component parts. This could only come about through a lengthy learning process from experience in reconciling conflicts. Two measures would be indispensable:

- first, recruitment and formation of a core body of people who would cultivate an empathetic understanding of forms of common sense other than their own – who could bridge inter-subjectivities;
- and second, promoting development of civil societies capable of articulating the basic sentiments and goals of the people who compose them.

Civil society is the force that develops the inter-subjective content of civilizations; and the core group which assumes the task of reconciliation of differences would have to keep abreast of these developments in the dynamics of civilizations.

This concept of a structure for world order is far from being an institutionalized form of global governance. It envisages a weak centre embodying certain accepted common principles in a world fragmented among peoples guided by different sets of social practices and goals. Such a pluralistic framework of weak centre in a fragmented whole has precedence in world history – in the European medieval Papacy, and in periods of Chinese history, for example. Such a structure would not displace the nation-state system or the international economy. It would provide the framework of principles within which the state system and economic relations could be regulated.

Struggle among social forces is the principal dynamic of change in societies. In the European tradition, this was understood by Giambattista Vico at the beginning of the eighteenth century and by Karl Marx in the nineteenth. This perception remains just as valid at the beginning of the twenty-first century. The nature of class conflict is, however, changing, no longer tied so closely to property in the means of production as Marx saw it, but expanding to include other forms of dominance and subordination and of particular interests versus the general welfare. The arena of social struggle lies in civil society which is why developments in civil society are the key to understanding civilizational changes.

Certain common principles can be affirmed as starting points for thinking an inter-civilizational world:

- mutual recognition of difference;
- maintenance of the biosphere upon which all forms of life depend;
- avoidance of violence in dealing with conflict and especially in the use of weapons of mass destruction;
- mutual support in promoting social equity, reversing the current trend towards social polarization;
- suppression of organized criminal activity that becomes an occult political and economic power;
- and consensual understanding of basic human rights.

Human rights is a particularly problematic case in the search for common understanding among coexisting civilizations. The conflict over Kosovo brought it to the fore and underlined the difficulties. Despite political rhetoric, there are no pure cases free of ambiguity and inconsistencies. Why is human rights a justification for intervention in one instance, while similar instances are ignored – for example, the war in Chechnya, the oppression of Kurds, the genocide in Rwanda, or the dispossession of Palestinians? The answer in every case lies in power relations, not morality.

In the European Enlightenment tradition rights are represented as innate in the human being and universal to a common human nature. This is the basis for much Western political rhetoric. In an historical mode of thinking, rights are not innate, they are the product of people's historical struggles which become enshrined in their common sense; and human nature is not uniform and universal, but is formed differently by different histories. This historical mode of thinking is more attune to understanding a multi-civilizational world.[18] From it we may derive the proposition that somewhat different concepts of human rights will be formed by the histories of different civilizations, arising in each case out of the conflicts that have shaped those civilizations, and that they will reflect the cosmologies, the relationship of humanity to nature, and the balance between individual and community characteristic of those civilizations.

The challenge in a multi-civilizational order is to find means of encouraging popular forces struggling for an entrenchment of human rights in *their* society without appearing to impose one civilization's norms upon another. An externally imposed order would remain fragile, vulnerable to the charge of imperialism.

To evoke the idea of a multi-civilizational world order is to affirm that an alternative, even more than one alternative, to the one and final civilization of globalization is possible. This can be a rallying force – a myth if you like, and myth is a powerful social force – for those who resist the claims of a one civilization world and of the *pensée unique*. Greens, cultural nationalists, anti-imperialists, those who are disadvantaged and marginalized by economic globalization and other forms of domination including feminists and native peoples, all can find reason to support this view of the world which allows for the expression of diversity and the exploration of alternative possibilities for social and economic development.

At this moment in world history, it is not sufficient either to celebrate or to deplore the dominant tendencies as they may be perceived by a dispassionate external observer. This would leave an impression of inevitability. A critical approach will seek out the contradictions in those tendencies which would open the possibility of action towards alternative futures. It would also try to think through what desirable alternatives might look like and anticipate reconciliation among differing visions of the future rooted in the aspirations of particular groups and peoples.

Existing institutions can play a role in this process – states, international institutions, universities, churches, non-governmental organizations, and diplomacy – but in and of themselves these are not the forces to build a world climate for coexistence among civilizations. They can be agencies used to this end, but a broader force must be present to activate and orient them. Behind these institutions is the climate of human purposes and attitudes that would be necessary to make these institutions work to that end. In the past, critical moments like the end of a great war have generated surges of collective motivation that pushed institutions in new directions. At present, one may well ask where such a movement could come from. Possibly, the motive force could arise from deeper awareness across civilizations of their common fragility in the face of threats to the biosphere, from the dangers to all from increasing social polarization, and from the existence of uncontrolled weapons of mass destruction; and at the same time from awareness of the possibility of transcending these impending disasters through consensual action taken in mutual recognition of and respect for differences.

The two critical factors in arousing this awareness – the strengthening of civil societies as the substrata of civilizations and the existence of a core body of people capable of linking civilizations in mutual understanding – cannot be reduced to institutional formulas. They can come about only through a conscious shaping of minds towards those ends. The European medieval monastic movement or the formation of the mandarin class in China are suggestive historical precedents, but differ from the present world situation in so far as each of those past movements led to a single civilizational perspective. The present challenge is to encourage the formation of *organic intellectuals* (to use Gramsci's term) who can *both* articulate the visions of possible future societies drawing upon the experience of different existing social formations *and* become links among these different visions and movements.

In today's world more and more people have acquired experience that lends itself to this task and many of them may be prepared to assume the responsibility of participating in a collective endeavour. Among teachers, aid workers, journalists, peace activists, environmentalists, diplomats and international civil servants, as examples, some individuals see the world not only through the perceptual lens they grew up with, but can also, by reflecting upon their own uniqueness, imagine how other people they have experience of perceive the world. Such individuals are capable of thinking and acting in terms of a coexistence of different forms of common sense. The network linking them together in a global movement might arise quite informally out of the contacts inherent in their daily work. Institutionalization might follow.

Academic educators may be inspired to study comparatively the different forms of 'common sense' that coexist and to trace their origins and developmental patterns. Activists may use this knowledge to show how diversity need not mean conflict. Journalists may in their reporting analyse the different senses of 'reality' that constitute situations of conflict, while avoiding lending themselves to making propaganda for one 'true' position.

Diplomats may focus on genuine reconciliation which takes account of differing perspectives rather than scoring a win for the institution they work for.

Such a movement could both work through existing institutions and generate new institutional forms. Will the impetus for it come from aversion to the dogmas and effects of globalization? Perhaps in part. Or would some more dramatic catalyst, some global catastrophe, be ultimately required to bring together the forces that could activate the movement?

Epilogue

The two visions of the future discussed in this book are neither of them predictions. They are both tendencies that express the aims of many people. What happens will come about through a sequence of unpredictable interacting events. People make history, but not in conditions of their own choosing. The constraining factors are present; but none of them is the ultimate determinant. Neither vision will be fulfilled. Both will have a role in shaping the future of the world.

Concentrated power strengthens the one-civilization vision, the combined power of military force, economic pressure and communications influence. This concentrated power centres in the United States and extends into much of the rest of the world through the acquiescence and subservience of allied and dependent governments, armed forces and intelligence services. This has constituted the twenty-first-century version of Empire pictured by Hardt and Negri (2000).

The United States has innovated a new mode of warfare, corresponding to the structure of Empire, that has global reach. It consists in aerial bombardment by the US air force with limited numbers of US special forces in ground support mainly to guide the air attack; and a ground follow-up to bombardment by subsidized local rebels and participation by some allied ground troops. The new mode was initiated experimentally in the attack on Serbia and perfected in the attack on Afghanistan. It stands as a warning to active opposition anywhere to the American vision of world order.

Deployment of this military force in particular situations requires compromise by the United States with other states whose cooperation or acquiescence may be required – with Russia in the case of Afghanistan in order to give US forces free passage in Central Asia, and with Pakistan as a base and staging ground. The quid pro quo comes in the form of a reversal of previous US policy – suspending criticism of Russia's action in Chechnya and reversing the embargo on Pakistan, imposed because of its nuclear testing, together with providing financial subsidies. Empire is not all-powerful and must negotiate the application of its power in any particular place; but Empire has sufficient resources to back its negotiating strategy.

Economic pressure is a continuing force behind the political goals of

Empire. The size of the US economy and the extent to which the rest of the world economy has become locked into the structures of globalization preclude overt deviation by significant others. The economics of globalization sustains the military power of Empire; and it is now, more than before, clear that military power, whether directly applied or held in reserve, is indispensable to economic globalization.

Communications are a necessary and integral part of this combined power. Communications technologies have, of course, increased enormously the ability to project ideas and sentiments; and the predominant communications power is rooted in US media. Other cultures fight a rearguard resistance to the latent monopoly in communications of the centre. At the root of communication is language and the bias incorporated into language. Technology is merely the way this bias is projected.

Two words have been particularly important in shaping the bias of communication: 'terrorism' and 'democracy'. President George W. Bush made 'terrorism' the distinguishing mark between 'we' and 'they'. It was not an original usage. 'Terrorism' was the term applied by Israeli leaders to the Palestinian resistance. Bush's 'war against terrorism' gave it a global extension.

In part, this was an emotional reaction to the attack of September 11, 2001, on the World Trade Center in New York and on the Pentagon. Americans in their homeland had heretofore been invulnerable to attack by others. Other peoples have experienced attacks on civilian populations. The atomic bombs on Hiroshima and Nagasaki destroyed many more lives than were lost on September 11. The massacres in the Warsaw ghetto and in the division of India and Pakistan, and the slaughter of women, children and old men in the Palestinian camps of Sabra and Chatila have left legacies of outrage, as have the acts of violence that have accompanied civil conflicts everywhere. But this was new to America, and a flagrant affront to the prestige of the sole remaining super power, to the centre of world power. In the days of British empire it was said that it was dangerous to twist the lion's tail. (Post-imperial Brits have become more used to this kind of violence in the long struggle over northern Ireland.) The emotional reaction in America was all the more emotionally charged. 'Terrorism' was the word used to mobilize a collective reaction.

'Terrorism' also had the function of defining a conflict that was not primarily among states, but essentially between people holding totally opposed views of the world, with whom there could be no negotiation of differences. States became accessories in the struggle, Afghanistan because its regime harboured the al-Qaeda network and allowed training of people who would carry out attacks against assets, symbols and populations of the enemy. This kind of conflict, in which states are auxiliaries to amorphous forces, has nullified the traditional concept of warfare and the rules of war evolved over the centuries in the inter-state system. The 'war against terrorism' is not legally a war. The President of the United States has rhetorically called it a war; but for the United States to be properly at war, the US Congress must declare war and it has not. The US military have determined that captured enemy soldiers are not prisoners of war but 'unlawful combatants'. The same epithet could be applied to the United States. The treatment of prisoners is now totally dependent upon the will of the super power. 'Terrorism' suspends all concepts of law in the relation of attackers and attacked. The new pattern of imperial conflicts goes on outside of any legal framework in a new global state of nature. The central power suffers no legal constraints.

Furthermore, defence against 'terrorism' leads to new levels of police sur-veillance and restrictions on movements of people. The essentially non-territorial nature of conflict among people with opposed visions of the world leads to an attempt by states to reinforce territorial power over people. Surveillance and coercion attempt to compensate for the weakening of the legitimacy of political institutions that gives rise to irregular forms of violent conflict. The state moves towards becoming a panopticon, the ultimate in total control over people.

Opposition to 'terrorism' becomes a justification by Russia for its actions in Chechnya, by China for its actions in Tibet and its internal acts of repres-sion, and by President Mugabe of Zimbabwe for his repression of opposition. As American world power models itself on Israel's repression of Palestinian resistance, others invoke the US model as justification of their own repressive actions.

'Democracy' is the rallying cry in the 'war against terrorism'. The word does not bear any very precise definition. Connotations rather than definition give it meaning. One connotation is the 'American way of life' as a universal aspiration; it puts most weight upon the material affluence of individuals rather than upon collective social protection or the complexities of the US electoral system. A related connotation is free market capitalism. The link of 'democracy' with civil rights, however, is being eroded by the focus on 'ter-rorism'.

On the threshold of the twenty-first century, the one-civilization vision has the preponderance of military, economic and communications power behind it. But its dialectical contradiction is alive and active in the vision shared by less powerful people of a more decentred and plural world of coexisting and developing civilizations, of alternative ways to live and to develop. The future of this alternative vision depends upon the resilience of people at ground level in contesting the power of Empire and its projections around the world.

The resistance of people is abetted by the residual power of some states to endorse options contrary to the designs of the central world power. The con-solidated central power is undermined by a variety of factors:

* The geopolitics of oil and gas complicates the project of Empire in Central Asia and the Middle East.
* The links of Russia, China, Japan and Europe to global capitalism are both constraining and at the same time divergent.

- Concern for the sustainability of the biosphere, neglected by the central power, gains support among people everywhere.
- The fragility of global finance, which is manifest in crises that leave people destitute and magnify the polarization of wealth and poverty within and among countries, erodes belief in social order and world order.
- The key words – terrorism and democracy – that enshrine the established order in the hearts of people are turned inside out by lived experience. They become replaced by new meanings, resistance to oppressive domination and initiatives from the base of society to create an alternative social order.

The vision of a plural world is not likely to be advanced by catastrophic events or a victory of arms. The military force of Empire is too powerful. Empire will have to decay from within by erosion of legitimacy in the minds of people. Violence has only a symbolic effect – it shows that resistance exists and that military, economic and media power cannot totally suppress that resistance.

The dominant vision of Empire will only recede through the gradual molecular growth of support for alternative visions. A strengthening of civil society and citizen participation everywhere is the surest way for this to come about. Nowhere is this movement more important and perhaps more difficult to achieve than in the heartland of Empire. The one-civilization vision was restimulated in the United States by reaction to the attack of September 11 and that stimulus was instantly relayed abroad. The rapid, triumphant and repressive reaction of the 'war against terrorism' could reveal to the world, and also to many people in the heartland, the contradiction between the ideals of a 'free world' and the chaos created by the measures taken in its name. From this experience the prospect of a more diverse world could gain strength. The plural world is latent within the structures of globalization and Empire.

Notes

2 Reflections and transitions

1 From Hegel's preface to his *Philosophy of Right*, trans. T. M. Knox, Oxford: Oxford University Press, 1952, p.13. 'Philosophy . . . appears only when actuality is already there cut and dried after its process of formation has been completed'.

2 Nishida Kitaro (1870–1945) was, as professor of philosophy at the Kyoto Imperial University, the foremost establishment philosopher in Japan during the first half of the twentieth century (Nishida, 1937). His translator into English writes that his works 'reflect a level of serious intercivilizational encounter in the twentieth century which perhaps still has no counterpart in our own occidental culture' (p. 2). His thought focused on history and religion and he saw the world as composed of societies reflecting the world through their own cultures like Leibnizian monads. He wrote: 'The content of the historical world's self-transformation is culture; and the religious always functions as its ground.' (p. 117). His disciples of the 'Kyoto School' were associated with the pre-war and wartime ideology in Japan and fell into disrepute during the post-war occupation of Japan. Interest in his work has revived in Japan as a Japanese version of 'post-modern' thinking. It is sometimes associated with the revival of Japanese nationalism, partly in reaction to globalization, partly to the post-war 'modernization' under the occupation regime.

3 This imposed identity takes too literally the irony in my phrase (Cox, 1986). 'Were it not for the contradictory diversity of Marxist thought [this writer] would be glad to acknowledge himself (in a parody of Reaganite rhetoric) as your friendly neighbourhood Marxist-Leninist subversive.' A companion comment is that I have 'bowdlerized' Marxism. Is this intended to suggest that, like Dr Thomas Bowdler with reference to the works of Shakespeare and Gibbon, I have sought to make Marx's work conform to the 'community standards' of a present-day puritanical society, i.e. in which 'community values' abhor anything like class struggle? 'Bowdlerize' with reference to Marxism might more appropriately characterize the 'Third Way'.

4 See Althusser in Althusser and Balibar, 1970: 'It has been possible to apply Marx's theory with success because it is "true"; it is not true because it has been applied with success' (p. 59).

5 Braudel (1980): 'I have sometimes compared models to ships. What interests me, once the boat is built, is to put it in the water to see if it will float, and then to make it ascend and descend the waters of time, at my will. The significant moment is when it can keep afloat no longer, and sinks' (p. 45). And 'Marx's genius, the secret of his long sway, lies in the fact that he was the first to construct true social models, on the basis of a historical *longue durée*. These models have been frozen in all their simplicity by being given the status of laws, of a preordained and automatic explanation, valid in all places and to any society. Whereas if they

were put back within the ever-changing stream of time, they would constantly reappear, but with changes of emphasis, sometimes overshadowed, sometimes thrown into relief by the presence of other structures which would themselves be susceptible to definition by other rules and thus by other models. In this way, the creative potential of the most powerful social analysis of the last century has been stymied. It cannot regain its youth and vigor except in the *longue durée*. Should I add that contemporary Marxism appears to me to be the very image of the model in its pure state, with models for models' sake' (p. 51).

6   Georges Sorel (1941, pp. 159–61) observed that in every complex body of knowledge there is a clear and an obscure region, and that the latter is the more important. In ethics, the clear region deals in maxims for equitable relations among people; the obscure region is sexual relationships. To understand it thoroughly you must have lived in a society. In legislation, the regulation of contracts and debts is the clear part; family relations, the more obscure and, at the same time, the more basic for the understanding of a people. In economics, he went on, the easy part concerns exchange; production, the more obscure and difficult.

7   Baker (1999) is a good example of such empirical work.

8   In partial rebuttal I can refer to my article 'Production and security' (1993) which discussed the growing importance of US military in relation to economic power in the post-Fordist era.

9   On panopticism, see Foucault (1979) and S. Gill (1997).

10 René Passet (1979) works towards a reconciliation of economic logic with the logic of the life sciences. The works of Edgar Morin (1977) and of Fritjof Capra (1996) are also relevant.

11 Some of my critics have juxtaposed culture to production as determinants of social change. I do not see these as opposites or alternatives. Culture is a productive force and can be grasped as such through historical materialism as I understand it.

12 Huntington (1996), writes (pp. 304–7): 'Far more significant than economics and demography are problems of moral decline, cultural suicide, and political disunity in the West . . . Western culture is challenged by groups within Western societies. One such challenge comes from immigrants from other civilizations who reject assimilation and continue to adhere to and to propagate the values, customs, and cultures of their home societies . . . In the name of multiculturalism [a small but influential number of intellectuals and publicists] have attacked the identification of the United States with Western civilization, denied the existence of a common American culture, and promoted racial, ethnic, and other subnational cultural identities and groupings . . . The clash between the multiculturalists and the defenders of Western civilization and the American Creed is, in James Kurth's phrase, "The *real* clash" within the American segment of Western civilization.'

13 I have tried to maintain this balance between the hegemonic and potentially counter-hegemonic roles of international organization. In Cox (1980) I wrote: '[I]nternational organization can now be redefined as the process of institutionalizing of hegemony. International institutions universalize the norms proper to a structure of world power, and that structure of power maintains itself through support of these institutions. In that sense institutions are a ballast to the status quo. But international institutions may also become vehicles for the articulation of a coherent counter-hegemonic set of values. In this way they may become mediators between one world order and another' (p. 377):

The UN conference on racism in Durban, September 2001, demonstrated how the United Nations can be a vehicle for the expression of bitter sentiments hostile to the status quo. Whether the experience will strengthen the UN's ability to lend itself to this role or will stimulate major powers to restrain such initiatives in future remains to be seen.

14 See, for instance, the article by Robert Fisk, correspondent for *The Independent*, entitled 'Now, who are the war criminals?' about the war in Afghanistan, (re)published in *The Globe and Mail* (Toronto), 30 November 2001.

15 Hozic (1999) argues that the US entertainment industry, America's cultural weapon, has been merging with the military-industrial complex.

16 From among this literature I would signal in particular Gills, ed. (2000), Mittelman (2000), O'Brien *et al.* (2000), Arrighi *et al.* (1989), Stavenhagen (1997), Scott (1993), and Sandbrook (2000).

3 Vico, then and now

1 Geoffrey Barraclough (1955) was one of the first to articulate in the English language this sense of the need for a new history. He wrote 'already long before 1939 a few historians, such as Herbert Butterfield (1951), had begun to look at the past with a new vision. But for most of us it was the impact of war that opened our eyes to the limitations, and in some cases to the falsifications, of the history we had learnt and taught ... In this sense it was only a pardonable exaggeration to say that, for me, it was the Russian victory at Stalingrad in 1943 that made a total revision of European history imperative' (p. 9). He began to think of history in terms not so much of continuity as of 'turning points' when society swings 'upwards, out of its existing course, onto a new plane' (p. 7). Barraclough (1964) developed this point. In France, the war produced the work of the *Annales* school represented by Fernand Braudel's masterly *La méditerranée et le monde méditerranéen à l'époque de Philippe II* (1966) and his essay 'Histoire et sciences sociales: la longue durée' (1980 [1958]). Professional historians were influenced by events to rethink the methods and purposes of historical scholarship. The need was evident even for a student.

2 He wrote: 'The practical requirements which underlie every historical judgment give to all history the character of "contemporary history" because, however remote in time events there recounted may seem to be, the history in reality refers to present needs and present situations wherein those events vibrate' (p. 17).

3 Vico's works referred to in this text are *The New Science of Giambattista Vico*, from the third edition (1744), translated by Thomas Goddard Bergin and Max Harold Fisch (Ithaca: Cornell University Press, 1948), referred to in the text as '*NS*' with the paragraph number; and *The Autobiography of Giambattista Vico*, translated by Max Harold Fisch and Thomas Goddard Bergin (Ithaca: Cornell University Press, 1944) referred to in the text as *Autobiography* with the page number.

4 Goethe had encountered Vico's *New Science* on a visit to Naples in March 1787, see Fisch and Bergin's, *Introduction to Autobiography*, p. 68. Berlin (1980, p. 91) thought Goethe probably did not bother to read it.

5 In the *Autobiography* Vico writes: 'others were concerned with the various parts of knowledge, but his [Vico's] should teach it as an integral whole in which each part accords with every other and gets its meaning from the whole' (p. 199). Leon Pompa in his masterful textual analysis of *The New Science* puts the main emphasis on Vico's aim to produce a science. Pompa distances himself from what he calls the 'humanist' interpretation of Collingwood and Berlin who place the emphasis on man creating history. If men transform themselves through their own creative actions, this, Pompa argues, can only be through the operation of the laws of the 'ideal eternal history', i.e. through the historico-sociological process Vico's science has revealed (Pompa, 1990, pp. 223–5). Pompa allows that there is an inductive empirical basis at the origin of Vico's generalizations; but once incorporated into his science any prior inductive support for them becomes irrelevant; the 'ideal eternal history' becomes a deductive hypothesis with the status of an historical law

(pp. 110–11, 148). Louis Althusser (Althusser and Balibar, 1970) made a similar argument about Marx: 'It has been possible to apply Marx's theory with success because it is 'true'; it is not true because it has been applied with success' (p. 59).

6 Pompa (1990) among others is troubled by the pessimism inherent in the 'barbarism of reflection' and tries to argue that it is inconsistent with Vico's scientific achievement (pp. 201–21). Like Croce, Pompa sees an inherently progressive rational nature of the process whereby institutions and human nature change. Perhaps the implication of inconsistency comes from Pompa's attributing to Vico a belief in a fixed basic human nature, what Pompa calls absolute common sense at the root of the relative common sense which has differentiated customs through time and space. *Absolute* common sense is linked by Pompa to the three principles through which Vico begins his ideal eternal history – religion, marriage and burial (pp. 34–5). I find no basis in *The New Science* for Pompa's distinction between absolute and relative common sense, ingenious though it is. Perhaps Pompa's error here is to attribute a fixed character to what was a beginning in a long process of change. Vico surely had in mind, in envisaging the 'barbarism of reflection', that reason gradually undermines the social cohesion established through these principles of social order through its accompanying sense of irony; and that reason quite possibly would not be powerful enough to create new principles of social cohesion. The progress of reason is often evidenced by scientific and technological progress; but who can escape the twentieth-century contradiction between technological sophistication and moral turpitude?

7 Southern (1962, p. 23) traces the saying as far back as the tenth century in Islam. Frederick no doubt derived it from a Muslim source.

8 All books published in Naples were required to include letters certifying that the work offered no challenges to Catholic orthodoxy or the authority of the state. Sometimes the letter writer would receive the Dedication in the book. It was possible to evade this procedure by having your book actually published in Naples, but with a title page saying it was published in another city, for example Cologne. It should obviously be a Catholic city, not Geneva or Amsterdam (Stone, 1997, pp. 17, 65–6, 217).

9 Giannone's history described Naples' rise as the greatest power in the middle of the Mediterranean area, with a creative community of scholars, and its subsequent fall as due to Papal and priestly power and the drag on the economy imposed by the Church – a theme congenial to Enlightenment opinion and popular with English booksellers.

10 When the House of Bourbon replaced the House of Hapsburg in Spain, there were repercussions in Naples. One faction of the Neapolitan nobility formed a conspiracy to seize power and proclaim an aristocratic republic, or, if that failed, to invite Austrian Hapsburg rule. The conspiracy (1701/2) was crushed and the conspirators who escaped went into exile. Vico was commissioned to write a history of the conspiracy. The originality which he allowed himself departed somewhat from the expected political justification. His analysis linked the political conflict to the social divisions of Naples. It was not published in Vico's lifetime and he makes no mention of it in his *Autobiography*, so presumably it was for him a political *faux pas*. Vico subsequently contributed to a volume celebrating the new Bourbon ruler, which may have helped protect his position. During the War of the Spanish Succession, the Bourbons were driven out of Naples by the Austrian Hapsburgs in 1707. The survivors of the conspiracy returned as heroes. Vico prepared inscriptions for those who died in the conspiracy. The Bourbons came back again in the War of the Polish Succession in 1734 and Naples became an independent kingdom. Vico contributed to the ritual volume of poems celebrating the new ruler; and he finally had his reward – the post of official court historiographer (Stone, 1997, pp. 138–9, 294, 309).

11 The final paragraph (*NS*, 1112) in the third edition of *The New Science* is unequivocal: 'To sum up, from all that we have set forth in this work, it is to be finally concluded that this Science carries inseparably with it the study of piety, and that he who is not pious cannot be truly wise.'

12 James C. Morrison (1979) argues that Vico's own writing in *The New Science* and his emphasis on irony gives the clue as to how he should be interpreted. The 'idea of divine providence is for Vico simply a metaphor for the irony of history'.

13 Bergin and Fisch, Introduction, *Autobiography*, p. 84.

14 Gino Bedani (1989) espouses the ironic reading of Vico, i.e. that he was dissimulating his heterodox views with a pretence of piety. A more recent study, Lilla (1993) argues that Vico sought to make a theological bridge between the scholastics like St Thomas Aquinas and the moderns while rejecting the sceptics like Descartes and Hobbes. Lilla bases his argument on Vico's early work prior to *The New Science*. Perhaps he takes insufficient account of the 'modifications' of Vico's own mind, a development of his thinking between the early work and his discovery of his key to historical knowledge. Another recent work, Mazzotta (1999), leaves open the question of Vico's irony in his commitment to the idea of a Christian commonwealth (esp. pp. 222–3). Croce's (1910, p. 59) opinion is most emphatic: 'Vico, considéré dans sa biographie, fut un catholique très sincère et sans équivoque. Cependant, toute la pensée de Vico est non seulement anticatholique, mais antireligeuse. Car il explique comment se forment naturellement les mythes et les religions; et le fait qu'il renonce à ce principe d'explication en présence de l'histoire et de la religion hébraïque, s'il fut subjectivement timidité de croyant, prend objectivement la valeur d'une inconsciente ironie, semblable de cette ironie consciente de Machiavel, quand celui-ci renonçait à rechercher comment pouvaient bien se maintenir les Etats, si mal gouvernés, du pape, parce que, – disait-il – "ils sont régis par des raisons supérieures auxquelles l'esprit humain ne peut atteindre!"'

15 In his *Two Concepts of Liberty* (Oxford: Clarendon Press, 1958), Berlin wrote: 'In the end, men choose between ultimate values; they choose as they do, because their life and thought are determined by fundamental moral categories and concepts that are as much a part of their being and conscious thought and sense of their own destiny, as their basic physical structure. It may be that the ideal of freedom to live as one wishes – and the pluralism of values connected with it – is only the late fruit of our declining capitalist civilization: an ideal which remote ages and primitive societies have not known, and one which posterity will regard with curiosity, even sympathy, but little comprehension. This may be so; but no sceptical conclusions seem to me to follow. Principles are not less sacred because their duration cannot be guaranteed. Indeed the very desire for guarantees that our values are eternal and secure in some objective heaven is perhaps only a craving for the certainties of childhood or the absolute values of our primitive past. "To realise the relative validity of one's convictions", said an admirable writer of our time, "and yet stand for them unflinchingly, is what distinguishes a civilised man from a barbarian." To demand more than this is perhaps a deep and incurable metaphysical need; but to allow it to guide one's practice is a symptom of an equally deep, and far more dangerous, moral and political immaturity' (p. 57).

16 Vico made few references to Arabic thought and where he did he was somewhat dismissive. He remarked that Averroes's commentaries on Aristotle 'left the Arabs no more humane or civilized than they were before' (*Autobiography*, p. 121). He lumped the Arabs with Descartes in putting the emphasis on mathematics and physics to the exclusion of languages, history and poetry (*Autobiography*, p. 138).

17 I take this phrase from the title of Paul Hazard's *La crise de la conscience européenne*, 1680–1715 (Hazard, 1963).

18 Mazzotta (1999), writes: 'Vico is always outside of history and he lives as an

irreducible exile; yet, at the same time, the movement of the text and of his life leads him to ever-deepening awareness of the historical role of his project and life' (p. 29).

4 Universality, power and morality

1 Richard Rorty, as I read him, affirms that there is no core human nature, no residue once the creations of history have been peeled off, such as Vico thought, and that only the experience of pain is common to human beings (and to animals). In *Contingency, Irony, and Solidarity* (1989), Rorty sees no common nature in the past, but the possibility of creating one in the future.

2 Among the earliest exponents of this approach to the natural sciences was Jacques Monod (1970). His thinking was extended with implications for the social sciences by Edgar Morin (1982). An American overview is in Waldrop (1993).

3 Jung (1933, p. 241) wrote: 'When I first took this direction I did not know where it would lead. I did not know what lay in the depths of the psyche – that region which I have since called the "collective unconscious", and whose contents I designate as "archetypes".' Compare this with Vico (1970, para 334): 'To discover the way in which this first human thinking arose in the gentile world, we encountered exasperating difficulties which have cost us the research of a good twenty years. We had to descend from these human and refined natures of ours to those quite wild and savage natures, which we cannot at all imagine and can comprehend only with great effort.' Jung's brief definition is: 'We mean by collective unconscious, a certain psychic disposition shaped by the forces of heredity; from it consciousness has developed. In the physical structure of the body we find traces of earlier stages of evolution, and we may expect the human psyche also to conform in its make-up to the law of phylogeny' (1933, p. 165).

4 A few journalists and intellectuals who were well informed about the region resisted this tendency. Among them Robert Fisk of *The Independent*, the Canadian Paul Watson of *The Los Angeles Times*, and the veteran British correspondent Nora Beloff. Régis Debray was excommunicated from the French intellectual milieu by the gatekeepers of French intellectual orthodoxy for writing an open letter to President Chirac criticizing the way in which human rights were being made the justification for a NATO aggression.

5 The long text of the 'Agreement' is accessible on the internet at <http://www.balkan.cc/Files/Rambouillet/Html/Rambo-html%201.htm>. It was never widely distributed even among supposed parties to the 'agreement', let alone negotiated.

6 See IPA Institute for Public Accuracy News Release 16 April 1999 'Troubling questions about Rambouillet', at <http://www.accuracy.org/press_releases/PR041699.htm>

7 See the report 'Rwanda: The Preventable Genocide' prepared by Stephen Lewis and five other 'eminent persons' for the Organization of African Unity (*The Globe and Mail*, 8 July 2000).

8 Red Tory is a peculiarly Canadian political designation. It refers to supporters of the Progressive Conservative Party of Canada who maintain the traditional conservative concept of society as an organic whole in which all elements have a social responsibility towards each other and who see the national whole as representing certain values to be protected, including the livelihood of farmers and fishermen. Red Tories have supported social welfare and assistance to Third World countries. They have opposed 'neo-conservatism' of the Thatcherite kind with its individualism that denies the reality of society and extols free trade. They are also strong environmentalists.

9 This is affirmed in the testimony of a Canadian career military officer, Roland Keith, who was a member of the Kosovo verification mission of the OSCE. It is also the evidence of a few Western journalists who remained in Kosovo after the bombing began, notably Robert Fisk of *The Independent* and the Canadian Paul Watson of the *Los Angeles Times*. For these observers, the massive attack upon and removal of the Albanian Kosovar population began after the bombing started on 24 March. Roland Keith has suggested that a strengthening of the observer verification presence together with a continued presence of foreign reporters would have been a deterrent to mass expulsions if supplemented by other pressures and incentives by concerned European governments.

10 See Richard Gwyn, 'No genocide, no justification for war on Kosovo', *Toronto Star*, 3 November 1999; and Lewis MacKenzie, 'Where have all the bodies gone?', *The Globe and Mail*, 9 November 1999.

11 Edward S. Herman and David Peterson, 'Kosovo: one year later: from Serb repression to NATO-sponsored ethnic cleansing' *Znet Commentaries,* 23 June 2000. The power relationship between the UN administration and the retreaded KLA was illustrated in an incident involving a Canadian citizen of ethnic Albanian origin who was employed by the UN in Kosovo in prison administration. He had to be spirited out of Kosovo by the UN after receiving death threats for refusing to hire former KLA members as prison guards (Andrew Mitrovica, *The Globe and Mail*, 27 June 2000).

12 Two indications are (1) a move towards centralized budgetary control which has long been a US objective and one generally opposed by poor countries that press for more UN services, and (2) the giving of fuller access to multinational corporate interests in the formation of UN policy.

13 Canadian diplomacy played a role in facilitating NATO penetration in Ukraine. ('With its 1.5 million Ukranian Canadians and its non-threatening image, Canada was a logical choice for NATO's co-ordinating job', wrote Geoffrey York in *The Globe and Mail*, 24 June 2000.) Canadian diplomacy has cherished the idea of being a support to the United Nations and being independent of, and an influence upon, the United States. In the final analysis on issues which the United States deems vital, Canada has always aligned itself with US policy irrespective of whether the United Nations was involved. Canada could take a different view from the United States on the abolition of land mines and the creation of an international criminal court, but not on NATO or Kosovo.

14 On China's reaction, see Frédéric Bobin in *Le Monde*, 22 June 1999, in which the perceived threat of encirclement coming after the bombing by US/NATO of the Chinese embassy in Belgrade (which no one in China accepts to have been an 'accident') was represented by the United States and NATO as one more case of 'collateral damage'.

5 Power and knowledge: towards a new ontology of world order

1 Giambattista Vico (1970 and Chapter 3 above) may be regarded as the first *counter*-modernist (neither a pre-modernist nor a post-modernist). It was very clear to him that the human mind was not adapted to understanding the 'truth' of the universe. It was, however, he thought, well adapted to understanding the processes of historical change.

2 Carr's reputation as a realist among students of international relations has come to rest mainly on his *The Twenty Years' Crisis, 1919-1939* (1946). His essay *Nationalism and After* (1945) illustrates his broad understanding of economic, social, and ideological transformation shaping the nature of states and of world

order. Much of the rest of his work, *The Romantic Exiles* (1949), for instance, and his studies of Dostoyevsky, Bakunin and Marx, as well as his essay *What is History?* (1964) and his history of the Soviet Union, demonstrate the breadth of his approach. For a balanced view of Carr's work see Michael Cox (2000).

3 Drucker (1986: 783) wrote: '[I]n the world economy of today, the "real" economy of goods and services and the "symbol" economy of money, credit, and capital are no longer bound tightly to each other; they are, indeed, moving further and further apart.'

4 For a fuller story of financial antics of the 1980s, see Strange (1986).

5 The phrase is attributed to Claude Cheysson, in Lorenzo Consoli, 'Lomé, with the "useless" in mind', *Cooperazione* (English edn) 113, April 1992: 46–7. Cited in Cheru (1997).

6 The United Nations used to be differentiated from the international economic agencies (World Bank, IMF, and now WTO) which have operated within a neo-liberal logic. The UN was seen as more open to the expression of heterodox views about world economy, particularly in the interest of less developed countries. However, the success of the United States in securing the election of Kofi Annan as Secretary-General after excluding Boutros Boutros Ghali from re-election led to a shift in the United Nations towards alignment with the neo-liberal policy orientation. The new Secretary-General, when he appointed Maurice Strong as his aide to reorganize the secretariat, seemed initially to be moving towards centralizing budgetary control which the United States had always sought, and towards giving fuller access to multinational corporate interests in the formation of UN policy.

7 Bull (1977, pp. 254–5) projected a 'new medievalism' as a possible form of future world order. See also Strange (1996) and Badie and Smouts (1992). On this theme of the increasing complexity of world politics and the obsolescence of conventional boundaries and distinctions, see also Rosenau (1997).

8 I take the notion of 'nature's veto' from Harries-Jones, Rotstein, and Timmerman (1992); see also their 'A signal failure: ecology and economy after the earth summit' in Schechter, ed. (1999).

9 René Passet (1979) works towards a reconciliation of economic logic with the logic of the life sciences. The works of Edgar Morin (1982) and of Fritjof Capra (1996) are also relevant.

10 I am indebted to Yoshikazu Sakamoto for the concept of 'civic state'. See Chapter 6, n. 3.

6 Civil society at the turn of the millenium: prospects for an alternative world order

1 References in the text to the *Prison Notebooks* are taken from Gramsci (1971), subsequently referred to as *PN*.

2 There is a current of 'political Marxism' expressed by Wood (1995) which is very critical of the hopes of some people on the left that civil society will play an emancipatory role. In her view, civil society retains its original identity with the bourgeois order. This originated with the conceptual distinction made in bourgeois ideology between politics and economics, creating the illusion that economics, the realm of civil society, was not an arena of politics, that is to say, of power relations. This mystification of private power has made possible the acceptance and reproduction of the bourgeois social order. She writes: 'It is certainly true that in capitalist society, with its separation of "political" and "economic" spheres, or the state and civil society, coercive public power is centralized and concentrated to a greater degree than ever before, but this simply means that one of

the principal functions of "public" coercion by the state is to sustain "private" power in society.' (p. 255). Her charge against the current appeal to civil society by the 'new social movements' and post-modernism is that it occludes the reality of class domination and fragments the opposition to the bourgeois order into a variety of distinct struggles for 'identity', thereby perpetuating capitalist domination.

Rosenberg (1994) transposes Woods's reasoning to international relations, arguing that the classical Westphalian concept of state sovereignty and the balance of power mystify the reality of power in the capitalist world order. The 'public' sphere of the state system is paralleled by the 'private' sphere of the global economy; and the state system functions to sustain 'private' power in the latter, the 'empire of civil society'.

'Political Marxism' provided a cogent argument with regard to the 'top-down' meaning of civil society, and in its critique of a post-modernism in which indiscriminate deference to identities implies a fragmentation and therefore weakening of opposition to the dominant order. The argument is more questionable in its apparent rejection of the Gramscian 'war of position' as a counter-hegemonic strategy for the conquest of civil society and for the transformation of civil society in an emancipatory direction. Two key points in the 'political Marxist' thesis that bear re-examination are: (1) the positing of capitalism as a monolithic 'totalizing' force which excludes the possibility of historicizing capitalism so as to perceive that it is subject to historical change and can take different forms; and (2) the freezing of the concept of 'class' in a nineteenth- and early twentieth-century form with a two-class model juxtaposing bourgeoisie and proletariat which obscures the ways in which changes in production have restructured social relations, especially during recent decades (see Chapter 5, pp. 84–5).

3 I take the term 'civic state' from Yoshikazu Sakamoto, in personal correspondence. See also his article 'Civil society and democratic world order', in Gill and Mittelman, eds (1997, pp. 207–19).

4 See, for example, Held (1995). Schechter (1997) contains a critical review of literature on 'global civil society'. Even the most optimistic writers regard 'global civic society' in the emancipatory sense as something to be achieved, not as something that already exists. In the 'top-down' hegemonic sense, by contrast, Rosenberg (1994) refers to the 'empire of civil society' as control by global capitalism. In the same sense, but without the Marxist theoretical framework, Strange (1989) wrote about a 'non-territorial empire'.

5 Macdonald (1997) gives a useful classification of 'ideal types' of NGOs according to their consequences for maintenance or transformation of social and political order. She suggests three types: neo-conservative, liberal-pluralist, and post-Marxist (or Gramscian) (pp. 15–23). With regard to opposition between dominant and subordinate groups within the labour movement, see Cox (1996a).

6 Madeuf and Michalet (1978) made the distinction between the international economy (understood as flows of goods, payments, and investments across frontiers) and an emerging form of economy in which production was being organized on an integrated basis among entities located in a number of countries. In the English translation of their article, which was written in French, the emerging economy was called the 'world economy', which accords with the French term applied to the process generating it, *mondialisation*. The term 'global economy' is commonly used now in English to designate the organization of production and finance on a world scale and 'globalization' as the process generating it. Of course, much of the world's economic activity still goes on outside this global economy, albeit increasingly constrained by and subordinated to the global economy. I reserve the term 'world economy' for the totality of economic activities of which the global economy is the dominant part. The impact of the globalization process on power relations among social forces and states, and the formation of institutions

designed to entrench the global economy, or in stimulating resistance to it, is the realm of 'global political economy'.

7 The first World Social Forum, convened in Porto Alegre in January 2001, brought together 10,000 delegates from social movements around the world to develop thinking and action towards an alternative world social order – 'globalization from below'. It met at the same time and in virtual confrontation with the World Economic Forum at Davos that brought together corporate executives and political leaders. The second World Social Forum in January 2000, also in Porto Alegre, attracted over 60,000 participants.

8 Professor Tamotsu Aoki, a cultural anthropologist, Research Centre for Advanced Science and Technology, University of Tokyo, at a symposium convened jointly by the International House of Japan and the Friedrich-Ebert-Stiftung, Tokyo, 26 September 1996.

9 Yoshikazu Sakamoto, Professor emeritus of international relations, Tokyo University and Young-Ho Kim, Professor at Kyungpook National University, South Korea, at a symposium on Prospects for Civil Society in Asia, International House of Japan, Tokyo, 24 September 1996

10 The 'Asianization' idea is presented in Funabashi (1993). The notion of a regional civil society is discussed in Bernard (1996). For a critical assessment, see Iida (1997b).

11 See various writings of János Kornai, including Kornai (1980a and 1980b); also Brus and Kowalik (1983); and Cox (1991).

12 Robinson (1996a) contains case studies of the Philippines, Chile, Nicaragua, Haiti, South Africa and the former Soviet Union; see also Robinson (1996b).

13 Amilcar Cabral (1979) was a particularly articulate leader who expounded in theory and practice the position that popular participation in revolutionary action and cultural change were essential for African peoples to raise themselves out of imperialist domination. Although, following Cabral's assassination by agents of Portuguese colonialism, the momentum of his movement stalled, the historian Basil Davidson (1994, pp. 217–43) thinks that Cabral's success in mobilizing Africans to make their own history has left its impact and example to inspire a renewed movement. Cabral's speeches and writing have striking similarity to Gramsci's thought.

14 Davidson (1992) envisaged the possibility that more participatory politics in Africa might develop within the framework of market economics, but concluded rather pessimistically: 'How far the developed world of multinational concentrations of power will bring itself to tolerate this devolutionary politics of participation, and its democratic implications, is [a] question to which, at present, we do not have an answer' (p. 225). The fall of the Mobutu regime in Zaire and its replacement by the Democratic Republic of the Congo under Laurent-Désiré Kabila did not really test Davidson's proposition. Kabila's victory was achieved by military means with considerable support from Ugandan and Rwandan military forces. The struggle seemed to take place over the heads of the vast majority of Zaire's population which has evolved techniques of survival in communities that have avoided involvement with the state and the formal economy. Although these elements of autonomous civil society do exist, they have not yet been able to evolve a real politics of participation that could be the foundation for a new state (Braeckman, 1997). Davidson (1994, pp. 261–2) seemed more optimistic about the long-range potential for the development of civil society and 'the elaboration of a culture capable of drawing the civilization of the Africans out of the fetters into which it has fallen, and of giving that civilization, in its multitudinous aspects and varieties, a life and meaning appropriate to its present tasks and destiny.'

15 The American sociologist Robert D. Putnam has suggested that civil society in the United States has lost much of the spirit of association once noted by Tocqueville

as its salient characteristic. He sees this as being replaced by non-participation in group activities and a privatizing or individualizing of leisure time. He calls this a decline of 'social capital' which refers to networks, norms, and social trust that facilitate coordination and cooperation for mutual benefit. See Putnam (1995). The same author has made a study about social capital in Italy: Putnam with Robert Leonardi and Raffaella Y. Nanetti (1993).

7 The covert world

1 One analysis of the interaction of covert and overt worlds is in a case study of Thailand, Pasuk Phongpaichit, Sungsidh Piriyarangsan, and Nualnoi Treerat, 1998.

2 The history of addiction is instructive (Lowes, 1966). In the United States it began with the civil war – the first war fought with modern arms and mass troops – when the wounded, in the absence of modern anaesthetics, were treated by morphine. To this source of addiction was added the sale of morphine-filled unregulated medication by itinerant salesmen during the nineteenth century, particularly in the American west; and then, in the twentieth century, the demand for heroin generated from despair among the marginalized in urban ghettoes.

3 Galbraith (1992), p. 45, noted that in the United States the number of private security guards was greater than the number of publicly employed police.

4 UN peace-keeping and peace-enforcement missions have run into obstacles. The United States has been unwilling to commit troops in Africa after suffering losses in Somalia. Other Western countries were also unwilling to intervene to stop the Rwanda genocide. Inadequately trained and equipped troops from other African countries placed under UN command in Sierra Leone were made prisoner by insurgents. These experiences have led to some suggestions that the well-trained and well-equipped mercenaries available on the world market could be more effective in pursuing UN goals. On the proliferation of mercenary troops generally, see Jacques Isnard, 'Le retour des mercenaires', *Le Monde*, 28 May 1998. On the question of the United Nations employing mercenaries, see Sebastian Mallaby, 'Think again: renouncing the use of mercenaries can be lethal', *International Herald Tribune*, 5 June 2001, reprinted from the *Washington Post*.

5 Attitudes towards sects differ on the two sides of the Atlantic. Americans are inclined to consider the existence of sects as a matter of religious freedom. Europeans have been more disposed to consider sects to be evidence of social malaise and even as agents of American penetration. The European activities of such groups as the Church of Scientology and even the Mormons (Church of Latter Day Saints) have been suspect in Europe. See Henri Tincq, 'Les sectes, métastases d'un corps social malade', *Le Monde*, 29 March 1997; Fouchereau (2001); and Henri Trincq, 'Les sectes et la République', *Le Monde*, 20 June 2001. A more nuanced view is to be found in a special issue of the Protestant journal *Réforme*, May 2001.

6 Transnational concern to combat financial corruption was discussed by thirty-five judges from Switzerland, Italy, France and Spain in Geneva in September 1994. They warned that corruption was threatening the functioning of democratic institutions, opening the way for organized crime and perverting competition on the free market (*Tribune de Genève*, 11–12 September 1994). More recent analysis of the financial corruption issue and of the work of Transparency International, a non-governmental organization supported by corporations and the World Bank, is to be found in Abramovici (2000) and Wang and Rosenau (2001).

7 Mittelman and Johnston (1999) introduce the concept of the 'courtesan state', i.e. a state that is beholden to more powerful interests in the global political economy.

The 'courtesan' condition manifests itself by tolerance of activities within its own jurisdiction that are formally illegal, but bring benefits to the country as well as to the covert interests that control them. Instances could be state toleration of the transnationally organised sex industry in eastern Asia, and the activities of the cocaine cartels in Latin America that play a key role in the balance of payments of some countries. Williams (1999, pp. 200–1), in attributing the growth of organized crime to the weakness of states, also indicates that organized crime has established a 'symbiotic relationship' with states so that it does not aim to destroy states, but rather to preserve the 'symbiotic relationship'.

8 The Mafia was an obstacle to the authority of the Fascist state in southern Italy. An adaptation by both parties to this potential conflict was achieved by the absorption into the black shirts of the more prominent mafiosi, leaving the lesser mafiosi vulnerable to arrest by the police.

9 Chesneaux suggests that the term *fei* represents more than just bandit and applies to people wholly opposed to the established social order. The Chinese equivalent of 'secret society', he suggests, may be a neologism translated into Chinese, possibly via Japanese, from the European term which covers organizations like the Freemasons and Rosicrucians. The point is that the term 'secret society' does not adequately represent the Chinese phenomenon which was the existence of an 'anti-society', or, in the terms drawn above from Vieille, a 'social movement' reacting to 'chaos' (Chesneaux, 1971, pp. 187–8; Chesneaux, 1972, p. 2).

10 Chesneaux writes: 'what is specifically original about the secret societies is that they were organized into a complex mass of rites and beliefs which were considered pernicious by Confucian scholars. They associated them with a politico-social dissidence either real or likely to become so, and which did in fact regard itself as the antithesis of the official system of thought and social organization' (Chesneaux, 1971, p. 67). The eschatological or millenarian ideas that the secret societies borrowed from Buddhism bear a remarkable similarity to those of Joachim of Floris, the twelfth century Calabrian abbot, whose concept of the third and final era, the era of the Holy Ghost, when the external constraint of institutions will give place to mystical unity, was very much like the *kalpa* of mystical Buddhism.

11 Runciman (1958) writes: 'Amongst a people so given to secret societies as the Sicilians one cannot hope for documents describing a plotter's organization to survive; and in an island where oral traditions linger long one must place some faith in them' (p.292). And: 'Charles was wrong to disregard the Sicilians and John of Procida [the principal agent of the Aragonese conspiracy] right to seek their support. Of all the peoples of Europe they are the most adept at conspiracy. Their loyalty to the Secret Society is only equalled by their loyalty to the honour of the family. They provided a perfect field for John and his fellow plotters to cultivate. Their grievances against Angevin rule were real and intense; they could be trusted to welcome a deliverer. But the good conspirator works in silence. Apart from the legendary tales of John's journeys there are no records of the manner in which the island conspiracy was organized. Everything was done in secret. It is certain that the agents from Aragon were working in the island. It is certain that arms were smuggled in. It is equally certain that the conspirators were in close touch with Constantinople, from which they received money with the promise of more to come, should all go according to the plan' (p. 212).

12 The Neapolitan *Camorra*, of more recent origin, appears to have a more centralized organization (Hobsbawm, 1965, pp. 33, 53–6).

13 Arlacchi (1986) writes about one of the regions of Calabria, the Plain of Gioia Tauro, during the impact of unification in the late nineteenth century. This was, he says, a society with a complex of subcultures that were in a state of perpetual decomposition and recomposition: 'The behaviour and power of the mafia

constituted in fact the specific reaction of the society of permanent transition to the powerful centrifugal forces generated within the sphere of its economic life. The essential feature of the mafia phenomenon was not that it was an organization nor a social movement with specific ends and programmes . . . but it was the point of convergence of a series of diverse tendencies in the society itself: the self-defence of a traditional society against threats to its traditional mode of life; the aspirations of the various groups which composed it towards a "freezing" and control of the undulating movements which distorted every institution and destroyed all security; personal ambition and the hopes of active and ruthless individuals' (p. 111).

14 The Nigerian 'mafia' was enlarged as a consequence of a dramatic drop in oil prices which left many members of an educated Nigerian diaspora jobless and available as recruits to a transnational criminal network (Mittelman and Johnston, 1999, p. 111; Williams, 1999, p. 196).

15 The US historian Roger Morris writes about the lavish financing of William Clinton's campaigns for governor of Arkansas and for the presidency of the United States by business circles connected with organized crime. President Clinton's last acts, pardoning some of those supporters who had been involved in criminal activities, provoked journalistic comment but passed without public outcry, no doubt because of the wide public support for Clinton's presidency (Roger Morris, 'Don't pardon corruption', *The Globe and Mail*, Toronto, 7 March 2001: also Roger Morris, *Partners in Power: The Clintons and Their America*). For comment on the less colourful relationship between money and politics in Tony Blair's Britain, see Patrice Claude, 'Tony Blair et l'argent', *Le Monde*, 17 February 2001.

16 'Reform' is a word that has been appropriated by the discourse of globalization in which it has the meaning of removing the state from intervention in economic processes. Its counterpart is the trimming of social protection. 'Reformers' are the agents promoting the achievement of the neo-liberal economy.

17 I draw here upon George Sorel's concept of the 'social myth' which mobilizes revolutionary force (Sorel, 1941). Sorel's myth creates a sense of cleavage between those ensconced in the established order and those who would change it. Their confrontation is imagined as a 'Napoleonic battle' in which the two forces are confronted in a catastrophic collision. The outcome in reality does not introduce a wholly new order but the energies it mobilizes, in Sorel's thinking, can achieve great things.

8 Civilizations: encounters and transformations

1 Huntington, along with Zbigniew Brzezinski, has been a theoretician of the Cold War. The two gave a joint seminar at Columbia University which led to their co-authorship of *Political Power: USA/USSR*, New York: Viking Press, 1965.

2 Similar fears of mass migrations from east and south are current in Europe, rooted in right-wing opinion but having a wider currency. They encourage an image of defence against the barbarian hordes, and make an issue of civilization in the form of a confrontation with Islam. European scholars have taken up the challenge to refute this depiction of the world. See Didier Bigo (1996).

3 It should be added that in Fukuyama's vision the triumphant culmination of the Hegelian dialectic foreshadows a Nietzschean pessimism concerning the kind of human life that would be attained – the contemptible 'last man' who exchanges creativity and struggle for a passive security.

4 Martin Weber, 'The "Otherness" of the Muslim', *Swiss Review of World Affairs* (a journal that published English translations of articles from the *Neue Zürcher Zeitung*), January 1994.

5 Arnold Hottinger, 'How dangerous is Islam' in ibid.

6 Victor Kocher, 'Continued instability in the Persian Gulf' in ibid.

7 A similar argument was put forward by two political scientists of Islamic background, Ahmed Samatar and Mustapha Kamal Pasha, in a paper for a symposium on globalization held at American University, Washington DC, in 1994. They reject the essentialist view of Islam as being fundamentally anti-modern, an idea which is, they observe, encouraged by the ideology of globalism. Faith, they argue, is the last bastion of communities under stress from the polarization of wealth and poverty produced by economic globalization. The community of faith, in this case the Islamic ummah, represents a principle of solidarity and regulates social relations in a community that cannot look to the state for support.

8 Yale University became embroiled in intramural controversy over a grant of $20 million made by a Texas oil magnate alumnus in 1991 for studies in Western Civilization. The money was returned to the donor in March 1995 after the university administration concluded the issue could not be resolved. [See *The Globe and Mail* (Toronto) 24 March 1995, quoting from an editorial of 14 March 1995 in *The Wall Street Journal*.] There was no statement as to what the issue actually was, but one may infer it had to do with the politicization of the very concept of Western Civilization in the United States. The concept has been embraced by the intellectual right, e.g. William Bennett, as a call for return to 'traditional values' and is opposed by many on the left as an attempt to glorify 'dead white males'. This scholarly atmosphere is hardly congenial for the study of civilizations (Western or other) in the United States.

9 Similarly, Christian civilization can be dated from the fourth century, following a long phase of mingling of peoples, interaction and syncretic borrowing among competing oriental religions in Europe, and an institutionalization of the church on the model of the Roman Empire. External and internal proletariats, to use Toynbee's terms, provided the stimulus for this amalgam.

10 Habermas (1973) wrote: 'Capitalist societies were always dependent on boundary conditions they could not themselves produce; they fed parasitically on the remains of tradition . . . Bourgeois culture was never able to reproduce itself from itself. It was always dependent on motivationally effective supplementation by traditional world-views' (pp. 76–7). One businessman imprisoned in Italy's *mani pulite* investigation of business-political corruption was reported as saying that corruption and illicit political funding was necessary to sustain capitalism and the free market (*La Repubblica*, 2 October 1993, p. 6).

11 Fitzpatrick (n.d.) argues that Mongol penetrations into China were a more practically significant force for political unification than was the ideal of unity in traditional Confucianism. Yoshikazu Sakamoto has pointed out to me that the Chinese absorbed and civilized their invaders. On the impact of nomads on Europe, see McNeill (1964).

12 The conclusion to Innis's *The Fur Trade in Canada* (1962) begins: 'Fundamentally the civilization of North America is the civilization of Europe and the interest of this volume is primarily in the effects of a vast new land area on European civilization' (p. 383).

13 In Innis's obituary on Cochrane (1946), he underlined Cochrane's commentary on Thucydides, from whom he saw the dynamic of history as 'the relationship between the ideals of men, on the one hand, and, on the other, the material circumstances upon which their satisfaction depends'.

14 William Aberhart was an evangelical preacher in Alberta in the 1930s who espoused the doctrine of social credit derived from the British Major Douglas and made it into a prairie populist movement that won him election as premier of Alberta. The movement had something of the radical right-wing overtones of

some contemporary European movements, especially in its condemnation of 'international Jewish bankers'. Father Charles Coughlin was an anti-semitic broadcaster with fascist tendencies in the United States during the same period.

15 The reference here is to Marshall McLuhan's celebrated aphorism: 'The medium is the message.' McLuhan, a colleague of Innis at the University of Toronto, was inspired by Innis's work and the two are often linked in the development of communications theory.

16 Jacob Burckhardt (1943), whose work Innis sometimes referred to, divided his reflections on history into state, religion and culture, which has a certain parallel with Innis's state, church and communication.

17 For an analysis of structural change in the Italian state/society complex during this period, see Guzzini (1994) and Amyot (1995).

18 Innis (1991) in 'A plea for time' (p. 80) refers negatively to individualism.

19 An Asian respondent to Huntington's 'clash of civilizations' thesis, Kishore Mahbubani (1993), a senior official of Singapore, viewed Huntington's essay as evidence of a 'siege mentality' in the West. There is, he wrote, 'a fatal flaw that has recently developed in the western mind: an inability to conceive that the West may have developed structural weaknesses in its core value systems and institutions'. This echoes Innis's (1991, p. 14) phrase, 'Each civilization has its own methods of suicide.'

20 Georges Sorel (1941), concerned with the same problem, came up with myth. But myth, like *virtù* and *'asabiya*, has no explicit content. There is no formula for evoking it.

9 Conceptual guidelines for a plural world

1 For the context of this work, see Hughes (1952).

2 See McNeill (1989). McNeill's *magnum opus, The Rise of the West* (1963), obviously entitled as a rejoinder to Spengler's *Decline of the West*, was expressive of the American *hubris* of the post-war decades. His theme was that the principal factor promoting historical change is contact with foreigners possessing new and unfamiliar skills. Civilizations result from a diffusion of skills and knowledge from a central point, such as the United States appeared to be following World War II. Twenty-five years later, in a more reflective mood, McNeill (1989) came to regard this thesis as 'a form of intellectual imperialism'.

3 Braudel's *Grammaire de civilisations* was first published in 1963, designed as a text for use in French secondary schools, but was never authorised by the education authorities. It was translated and published in English, as *A History of Civilizations*, only in 1994. Other works by Braudel were published in English translation from the late 1970s.

4 On inter-subjectivity, see Taylor (1965). Collingwood (1946) called this process 'rethinking the thought of the past'. He applied this notion to different temporal epochs in a continuous history, but it is equally applicable to different cultures or civilizations. Indeed, it is the method used and advocated by Vico (1970, para. 338), who wrote that his effort to discover the way in which the first human thinking arose 'cost us the research of a good twenty years', in which it was necessary 'to descend from these human and refined natures of ours to those quite wild and savage natures, which we cannot at all imagine and can comprehend only with great effort'.

5 Vico did not use the word 'civilizations' more than a century before it became current in European discourse. Rather he spoke of 'nations', although with a meaning very different from that of nineteenth- and twentieth-century nationalisms. 'Nation' for him meant an entity with a common origin and a common set

of institutions, in the sense of common social practices, not formal institutions; and a common language, not in the sense of English or French but as a common means of communicating meaning, or what we have here called 'inter-subjectivity'.

6 'In a rock stratum are embedded crystals of a mineral. Clefts and cracks occur, water filters in, and the crystals are gradually washed out so that in due course only their hollow mould remains. Then come volcanic outbursts which explode the mountain; molten masses pour in, stiffen, and crystalize out in their turn. But these are not free to do so in their own special forms. They must fill up the spaces that they find available. Thus there arise distorted forms, crystals whose inner structure distorts their external shape, stones of one kind presenting the appearance of stones of another kind. The mineralologists call this phenomenon *Pseudomorphosis*.

'By the term "historical pseudomorphosis" I propose to designate those cases in which an older alien Culture lies so massively over the land that a young culture born in this land, cannot get its breath and fails not only to achieve pure and specific expression-forms, but even to develop fully its own self-consciousness. All that wells up from the depths of the young soul is cast in the old moulds, young feelings stiffen in senile works, and instead of rearing up its own creative power, it can only hate the distant power with a hate that grows to be enormous.'

7 The tragedy of the Russian pseudomorphosis, in Spengler's analysis, has been the continuing dominance of Western imported thought over a suppressed and barely articulate Russian spirit. By analogy, the current 'market reformers' are but an extension of the Western-inspired communist managers, themselves natural successors to Peter the Great's modernization. Those with a longer historical perspective might trace the phenomenon back to the Varangians! In the post-communist débâcle, opposition to the advocates of 'shock therapy' have revived awareness of non-Western *narodnik* sentiment. One literary instance is in a revived interest in the work of Nicholas Berdyaev (1947).

8 'The crisis is far deeper than the ordinary; its depth is unfathomable, its end not yet in sight, and the whole of the Western society is involved in it. It is the crisis of a Sensate culture, now in its overripe stage, the culture that has dominated the Western World during the last five centuries. It is also the crisis of a contractual (capitalist) society associated with it.' Against this prediction, it can be argued that the three decades following World War II saw a flourishing of the sensate culture, especially in American social science, and the collapse of 'real socialism' appears to negate a crisis of capitalism. In favour of it, it can be argued that the crisis was only postponed and that movements like post-modernism and deep ecology redefine the crisis in more meaningful contemporary terms.

9 As an instance of absolutist thinking, Louis Althusser has written: 'It has been possible to apply Marx's theory with success because it is "true"; it is not true because it has been applied with success' (Althusser and Balibar, 1970, p. 59). The French Catholic philosopher Jean Guitton, who had been Althusser's professor in his preparation for the *Ecole normale* and was his companion in *l'Action catholique*, remained his friend after Althusser's conversion to atheism and Marxism. The two maintained a close relationship and correspondence thereafter. In 1980, just before the psychiatric crisis in which he strangled his wife, Althusser came to Guitton with a premonition of human catastrophe which, he thought, could only be avoided by a union of Rome with Moscow. Reflecting on this strange and enduring friendship, Guitton wondered whether from his days with *l'Action catholique* to his role as foremost exponent of Marxism in post-1968 France, Althusser had fundamentally changed '*dans son intimité secrète et profonde*' (Guitton, 1988).

10 Soros expanded his article into a book (Soros, 1998). He returned to a revised critique of 'market fundamentalism' in Soros, 2000. For a critical discussion see Sidelsky (2001).

11 David Harvey (1989) sees a compression of time and space as the present condition. Time, he sees as privileged over space in social theories; and space over time in aesthetics. Space is compressed in the awareness of global interdependencies. The compression of time comes about through the shrinking of decision-making horizons into a non-historical present. (One might say, inspired by Innis, that time is being compressed into space.) Harvey's strongest point is that our consciousness of both time and space is dependent upon material processes: 'From this materialist perspective we can then argue that objective conceptions of time and space are necessarily created through material practices and processes which serve to reproduce social life . . . The objectivity of time and space is given in each case by the material practices of social reproduction, and to the degree that these latter vary geographically and historically, so we find that social time and social space are differentially constructed. Each distinctive mode of production or social formation will, in short, embody a distinctive bundle of time and space practices and concepts' (p. 204). Harvey relates present day concepts of time and space to the reorganization of production from Fordism to post-Fordism; the fragmentation of production processes in what he calls 'flexible accumulation' enhances the sense of the ephemeral.

10 Civilizations and world order

1 Harvey (1989) writes: 'Spatial and temporal practices are never neutral in social affairs. They always express some kind of class or other social content, and are more often than not the focus of intense social struggle . . . During phases of maximal change, the spatial and temporal bases for reproduction of the social order are subject to the severest disruption' (p. 239). He adds: 'As space appears to shrink to a "global village" of telecommunications and a "spaceship earth" of economic and ecological interdependencies – to use just two familiar and everyday images – and as time horizons shorten to the point where the present is all there is (the world of the schizophrenic), so we have to cope with an overwhelming sense of *compression* of our spatial and temporal worlds' (p. 240).

2 See, for example, Miller (1974) who writes: 'monotheistic thinking . . . fails a people in a time when experience becomes self-consciously pluralistic' (p. 7); and 'polytheism is not a matter of some new theology, sociology, or psychology. It is rather a matter of many potencies, many structures of meaning and being, all given to us in the reality of our everyday lives' (p. 65).

3 Kapra (1996) writes: 'Shallow ecology is anthropocentric, or human-centered. It views humans as above or outside of nature, as the source of all value, and ascribes only instrumental, or "use", value to nature. Deep ecology does not separate humans – or anything else – from the natural environment. It sees the world not as a collection of isolated objects, but as a network of phenomena that are fundamentally interconnected and interdependent. Deep ecology recognizes the intrinsic value of all living beings and views humans as just one particular strand in the web of life.

'. . . the emerging new vision of reality based on deep ecological awareness is consistent with the so-called perennial philosophy of spiritual traditions, whether we talk about the spirituality of Christian mystics, that of Buddhists, or the philosophy and cosmology underlying the Native American traditions' (p. 7).

4 Deibert (1997) argues compellingly for a non-reductionist theory of communication and civilizational change, developing the work of Harold Innis.

5 A few examples are Berger and Dore, eds (1996); Zysman (1996); Bernard (1999).

6 The American sociologist Robert D. Putnam (1995) has suggested that civil society in the United States has lost much of the spirit of association once noted by

de Tocqueville as its salient characteristic. He sees this as being replaced by a privatizing and individualizing of leisure time with non-participation in group activities. He calls this a decline of 'social capital' which refers to networks, norms, and social trust that facilitate coordination and cooperation for mutual benefit. The same author has made a study in collaboration with others about social capital in Italy: Putnam with Leonardi and Nanetti (1993). The Italian study contrasted with the American in finding stability in a northern Italy with a higher propensity for cooperative social interaction and a south where this was lacking – characteristics both of which had a long historical legacy. It may be recalled that Giambattista Vico (1970: paras 1102–6) in the early eighteenth century envisaged as a possible end stage in the cyclical evolution of civilizations a 'barbarism of reflection' more inhuman than the primitive 'barbarism of sense' among peoples who 'have fallen into the custom of each man thinking only of his own private interests'. Robert Putnam, Susan Pharr and Russell Dalton (2000) use opinion surveys to show a general decline in people's confidence in their political institutions, most marked in the United States, but noticeable in all of the rich countries (except for Iceland and Denmark). *The Economist* in its issue of 17 July 1999 began a series 'Is there a crisis?', enquiring why citizens of the mature democracies are losing confidence in their institutions.

7 Michel Albert (1991) presented the case for a 'Rhineland model' of capitalism confronting the Anglo-Saxon model, the former characterized by consensus, corporatism, long-term planning and a stabilizing relationship between banks and industry, the latter by a focus on short-term profits, shareholder dividends and stock markets facilitating predatory behaviour such as hostile takeovers.

8 Hans-Jürgen Bieling, 'European integration and industrial relations – a critique of the concept and strategy of "competitive corporatism"' (unpublished draft); also M. Rhodes, 'Globalization, labour markets and welfare states: a future of "competitive corporatism"?', in M. Rhodes and Y. Mény (1998); also Ignacio Ramonet (1999), and José Vidal-Beneyto (1999).

9 See Shigeto Tsuru (1993); Chalmers Johnson (1982); James Fallows (1994); and Chie Nakane (1973).

10 Professor Tamotsu Aoki, a cultural anthropologist, Research Centre for Advanced Science and Technology, University of Tokyo, at a symposium convened jointly by the International House of Japan and the Friedrich-Ebert-Stiftung, Tokyo, 26 September 1996.

11 Yumiko Iida (1997). Aum Shinryiko, a doomsday cult, attracted a large number of highly educated Japanese.

12 Bernard (1999) analyses the 'Asian crisis' in terms of the different forms of social class relations of production evolving in different Asian countries interacting with global finance. He argues that an alternative to foreign capital acquiring control of Asian economies, such as is likely to continue under IMF 'structural adjustment', could be popular support for an alternative conception of locally controlled and socially and ecologically oriented development based on a coalition of worker and peasant social forces, and with some middle-class support for something like a Tobin tax to curb speculative financial movements.

13 There is much recent reporting on the criminalization of Russian capitalism. See *Le Monde*, 21 August 1999; and *The Economist*, August 28–September 3, 1999. Grigory Yavlinski (1998), an advocate of economic liberalism, excoriated 'Russia's phony capitalism' citing George Soros as saying that in the process of privatization, first 'the assets of the state were stolen, and then when the state itself became valuable as a source of legitimacy, it too was stolen' (p. 69). This judgement relates especially to the corruption of the Yeltsin era. Putin's presidency has been characterized by ambiguity between the continuing influence of the Yeltsin-era oligarchy and attempts to construct a more powerful central state, the outcome of

which remains uncertain. The problem has been evident also in other countries of the former Soviet bloc which have too readily accepted the notion that state control of the economy was the evil. Sabina Neumann and Michelle Egan (1999) argue that 'the deliberate failure to establish a system of rules and enforcement over financial markets was the result of the belief that overregulation would cramp the natural growth of capitalism' (p. 190).

14 Nicholas Berdyaev (1947) is the classic statement. Tim McDaniel (1996) traces its history and its influence from Tsarist times, through the Soviet period, to Yeltsin's 'reforms'. McDaniel argues that the vision of the West held by Russian reformers was a mythical West defined as the opposite of the Soviet system, so that the idea of capitalism conceived by the reformers was both unlike real Western capitalism and totally divorced from traditional Russian morality and culture. It is notable that the evocation of the 'Russian idea' has parallels with a nationalist current in Japanese politics that appeals to an imagined past. See Yumiko Iida (1997).

15 George T. Crane (1999); Lily Ling (1996); and Gregory T. Chin (1999).

16 The 'battle in Seattle' refers to the anti-globalization, anti-multinational corporation demonstrations from a variety of groups that paralysed the World Trade Organization conference in Seattle, 30 November–3 December 1999.

17 Brian Urquhart, a former Undersecretary-General of the United Nations, described in his article 'The making of a scapegoat' (1999) how the United States manipulated the appointment process to the Secretary-Generalship of the United Nations in December 1996 so as to eliminate the reappointment of Boutros Boutros-Ghali, which had the support of all members of the Security Council except for the United States, and to secure the appointment of Kofi Annan. This article was a review of Boutros Boutros-Ghali's book *Unvanquished: A US-UN Saga* (1999).

18 This view of history is, I think, consistent with that of R. G. Collingwood (1946). In *The New Leviathan* (1942), Collingwood wrote: 'Civilization is a thing of the mind . . . an enquiry into its nature, therefore, belongs to the sciences of the mind, and must be pursued by the method proper to those sciences' (p. 280). I believe Collingwood rejected the term 'idealism' applied to his own work. My own thinking about historical materialism includes relating 'things of the mind' to the material context of thought, which I think is not inconsistent with Collingwood although not explicit in his work. Collingwood regards civilization as a process leading towards civility and away from barbarism. Writing during World War II, Collingwood was addressing 'German barbarism' which he saw as a recent growth, specifically Nazism; but the more general conception of tendencies towards civility or barbarity stands apart from the German question. He is quite clear as an historian that this process does not imply a 'one-civilization' outcome because 'the civilizing process . . . leads in different places and at different times to different results.' And: 'as men who create a particular society aim at creating a universal society but, owing to facts over which they have no control, find it turning under their hands into a particular society' (p. 288).

References

Abramovici, Pierre (2000), 'Les jeux dispendieux de la corruption mondiale', *Le Monde diplomatique*, November.

Albert, Michel (1991), *Capitalisme contre capitalisme*, Paris: Seuil.

Althusser, Louis and Etienne Balibar (1970), *Reading Capital*, trans. by Ben Brewster, London: Verso. The French original was published in Paris in 1968.

Amyot, G. (1995), 'The relative autonomy of the Italian state', *Studies in Political Economy*, 46 spring.

Andor, László (1996), 'Economic transformation and political stability in East Central Europe', *Security Dialogue*, 27 (2) June.

Arlacchi, Pino (1983), *Mafia, Peasants and Great Estates. Society in Traditional Calabria*, Cambridge: Cambridge University Press.

——(1986), *Mafia Business. The Mafia Ethic and the Spirit of Capitalism*, London: Verso.

Armstrong, Karen (1993), *A History of God*, New York: Ballantyne Books.

Arrighi, Giovanni, Terence K. Hopkins and Immanuel Wallerstein (1989), *Antisystemic Movements*, London: Verso.

Badie, Bertrand and Marie-Claude Smouts (1992), *Le retournement du monde. Sociologie de la scène internationale*, Paris: Presses de la Fondation Nationale des Sciences Politiques and Dalloz.

Baker, Andrew (1999), '*Nébuleuse* and the 'internationalization of the state' in the UK? The case of HM Treasury and the Bank of England', *Review of International Political Economy* 6 (1) spring: 79-100.

Bakhtin, Mikhail (1984), *Problems of Dostoyevsky's Poetics*, ed. and trans. Caryl Emerson. Introduction by Wayne C. Booth, Minneapolis: University of Minnesota Press.

Barraclough, Geoffrey (1955), *History in a Changing World*, Oxford: Blackwell.

——(1964), *An Introduction to Contemporary History*, Harmondsworth, Middlesex: Penguin

Becker, Carl (1932), *The Heavenly City of the Eighteenth Century Philosophers*, New Haven, CT: Yale University Press.

Bedani, Gino (1989), *Vico Revisited: Orthodoxy, Naturalism and Science in the Scienza Nuova*, Oxford and New York: Berg and St. Martin's Press.

Bendix, Reinhard (1960), *Max Weber: An Intellectual Biography*, New York: Doubleday.

Berdyaev, Nicholas (1947), *The Russian Idea*, London: Geoffrey Bles.

Berger, Suzanne and Ronald Dore, eds (1996), *National Diversity and Global*

Capitalism, Ithaca, NY: Cornell University Press.

Bergson, Henri (1945), *Essai sur les données immédiates de la conscience*, Geneva: Skira. Originally published in Paris in 1889. Translated into English as *Time and Free Will*.

Berlin, Isaiah (1958), *Two Concepts of Liberty*, Oxford: Clarendon Press

——(1980), *Vico and Herder*, London: Chatto and Windus

——(1991), *The Crooked Timber of Humanity,* London: Fontana Press

Bernard, Mitchell (1996), 'Regions in the global political economy: beyond the local-global divide in the formation of the eastern Asian region', *New Political Economy*, 1 (3) November.

——(1999), 'East Asia's tumbling dominoes: financial crisis and the truth about the regional miracle', in Leo Panitch and Colin Leys, eds. *The Socialist Register* 1999, London: Merlin Press.

Bieling, Hans-Jürgen (n.d.), 'European integration and industrial relations – a critique of the concept and strategy of "competitive corporatism"', Marburg: Philipps-Universität (unpublished).

Bigo, Didier (1996), 'Guerres, conflits, transnational et territoire', in Bertrand Badie and Marie-Claude Smouts, eds. *L'international sans territoire*, Paris: L'Harmattan, Culture & Conflits.

Boutros-Ghali, Boutros (1999), *Unvanquished: A US/UN Saga*, New York: Random House.

Braeckman, Colette (1997), 'Comment le Zaïre fut libéré', *Le Monde Diplomatique*, July.

Braudel, Fernand (1966), *La méditerranée et le monde méditerranéen à l'époque de Philippe II*, Paris: Armand Colin. First published 1949.

——(1979a), *Civilisation matérielle, économie et capitalisme, Xve-XVIIIe siècle*, Vol. I, *Les structures du quotidien*, Paris: Armand Colin

——(1979b), *Civilisation matérielle, économie et capitalisme, XVe-XVIIIe siècle*, Vol. III, *Le temps du monde*, Paris: Armand Colin.

——(1980), 'History and the social sciences: the *longue durée*', in Braudel, *On History*, trans. by Sarah Matthews, Chicago: University of Chicago Press, pp. 25–54.

——(1994), *A History of Civilizations*, trans. Richard Mayne, London: Allen Lane, The Penguin Press.

Brus, Wlodzimierz and Tadeus Kowalik (1983), 'Socialism and development', *Cambridge Journal of Economics*, 7.

Bull, Hedley (1977), *The Anarchical Society*, New York: Columbia University Press.

Burckhardt, Jacob (1943), *Force and Freedom: Reflections on History*, New York: Pantheon. The original German text was prepared from notes of Burckhardt's lectures in Basel in the 1860s and 1870s.

Bury, J. B. (1955), *The Idea of Progress: An Enquiry into its Origin and Growth*, New York: Dover Publications.

Butterfield, Herbert (1951), *The Whig Interpretation of History*, London: G. Bell and Sons.

Cabral, Amilcar (1979), *Unity and Struggle. Speeches and Writings of Amilcar Cabral*, New York: Monthly Review.

Capra, Fritjof (1996), *The Web of Life. A New Scientific Understanding of Living Systems*, New York: Doubleday Anchor.

Carr, Edward Hallett (1945), *Nationalism and After*, London: Macmillan.

——(1946), *The Twenty Years' Crisis, 1919–1939*, London: Macmillan.

——(1949), *The Romantic Exiles*, Harmondsworth, Middlesex: Penguin.

——(1964), *What is History?*, Harmondsworth, Middlesex: Penguin.

Carroué, Laurent (1997), 'Les travailleurs coréens à l'assaut du dragon', *Le Monde diplomatique*, November.

Cassel, Douglas (1999), 'The Rome Treaty for an International Criminal Court: a flawed but essential first step', *Brown Journal of World Affairs* VI (41), winter/spring. Available on http://www.iccnow.org/html/cassel199904

Chabod, Federico (1958), *Machiavelli and the Renaissance*, London: Bowes and Bowes.

Chandra, Satish (1997), 'The Indian perspective', in Cox, ed (1997), pp. 124–44.

Chatterjee, Partha (1986), *Nationalist Thought and the Colonial World: A Derivative Discourse*, London: Zed Books.

Cheru, Fantu (1989), *The Silent Revolution in Africa: Debt, Development and Democracy*, Harare and London: Zed/Anvil Press.

——(1997), 'Global apartheid and the challenge to civil society: Africa in the transformation of world order', in Robert W. Cox, *The New Realism: Perspectives on Multilateralism and World Order*, London: Macmillan for the United Nations University.

Chesneaux, Jean (1971), *Secret Societies in China in the Nineteenth and Twentieth Centuries*, trans. Gillian Nettle, London: Heinemann.

——(1972), *Popular Movements and Secret Societies in China, 1840–1950*, Stanford, CA.: Stanford University Press.

Childe, Gordon (1942), *What Happened in History*, Harmondsworth, Middlesex: Penguin.

Chin, Gregory (1999), 'Beneath the "miracle": explaining China's economic growth', paper prepared for the annual conference of the Canadian Political Science Association, Sherbrooke, Québec, June (unpublished).

Choudhury, Masudul Alam (2000), *The Islamic Worldview: Socio-Scientific Perspectives*, London and New York: Kegan Paul International.

Chouvy, Pierre-Arnaud (2000), 'Les chinois d'outre-mer des Tchou à Deng Xiaoping: des origines historiques et géographiques d'un phénomène migratoire plus que millénaire', http://www.cybergeo.presse.fr/essoct/texte/leschin.htm

Cochrane, Charles Norris (1944), *Christianity and Classical Culture: A Study in Thought and Action from Augustus to Augustine*, London: Oxford University Press.

Collingwood, R. G. (1942), *The New Leviathan, or Man, Society, Civilization and Barbarism*, Oxford: Clarendon Press.

——(1946), *The Idea of History*, Oxford: Clarendon Press.

Cox, Michael (2000), *E. H. Carr. A Critical Appraisal*, London: Macmillan.

Cox, Robert W. (1980), 'The crisis of world order and the problem of international organization in the 1980s', *International Journal*, XXXV (2) spring.

——(1986), Social forces, states and world orders: beyond 'international relations theory' and 'Postscript', both in Robert O. Keohane, ed., *Neorealism and its Critics*, New York: Columbia University Press. 'Social forces, states and world orders' was originally published in *Millennium* 10 (2), summer 1981.

——(1987), *Production, Power, and World Order: Social Forces in the Making of History*, New York: Columbia University Press.

——(1991), 'Real socialism in historical perspective', in Cox with Sinclair (1996).

——(1992), 'Towards a post-hegemonic conceptualization of world order: reflections on the relevancy of Ibn Khaldun', in James N. Rosenau and Ernst-Otto Czempiel, eds. *Governance Without Government: Order and Change in World Politics*, Cambridge: Cambridge University Press.

——(1993), 'Production and security', in David Dewitt, David Hagland, and John Kirton, eds, *Building a New Global Order: Emerging Trends in International Security*, Toronto: Oxford University Press.

——(1996), 'A perspective on globalization' in James H. Mittelman, ed. *Globalization: Critical Reflections*, Boulder, CO: Lynne Rienner.

——(1996), 'Labor and hegemony' and 'Labor and hegemony: a reply', in Cox with Sinclair (1996).

Cox, Robert W., ed (1997), *The New Realism: Perspectives on Multilateralism and World Order*, London: Macmillan for the United Nations University.

Cox, Robert W. with Timothy J. Sinclair (1996), *Approaches to World Order*, Cambridge: Cambridge University Press.

Crane, George T. (1999), 'Imagining the economic nation: globalization in China', *New Political Economy* 4 (2) July.

Croce, Benedetto (1910), *Ce qui est vivant et ce qui est mort de la philosophie de Hegel*, Paris. Available in Brown Reprint Library.

——(1945), *Politics and Morals*, New York: Philosophical Library.

——(1955), *History as the Story of Liberty*, trans. Sylvia Sprigge, New York: Meridian.

——(1964), *The Philosophy of Giambattista Vico*, trans. R. G. Collingwood, New York: Russell and Russell. First published 1913. Preface to the original Italian edition dated Sept. 1910.

Dahl, Robert A. (1971), *Polyarchy: Participation and Opposition*, New Haven, CT: Yale University Press.

Dahrendorf, Ralf (1959), *Class and Class Conflict in Industrial Society*, Stanford, CA: Stanford University Press.

Daix, Pierre (1995), *Braudel*, Paris: Flammarion.

Davidson, Basil (1992), 'Africa: the politics of failure', in Ralph Miliband and Leo Panitch, eds. *Socialist Register* 1992, London: Merlin Press.

——(1994), *The Search for Africa: History, Culture, Politics*, New York: Random House.

Davies, Paul (1996), *About Time: Einstein's Unfinished Revolution*, New York: Simon and Schuster.

Deibert, Ronald J. (1997), *Parchment, Printing and Hypermedia: Communication in World Order Transformation*, New York: Columbia University Press.

Drucker, Peter (1986), 'The changed world economy', *Foreign Affairs*, 64 (4).

Eisenstadt, S. N. (1993), *The Political Systems of Empires*, New Brunswick, NJ, and London: Transaction Publishers.

Elias, Norbert (1994), *The Civilizing Process: Sociogenetic and Psychogenetic Investigations*, trans. Edmund Japhrott, revised edn, Oxford: Blackwell.

Fallows, James (1994), *Looking at the Sun: The Rise of the New East Asian Economic and Political System*, New York: Pantheon.

Fisk, Robert (1990), *Pity the Nation: Lebanon at War*, Oxford: Oxford University Press.

Fitzpatrick, John (n.d.), 'The middle kingdom, the middle sea and the geographical pivot of history', unpublished paper, Flinders University, South Australia.

Foucault, Michel (1979), *Discipline and Punish: The Birth of the Prison*, trans. Alan Sheridan, New York: Vintage Books

Fouchereau, Bruno (2001), 'Les sectes, cheval de Troie des États-Unis en Europe', *Le Monde diplomatique*, May.

Fukuyama, Francis (1989), 'The end of history?', *The National Interest*, summer, pp. 3–18. Subsequently, this was expanded into a book *The End of History and the Last Man*.

——(1992), *The End of History and the Last Man*, New York: Avon Books.

Funabashi, Yoichi (1993), 'The Asianization of Asia', *Foreign Affairs*, 72 (5).

Galbraith, John Kenneth (1992), *The Culture of Contentment*, Boston, MA: Houghton Mifflin.

Geyl, Pieter (1955), *Debates with Historians*, London: B. T. Batsford.

Gill, Stephen (1997), 'Finance, Production and Panopticism: Inequality, Risk and Resistance in an Era of Disciplinary Neo-Liberalism', in Gill, ed., *Globalization, Democratization and Multilateralism*, London: Macmillan

Gill, Stephen and James H. Mittelman, eds. (1997), *Innovation and Transformation in International Studies*, Cambridge: Cambridge University Press.

Gills, Barry K. ed. (2000), *Globalization and the Politics of Resistance*, London: Macmillan.

Goetz, Anne Marie (1991), 'Feminism and the claim to know: contradictions in feminist approaches to women in development', in Rebecca Grant and Kathleen Newland, eds. *Gender and International Relations*, Milton Keynes: Open University Press.

Gorz, André (1982), *Farewell to the Working Class: An Essay on Post-Industrial Socialism*, trans. Michael Sonenscher, London: Pluto Press.

Gramsci, Antonio (1971), *Selections from the Prison Notebooks of Antonio Gramsci*, ed. Quintin Hoare and Geoffrey Nowell Smith, New York: International Publishers.

Green, Leslie C. (1997), 'War crimes, crimes against humanity, and command responsibility', at http://www.nwc.navy.mil/press/review/1997/spring/art2sp97.htm

Guéhenno, Jean-Marie (1993), *La fin de la démocratie*, Paris: Flammarion.

Guitton, Jean (1988), *Lire. Le magazine des livres*, No. 148 January.

Guzzini, Stefano (1994), *The Implosion of Clientalistic Italy in the 1990s: A Study of 'Peaceful Change' in Comparative Political Economy*, European University Institute, Florence: EUI Working Papers in Political and Social Sciences, No. 94/12.

Habermas, Jürgen (1973), *Legitimation Crisis*, London: Heinemann.

Hanochi, Seiko and Kinhide Mushakoji (1996), 'Human trafficking and human security: the case of modern Japan', for a conference organized by the Centre for Social Development Studies, Chulalongkorn University, September.

Hardt, Michael and Antonio Negri (2000), *Empire*, Cambridge, MA: Harvard University Press.

Harmes, Adam (2001), *Unseen Power: How Mutual Funds Threaten the Political and Economic Wealth of Nations*, Toronto: Stoddart.

Harries-Jones, Peter, Abraham Rotstein, and Peter Timmerman (1992), 'Nature's veto: UNCED and the debate over the earth' (unpublished paper, February).

Harries-Jones, Peter, Abraham Rotstein, and Peter Timmerman (1999), 'A signal failure: ecology and economy after the earth summit', in Schechter, ed. (1999).

Harvey, David (1989), *The Condition of Postmodernity: An Enquiry into the Origins of Cultural Change*, Oxford: Basil Blackwell.

Hazard, Paul (1963), *The European Mind (1680–1715)*, New York: Meridian. Trans.

J. Lewis May of *La crise de la conscience europénne*, Paris: Boivin, 1935.

Held, David (1995), *Democracy and the Global Order: From the Modern State to Cosmopolitan Governance*, Stanford, CA: Stanford University Press.

Helleiner, Eric (1996), 'International political economy and the greens', in *New Political Economy* 1 (1).

——(1999), 'State power and the regulation of illicit activity in global finance', in R. Friman and P. Andreas, eds., *The Illicit Global Economy and State Power*, New York: Rowman and Littlefield

——(2001), 'Regulating capital flight', *Challenge*, 44 (1) January–February.

Hellman, Judith Adler (1995), 'The riddle of new social movements: who they are and what they do', in Sandor Halebsky and Richard L. Harris, eds., *Capital, Power, and Inequality in Latin America*, Boulder, CO: Westview Press.

Hobsbawm, E. J. (1965), *Primitive Rebels: Studies in Archaic Forms of Social Movement in the 19th and 20th Centuries*, New York: Norton

——(1994), *The Age of Extremes: A History of the World, 1914–1991*, New York: Pantheon.

Hozic, Aida A. (1999), 'Uncle Sam goes to Siliwood: of landscapes, Spielberg and hegemony', *Review of International Political Economy* 6 (2) autumn.

Hughes, H. Stuart (1952), *Oswald Spengler: A Critical Estimate*, New York: Scribners.

Huntington, Samuel P. (1993), 'The clash of civilizations?', *Foreign Affairs* 72 (3).

——(1996), *The Clash of Civilizations and the Remaking of World Order*, New York: Simon and Schuster.

Ibn Khaldun (1967), *The Muqaddimah*, trans. Franz Rosenthal, abridged and ed. N. J. Dawood, Princeton, NJ: Princeton University Press, Bolingen Series. The original Arabic text was completed in 1377.

Iida, Yumiko (1977), 'Virtual kingdom and dreams of apocalypse: contemporary Japan mirrored in *Aum Shinrikyo*', paper presented at the Tenth Annual Conference, Japan Studies Association, Toronto, Ontario, October 3–5.

——(1997), 'Fleeing the West, making Asia home: transpositions of Otherness in Japanese pan-Asianism', *Alternatives* 22: 409-432.

IILS (1980), *Islam and a New International Economic Order: The Social Dimension, Geneva*: International Institute for Labour Studies.

Innis, Harold A. (1946), 'Charles Norris Cochrane, 1889–1945', obituary notice in *The Canadian Journal of Economics and Political Science* xii, 1 February.

——(1956), 'Decentralization and democracy', in Innis, *Essays in Canadian Economic History*, ed. by Mary Q. Innis, Toronto: University of Toronto Press, pp. 368–71.

——(1962), *The Fur Trade in Canada*, rev. edn, Toronto: Toronto University Press. Original published in 1930.

——(1980), *The Idea File*, ed. by William Christian, Toronto: University of Toronto Press.

——(1986), *Empire and Communication*, ed. David Godfrey, Victoria and Toronto: Press Porcépic. Original published by Oxford University Press, 1950.

——(1991), *The Bias of Communication*, Introduction by Paul Meyer and David Crowby, Toronto: Toronto University Press. Original published by Toronto University Press, 1951.

Johnson, Chalmers (1982), *MITI and the Japanese Miracle*, Stanford, CA: Stanford University Press.

——(2000), *Blowback: The Costs and Consequences of American Empire*, New York: Holt.

Jung, Karl (1933), *Modern Man in Search of a Soul*, New York: Harcourt Brace.

Kapra, Fritjof (1996), *The Web of Life: A New Scientific Understanding of Living Systems*, New York: Doubleday.

Kornai, János (1980a), *Economics of Shortage*, Amsterdam: North Holland.

——(1980b), 'Dilemmas of a socialist economy', *Cambridge Journal of Economics* 4 (2).

Kwong, Peter (1997), *Forbidden Workers: Illegal Chinese Immigrants and American Labor*, New York: The New Press

Lacoste, Yves (1984), *Ibn Khaldun: The Birth of History and the Past of the Third World*, London: Verso.

Lilla, Mark (1993), *G. B. Vico. The Making of an Anti-Modern*, Cambridge, MA: Harvard University Press.

Ling, Lily (1996), 'Hegemony and the internationalizing state: a post-colonial analysis of China's integration into Asian corporatism', *Review of International Political Economy* 3 (1).

Lovelock, J. E. (1979), *GAIA: A New Look at Life on Earth*, Oxford: Oxford University Press.

Lowes, Peter (1966), *The Genesis of International Narcotics Control*, Thèse No. 164, Université de Genève, Institut universitaire de hautes études internationales, Geneva: Imprimerie du Courrier.

Macdonald, Laura (1997), *Supporting Civil Society: The Political Role of Non-Governmental Organizations in Central America*, Basingstoke: Macmillan.

Machiavelli, Niccolò (1961), *The Prince*, trans. with an introduction by George Bull, Harmondsworth, Middlesex: Penguin Books. Original written 1513.

Madeuf, Bernadette and Charles-Albert Michalet (1978), 'A new approach to international economics', in *International Social Science Journal* xxx (2).

Mahbubani, Kishore (1993), in *Foreign Affairs* 72 (4): 10–14.

Malaparte, Curzio (1952), *The Skin*, trans. David Moore from *La Pelle*, London and Sydney: Alvin Redman.

Malone, David D. (2001), 'Uncle Sam's coalition of one', *The Globe and Mail*, December 11.

Marcos, Sous-commandante (1997), 'La 4e guerre mondiale a commencé', *Le Monde diplomatique*, August.

Marglin, Stephen A. (1974), 'What do bosses do? The origin and function of hierarchy in capitalist production', *Review of Radical Political Economy* 6 (2) summer.

Marx, Karl (1969), *The Eighteenth Brumaire of Louis Bonaparte*, based on the 2nd edn 1869, New York: International Publishers.

Mazzotta, Giuseppe (1999), *The New Map of the World: The Poetic Philosophy of Giambattista Vico*, Princeton, NJ: Princeton University Press.

McDaniel, Tim (1996), *The Agony of the Russian Idea*, Princeton, NJ: Princeton University Press.

McNeill, William H. (1963), *The Rise of the West: A History of the Human Community*, Chicago: University of Chicago Press.

——(1964), *Europe's Steppe Frontier, 1500–1800*, Chicago: University of Chicago Press.

——(1989), '"*The Rise of the West*" after twenty-five years', *Journal of World History* 1: 1–21 (University of Hawaii Press). This essay was republished in the 1991 re-edition of McNeill, *The Rise of the West*.

Miller, David L. (1974), *The New Polytheism*, New York: Harper and Row.

Mittelman, James H. (2000), *The Globalization Syndrome: Transformation and Resistance*, Princeton, NJ: Princeton University Press.

——(2001), 'Microresistance to globalization', preliminary unpublished manuscript.

Mittelman, James H. and Christine B. N. Chin (2000), 'Conceptualizing resistance to globalization', in James H. Mittelman, *The Globalization Syndrome: Transformation and Resistance*, Princeton, NJ: Princeton University Press.

Mittelman, James H. and Robert Johnston (1999), 'The globalization of organized crime, the courtesan state, and the corruption of civil society', in *Global Governance* 5: 103–26.

Mohanty, Chandra Talpade (1991), 'Under western eyes: feminist scholarship and colonial discourses', in Chandra T. Mohanty, ed. *Third World Women and the Politics of Feminism*, Bloomington: Indiana University Press.

Monod, Jacques (1970), *Le hasard et la nécessité*, Paris: Seuil.

Morazé, Charles (1957), *Les bourgeois conquérants*, Paris: Armand Colin.

Morin, Edgar (1973), *Le paradigme perdu: la nature humaine*, Paris: Seuil.

——(1977), *La Méthode*, Paris: Seuil.

——(1982), *Science avec conscience*, Paris: Fayard.

Morris, Roger (1996), *Partners in Power: The Clintons and their America*, New York: Holt.

Morrison, James C. (1979), 'How to interpret the idea of Divine Providence in Vico's *New Science*', *Philosophy and Rhetoric* 12 (4) fall. 256–61.

Mushakoji, Kinhide (1997), 'Multilateralism in a multicultural world: notes for a theory of occultation', in Robert W. Cox, ed., *The New Realism: Perspectives on Multilateralism and World Order*, London: Macmillan for the United Nations University.

Najman, Maurice (1997), 'Le grand virage des zapatistes', *Le Monde Diplomatique*, January.

Nakane, Chie (1973), *Japanese Society*, Harmondsworth, Middlesex: Penguin.

Neill, Robin (1972), *A New Theory of Value: The Canadian Economics of H. A. Innis*, Toronto: University of Toronto Press.

Neumann, Sabina and Michelle Egan (1999), 'Between German and Anglo-Saxon capitalism: the Czech financial markets in transition', *New Political Economy* 4 (2) July.

Nishida, Kitaro (1937), *Last Writings: Nothingness and the Religious Worldview*, translated with an introduction by David A. Dilworth, Honolulu: University of Hawaii Press.

O'Brien, Robert, Anne Marie Goetz, Jan Aart Scholte, and Marc Williams (2000), *Contesting Global Governance. Multilateral Economic Institutions and Global Social Movements*, Cambridge: Cambridge University Press.

Ownby, David (2001), 'Falungong and Canada's China policy', in *International Journal* LVI (2) spring.

Panikkar, K. M. (1953), *Asia and Western Dominance*, London: Allen and Unwin.

Pascal, Blaise (1910), *Thoughts*, translation of *Pensées* by W. F. Trotter, in The Harvard Classics, New York: P. F. Collier and Son.

Passet, René (1979), *L'économique et le vivant*, Paris: Payot.

Phongpaichit, Pasuk, Sungsidh Pinyaransang, and Nualuoi Treerat (1998), *Guns, Girls, Gambling, Ganja: Thailand's Illegal Economy and Public Policy*, Chiang Mai, Thailand: Silkworm Books.

Piaget, Jean (1965), 'L'explication en sociologie', in Piaget, *Études sociologiques*, Geneva: Droz.

Polanyi, Karl (1944, 1957), *The Great Transformation: The Political and Economic Origins of Our Time*, Boston, MA: Beacon Press.

Polanyi, Karl, Conrad H. Arensberg and Harry W. Pearson (1957), *Trade and Market in the Early Empires*, Chicago: Regnery.

Pompa, Leon (1990), *VICO: A Study of the 'New Science'*, 2nd edn, Cambridge: Cambridge University Press.

Pons, Philippe (1997), articles in *Le Monde*, 3, 15, 16 January.

——(1999), *Misère et crime au Japon du XVIe siècle à nos jours*, Paris: Gallimard.

Przeworski, Adam (1981), 'Democratic socialism in Poland?', in *Studies in Political Economy* 5, spring:. 29–54, esp. 37–41.

Putnam, Robert D. (1995), 'Bowling alone: America's declining social capital', *Journal of Democracy* 6 (1) January.

Putnam, Robert D. with Robert Leonardi and Rafaella Y. Nanetti (1993), *Making Democracy Work. Civic Traditions in Modern Italy*, Princeton, NJ: Princeton University Press.

Putnam, Robert, Susan Pharr, and Russell Dalton (2000), *What is Troubling the Trilateral Democracies?*, Princeton, NJ: Princeton University Press.

Ramonet, Ignacio (1999), 'Social-conformisme', *Le Monde diplomatique*, April.

Rhodes, Martin (1998), 'Globalization, labour markets and welfare states: a future of "competitive corporatism"?', in Martin Rhodes and Yves Mény, eds., *The Future of European Welfare: A New Social Contract?*, London: Macmillan.

Richardson, M. (1998), *International Herald Tribune*, 20-21 June.

Robinson, William I. (1996a), *Promoting Polyarchy: Globalization, US Intervention, and Hegemony*, Cambridge: Cambridge University Press.

——(1996b), 'Globalization, the world system, and "democracy promotion" in US foreign policy', *Theory and Society* 25: 616–65.

Rorty, Richard (1989), *Contingency, Irony, and Solidarity*, Cambridge: Cambridge University Press.

Rosenau, James N. (1997), *Along the Domestic-Foreign Frontier: Exploring Governance in a Turbulent World*, Cambridge: Cambridge University Press.

Rosenberg, Justin (1994), *The Empire of Civil Society: A Critique of the Realist Theory of International Relations*, London: Verso.

Runciman, Steven (1958), *The Sicilian Vespers*, Cambridge: Cambridge University Press.

Said, Edward (1978), *Orientalism*, New York: Random House.

——(1993), *Culture and Imperialism*, New York: Knopf.

Sakamoto, Yoshikazu (1987), 'The international context of the occupation of Japan', in Robert E. Ward and Yoshikazu Sakamoto, eds. *Democratizing Japan: The Allied Occupation*, Honolulu: University of Hawaii Press.

——(1995), 'The fifty years of the two Japans', *Medicine and Global Survival* June.

Sandbrook, Richard (2002), 'Globalization and the limits of neoliberal development doctrine', *Third World Quarterly* 21(6): 1071–80.

Scharf, Michael P. (1999), 'The politics behind the US opposition to the International Criminal Court', *New England International and Comparative Law Annual*.

Schechter, Michael G. (1997), 'Globalization and civil society', paper presented to the annual meeting of the Academic Council on the United Nations System (ACUNS), San Jose, Costa Rica.

——ed. (1999) *Future Multilateralism: The Political and Social Framework*, London: Macmillan for United Nations University.

Schumpeter, Joseph A. (1943), *Capitalism, Socialism, and Democracy*, London: George Allen & Unwin.

Scott, James C. (1993), *Everyday Forms of Resistance*, Yokohama: PRIME, International Peace Research Institute Meigaku. Occasional Papers Number 15.

Senghaas, Dieter (2002), *The Clash Within Civilizations: Coming to Terms with Cultural Conflicts*, London: Routledge.

Shaw, Martin (2000), *Theory of the Global State: Globality as an Unfinished Revolution*, Cambridge: Cambridge University Press.

Shelley, Louise (1995), 'Transnational organized crime: an immanent threat to the nation-state?, *Journal of International Affairs* 48 (1) January.

——(1996), 'Transnational organized crime: the new authoritarianism', paper presented at Law and Society meetings, Glasgow, Scotland, July.

Sidelsky, Robert (2001), 'The world on a string', *The New York Review of Books*, 8 March.

Sinclair, Timothy J. (1994), 'Passing judgement: credit rating processes as regulatory mechanisms of governance in the emerging world order', *Review of International Political Economy* 1 (1).

——(1997), 'Global governance and the international political economy of the commonplace', paper presented to the International Studies Association, Toronto.

Sorel, Georges (1896), 'Étude sur Vico', *Le Devenir Social* Nos. 9–11, October, November, December.

——(1941), *Reflections on Violence*, New York: Peter Smith.

——(1941), *Reflections on Violence*, trans. T. E. Hulme, New York: Peter Smith. Original French text first published in *Le mouvement socialiste* (1906). First publication in English, 1915. Republished as *Réflexions sur la violence*, Paris: Marcel Rivière, 1950.

——(1947), *Les illusions du progrès*, Paris: Marcel Rivière. Originally published 1908.

——(1971), *Le système historique de Renan*, Geneva: Slatkine Reprints.

Sorokin, Pitrim (1957), *Social and Cultural Dynamics*, rev. and abridged in one volume by the author, Boston, MA: Porter Sargent. Original four-volume edition published in 1937.

Soros, George (1997), 'The capitalist threat', *Atlantic Monthly*, February.

——(1998), *The Crisis of Global Capitalism*, New York: Public Affairs.

——(2000), *Open Society: Reforming Global Capitalism*, New York: Public Affairs.

Southern, R. W. (1962), *Western Views of Islam in the Middle Ages*, Cambridge, MA: Harvard University Press.

Spengler, Oswald (1939), *The Decline of the West*, trans. Charles Francis Atkinson, one volume edn, New York: Knopf (here, the English translation of the two-volume original work appears as one volume, paginated as two). The German original *Der Untergang des Abendlandes* appeared in July 1918. A two-volume English translation was published by Knopf in 1926 (Vol. 1) and 1928 (Vol. 2).

Spero, Joan (1977), *The Politics of International Economic Relations*, 1st edn. New York: St. Martin's Press.

Stavenhagen, Rodolfo (1997), 'Peoples' movements: the antisystemic challenge', in Robert W. Cox, ed., *The New Realism. Perspectives on Multilateralism and World Order*, London: Macmillan.

Stone, Harold Samuel (1997), *Vico's Cultural History; The Production and Transmission of Ideas in Naples, 1685–1750*, Leiden, New York and Cologne: E. J. Brill.

Strange, Susan (1970), 'International economics and international relations: a case of mutual neglect' in *International Affairs*, 46 (2).

——(1986), *Casino Capitalism*, Oxford: Blackwell.

——(1988), *States and Markets*, London: Pinter.

——(1989), 'Toward a theory of transnational empire', in E.-O. Czempiel and James N. Rosenau, eds., *Global Changes and Theoretical Challenges: Approaches to World Politics for the 1990s*, Lexington, MA: Lexington Books.

——(1990), 'The name of the game', in Nicholas X. Rizopoulos, ed., *Sea Changes: American Foreign Policy in a World Transformed*, New York: Council on Foreign Relations.

——(1996), *The Retreat of the State: The Diffusion of Power in the World Economy*, Cambridge: Cambridge University Press.

Taylor, Charles (1965), 'Hermeneutics and politics', in Paul Connerton, ed. *Critical Sociology*, Harmondsworth, Middlesex: Penguin.

——(1979), *Hegel and Modern Society*, Cambridge: Cambridge University Press.

Thompson, E. P. (1978), *The Poverty of Theory and Other Essays*, London: Merlin Press.

Tocqueville, Alexis de (1951), *De la démocratie en Amérique*, 2 vols., Paris: Gallimard.

Toynbee, Arnold (1946, 1957), *A Study of History*, two volumes prepared by D. C. Somervell summarizing Toynbee's ten-volume work, London: Oxford University Press for the Royal Institute of Internatonal Affairs. The first three volumes of the whole work were published in 1933. A volume entitled *Reconsiderations* reflecting upon criticisms of the work was published in 1961.

Tsuru, Shigeto (1993), *Japan's Capitalism*, Cambridge: Cambridge University Press.

Turbiville, Graham H. (1995), 'Organized crime and the Russian armed forces', *Transnational Organized Crime* 1 (4) winter.

UNRISD (1995), United Nations Research Institute for Social Development, *States of Disarray. The Social Effects of Globalization*.

Urquhart, Brian (1999), 'The making of a scapegoat', *The New York Review of Books*, 12 August.

Van der Pijl, Kees (2001), 'What happened to the European option for Eastern Europe?', in Andreas Bieler and Adam David Morton, eds., *Social Forces in the Making of the New Europe: The Restructuring of European Social Relations in the Global Political Economy*, London: Macmillan.

Vico, G. B. (1944), *The Autobiography of Giambattista Vico*, trans. Max Harold Frisch and Thomas Goddard Bergin, Ithaca, NJ: Cornell University Press.

——(1970), *The New Science of Giambattista Vico*, trans. from the 3rd edn (1744) by Thomas Goddard Bergin and Max Harold Fisch, Ithaca, NJ: Cornell University Press.

Vidal-Beneyto, José (1999), 'La social-démocratie privatisée', *Le Monde diplomatique*, July.

Vieille, Paul (1988), 'The world's chaos and the new paradigms of the social movement', in *Theory and Practice of Liberation at the End of the xxth Century*, Brussels: Bruylant.

Waldrop, M. Mitchell (1993), *Complexity: The Emerging Science at the Edge of Order and Chaos*, New York: Touchstone.

Wang, Hongying and James Rosenau (2001), 'Transparency International and corruption as an issue of global governance', in *Global Governance* 7: 25–49.

Weber, Max (1948), 'Politics as a vocation', in H. H. Gerth and C. Wright Mills, eds.,

From Max Weber: Essays in Sociology, London: Routledge and Kegan Paul.

——(1948), 'The social psychology of the world religions', in H. H. Gerth and C. Wright Mills, eds., *From Max Weber*, London: Routledge and Kegan Paul.

——(1948), *From Max Weber: Essays in Sociology*, ed. H. H. Gerth and C. Wright Mills, London: Routledge and Kegan Paul.

Williams, Phil (1999), 'The dark side of global civil society: the role and impact of transnational criminal organizations as a threat to international security', in Muthiah Alagappa and Takashi Inoguchi, eds., *International Security Management and the United Nations*, Tokyo: UNU Press.

Wilson, Edmund (1940), *To the Finland Station: A Study in the Writing and Acting of History*, New York: Harcourt Brace.

Wood, Ellen Meiskins (1995), *Democracy Against Capitalism: Renewing Historical Materialism*, Cambridge: Cambridge University Press.

Yavlinski, Grigory (1998), 'Russia's phoney capitalism', *Foreign Affairs*, May–June.

Zong Hairen (2001), 'Jiang Zemin said Falungong is meticulously planned event', Hong Kong Hsin Pao (Hong Kong Economic Journal), part 5 of excerpts from book *Zhu Rongji* in 1999

Zysman, John (1966), 'The myth of the "Global Economy": enduring national foundations and emerging regional realities', *New Political Economy* 1 (2) July.

Name index

Subject index

aboriginal people 62–3, 178, 186
absolute values 61
Afghanistan: CIA and Pakistan ISI in 120; criminal networks 121; new mode of warfare 189; Taliban xv, xvii; terrorism xiii; war in 35, 41, 74–5, 86, 176, 183, 190, 195 n. 14; *see also* terrorism: 'war against terrorism'
alienation xv, 50, 93–4, 181; and covert world 119–21; and globalization 116, 137–8
al-Qaeda 122, 190
alternative order xix–xxi, xxvi, 37, 85, 93, 192; in Asia 210 n.12; and the biosphere 87; and civil society 92, 96–8, 102, 115, 124; and civilizations 90; and communication 150; and European Left 152; to globalization 116, 136–8; more than one 186; and organic intellectuals 117; and secret societies 120; thinking alternatives 154; and time perspective 173
America xiii, xvii, 41; and globalization 90, 180; ideology of guns 122; pop culture 150, 181; American psyche 140; resentments towards xviii–xix; 'way of life' 180; world order vision 189; *see also* United States
anarchism 41, 60, 136
anarchy ('coming anarchy') 140–1
Argentina 83, 96, 112
arms trade 121, 135
'asabiya 143–4, 154, 164, 207 n. 20; *see also* Ibn Khaldun in Name index
Aum Shinrikyo 122, 135, 171, 210 n. 11
authoritarianism 110–11; and communication 149–50

'barbarism of reflection' *see* Vico in Name index
'battle in Seattle' 8, 123, 183, 211 n. 16
biosphere: in contradiction with real economy 107; Cox criticized re 5–6, 19 n. 3; deep ecology 170, 178, 208 n. 8, 209 n. 3; environmentalism 91, 110; and globalization 42, 86–8; Green movement 90; and international political economy 79; the larger context of international relations 38; opposing ecological degradation as common ground among different civilizations 155–6, 185, 187, 192; and pantheism 146; and social economy 183; and social movements 94; US unilateralism on ecological issues xviii, xix

Boxer Rebellion 127, 129
Buddhism xvi, 27, 127, 132, 204 n. 10

Canada 63, 67, 91, 147, 156, 199 n. 13
capitalism: and class 30; crisis of 101, 118; in 'end of history' thesis 139–40; forms of 42, 89, 108, 146, 166, 180–2, 210 n. 7; linked to free world 77; global capitalism xiii, xviii, 34, 96; and hegemony 100; ideology of 171; laws of motion of capital 153; and military power 21 n. 27; as monolithic force 89, 201 n. 2; primitive accumulation 128, 132, 134, 144; 'social capital' 202–3 n. 13, 209–10 n. 6; social market 73, 108, 146; structural power of 81
Central Asia xiv–xv, xvii–xviii, 35, 74–5, 144, 169, 191
chaos: chaos theory 60; and covert world 126–7; from globalization 142; and legitimacy xv, xx; negative effects of established institutions 118–19, 125, 134, 136, 192
Chechnya xvii, 186, 189, 191
Chiapas 92, 103, 113, 123
China: and capitalism 167, 182; and civil society 110; Falungong 123, 128–9; mandarin class 187; Mongol conquerors 144; and NATO 184; and oil xiv; political economy 90, 146; repression in Xinjiang xviii; secret societies 126–9, 134; and war in Afghanistan 75; and war over Kosovo 42, 73, 199 n. 14; and war against terrorism xvii; world view 39
Christianity 51, 54; 'born again' Christians 138; missions as targets 127
Church, Roman Catholic 48–50, 111, 178, 196 n. 8 & 9
CIA (US Central Intelligence Agency) 120, 124, 135; and 'blowback' 138
citizenship 93, 141, 192; activism 95
'civic state' 92, 102, 200 n. 10, 201 n. 2
civil society: in Africa 113–14; in Asia 108–11; challenging globalization 103–4; changing meanings of 98–100; in confrontation with government and corporate leaders xix, 118; as counter-hegemonic force 91–2; Cox criticized re 8, 11, 23 n. 54; and dissidence 124; emancipatory role 200–1 n. 2; global civil society 8–9, 201 n. 4; inner strength of a civilization 183, 185, 187; and legitimacy 36; renaissance of 184;